Inclusive Teaching in a

Inclusive Teaching in a Nutshell is a visual, easy-to-read and honest guide for teachers who are looking for practical ways to adapt their teaching to meet the needs of all pupils. It provides a useful framework for thinking about inclusion and pupil engagement and encourages the reader to reflect on their classroom approaches. It explains how to provide an inclusive environment and ethos and offers straightforward explanations of common barriers to learning, and how these may present in the classroom.

Packed with ideas for every age group and designed to be easy to access and use, the book spans eight key themes, covering topics such as lesson planning, classroom environment, assessment and feedback and much more. Each section includes:

◆ explanations in accessible, digestible language

◆ a range of tried-and-tested strategies that teachers can adopt to improve pupil engagement and progress

◆ a summary of key content via one-page visual prompts

The book is an ideal scaffold for teachers working in any setting who want to personalise their approaches in the classroom and make the school experience of vulnerable learners more positive.

Rachel Cosgrove studied zoology before training as a teacher, and has taught in primary, special and secondary schools. She is a hugely experienced secondary SENCo and Assistant Head Teacher and now works as an independent education consultant, supporting schools with inclusive approaches and developing and delivering training in schools and other organisations. She works closely with Oxfordshire Virtual School for Looked After Children and Care Leavers and is also an associate consultant for nasen (National Association for Special Educational Needs). Her primary aim is to take the mystery out of inclusive teaching.

INCLUSIVE TEACHING IN A NUTSHELL

A VISUAL GUIDE FOR BUSY TEACHERS

RACHEL COSGROVE

First published 2021
by Routledge
2 Park Square, Milton Park, Abingdon, Oxon OX14 4RN

and by Routledge
52 Vanderbilt Avenue, New York, NY 10017

Routledge is an imprint of the Taylor & Francis Group, an informa business

© 2021 Rachel Cosgrove

The right of Rachel Cosgrove to be identified as author of this work has been asserted by her in accordance with sections 77 and 78 of the Copyright, Designs and Patents Act 1988.

All rights reserved. No part of this book may be reprinted or reproduced or utilised in any form or by any electronic, mechanical, or other means, now known or hereafter invented, including photocopying and recording, or in any information storage or retrieval system, without permission in writing from the publishers.

Trademark notice: Product or corporate names may be trademarks or registered trademarks, and are used only for identification and explanation without intent to infringe.

British Library Cataloguing-in-Publication Data
A catalogue record for this book is available from the British Library

Library of Congress Cataloging-in-Publication Data
A catalog record for this book has been requested

ISBN: 978-0-367-52125-7 (hbk)
ISBN: 978-0-367-36325-3 (pbk)
ISBN: 978-0-429-34532-6 (ebk)

Typeset in Futura
by Apex CoVantage, LLC

Cover design by: Sue Carver

Printed and bound in Great Britain by Bell & Bain Ltd, Glasgow

Contents

	Acknowledgements	vi
CHAPTER 1	Setting the scene	1
CHAPTER 2	It's all in the planning	17
CHAPTER 3	It's all in the classroom	33
CHAPTER 4	Accessible assessment and feedback	125
CHAPTER 5	Outside the classroom	145
CHAPTER 6	Working with parents and carers	155
CHAPTER 7	Strategies for learners – the nuts and bolts	163
CHAPTER 8	Staff energy	247
	Appendices	253
	Bibliography	261

Acknowledgements

A huge thank you to the wonderful Inclusion Department at The Warriner School for all their compassion, brilliance and insight over the years. Thanks especially to Selina Chard for all the hours problem solving, ideas storming and generally putting the world to rights, and to Janet Worthington, who always made me look organised! Thanks to Mark Corness and Emma Masefield, with whom I have enjoyed many fruitful discussions about inclusive practice. Thank you for the team at Routledge for believing that this would make a book. Love and thanks to my family, especially my husband, Peter, and my children Sam, Jeni and Ross, who have patiently listened for years to my teaching stories and been so understanding about my devotion to the job. To all the pupils I have had the privilege of working with, it has never been boring – you are the reason I have written this book for teachers.

Finally, thanks to Lawrence Todd, a lovely cover teacher, who happened to mention that I should write a book with some of the material I had shared at school – he said he would buy it. Well, here it is!

Chapter 1

Setting the scene

INTRODUCTION	3
TEACHER EXPECTATION	9
HOW TO USE THIS BOOK	12
GLOSSARY OF STRATEGIES	14

Setting the scene

Introduction

Inclusive teaching is about planning and creating great lessons in which everyone can learn and engage. The inclusive approach meets everyone in class where they are, and allows teachers to provide choices and options for pupils in how they absorb information, how they make sense of it and how they express or record what they have learned. Pupils might struggle with the content of the curriculum; they might struggle with the way it is being taught or the method by which they are expected to show their understanding. Inclusive teaching pays attention to social and emotional outcomes as well as academic progress. Pupils may not believe they can be successful; thus, teacher expectation plays a huge part in generating pupil self-belief and resilience, and expectation lifts that inclusive ethos.

Pupils vary widely and develop at different rates. Inclusive teaching is about recognising strengths and barriers to learning so that we can adapt, remove or work around the barriers. The barriers to learning that teachers are most likely to come across include attention difficulties; language and communication difficulties; poor working memory or slow processing speed; literacy and numeracy difficulties; and social and emotional difficulties. Some pupils will have specific needs identified, and this can be helpful when you are making decisions about how to support in class, but many pupils will have a range of needs – subsequently, the 'label' only tells you part of their story. There will be also pupils in every class whose needs have gone unidentified because they have good coping strategies. Good teaching involves responding to each pupil, each lesson, each topic, and over time tweaking content and delivery to get the best out of everyone. Inclusive teaching benefits all pupils.

One of the big influences on learning is prior experience. If a pupil has had lots of challenges in their life or has had previous poor experience of school, they may have gaps in their knowledge, already see themselves as unsuccessful learners and accordingly be less resilient. Good teaching makes a huge difference to pupils who have any kind of additional needs, and it is always worth keeping a totally open mind about the potential of pupils, because **lack of inclusive teaching** itself can be a barrier.

Who needs inclusive teaching?

In England, a child or young person has a **special need** if they have a learning difficulty or disability which means they need different and/or additional provision

Setting the scene

in school, compared to other pupils of the same age. Terminology regarding special needs and additional needs vary between England, Wales, Scotland and Northern Ireland, but are similar in ethos and responsibilities. Definitions of special needs outside the UK similarly reference the need for additional assistance or accommodations.

In England, there are four categories of special need:

Cognition and Learning – Learning needs (moderate or severe) and specific learning difficulties (dyslexia, dyscalculia and dyspraxia)

Communication and Interaction – Speech and language needs and autistic spectrum disorder

Social, Emotional and Mental Health Difficulties – Including conditions such as attention deficit hyperactivity disorder (ADHD) or attachment disorder

Sensory and Physical – Vision impairment, hearing impairment and physical difficulties

How might we identify pupils with special or additional needs?

All pupils are expected to make progress, and pupils progress at different rates, but inadequate progress may be the first step to identifying a special need. If staff are concerned that, despite high-quality teaching and intervention, a pupil is not making expected progress and there may be a barrier to learning, the school's special educational needs (SEN) coordinator should be consulted. A pupil may be placed on the SEN register at SEN Support (K) if there is enough evidence that they need additional and/or different provision.

When a pupil presents with very significant needs that may be complex (i.e., more than one area of difficulty) and may require more extensive support or a specialist placement, a request can be made for a statutory assessment. A multiagency team, including an educational psychologist, will look at the request and then either agree to process the plan further, or pass it back to the school to use the services already available in the local authority and school to meet the pupil's needs. An Education Health Care Plan is a legal document that sets out the sort of provision a school must make for the pupil.

Many pupils with a **disability** are on the SEN register, but some pupils with a disability may not be designated as having special needs. Teachers are required to plan for them and ensure equality of access. Inclusive teaching is paramount for ensuring that the disability does not become a barrier to progress.

Setting the scene

Pupils with **medical needs** are potentially vulnerable learners in school. Pupils with chronic or significant medical conditions may be impacted by their condition both physically and emotionally, and school may present many challenges for them. Attendance may be affected by appointments or illness, or pupils may be at home for long periods of time, resulting in social isolation. Not feeling 100% can affect concentration levels, and certain conditions can affect cognitive processes. Pupils may feel misunderstood or judged and may not be able to fully participate in the range of activities on offer.

Pupils whose first language is not English may be vulnerable learners, and may need extra consideration and support in school. In addition to the language barrier, pupils may be asylum seekers or refugees and therefore dealing with emotional or physical trauma.

Pupils whose birthdate makes them younger than most of their peers, often means they start school less mature than most of their peers or have had less experience of being in education compared to other children. It is important to monitor expectations about how younger pupils are doing, due to the fact that teachers can make judgements about their progress which do not take their developmental stage into account.

Experience outside school can have a big impact on the wellbeing of pupils and increase the likelihood that they will be vulnerable to underachievement. Disadvantage can be experienced in many ways. **Looked after and previously looked after children** will have had a very different experience compared to other pupils; they may have moved home and school several times, and additionally may be impacted by trauma or attachment issues. Pupils who are **young carers** will be balancing school life with other duties. Pupils with **challenging family or community circumstances** may have experienced poverty, family breakdown, abuse or neglect, domestic violence, the impact of crime or exploitation. The baggage that many pupils carry with them can have a massive effect on their social and emotional development and their potential academic capacity.

What is inclusive teaching?

The best intervention is what happens in the classroom through high-quality inclusive teaching. Inclusive teaching offers a more positive and engaging experience for vulnerable learners. Inclusive teachers consider everyone's needs and strengths, and strive to package their curriculum in a way that all pupils can access and engage in. Engagement is a key component in a pupil's motivation and resilience.

Inclusive teaching should be **ambitious** for pupils. Pupils should have the opportunity to engage with a wide curriculum, but this curriculum needs to be

Setting the scene

appropriate and accessible. It is not okay for pupils to be in lessons where the level is way outside their reach. If the gaps for pupils are too wide, they switch off and start to identify as unsuccessful learners. In inclusive classrooms, the teaching can be adapted so that tasks are open ended and scaffolded or supported. The content can be explicitly taught in order to close the gaps, or the content can be worked around – e.g., for pupils working significantly below the level of the class, a parallel but equally valuable set of objectives can run alongside the main lesson. An ambitious curriculum should set no limits on the potential journey for each pupil. An ambitious curriculum should also recognise that sometimes the teacher must take a step backwards to reinforce previously covered skills or knowledge, abandon content because it is not relevant at the stage the pupil is at, or steam ahead because the pupils have made amazing progress and reached a higher level than they had originally planned for. An ambitious curriculum is responsive to each cohort.

Structure and routine are very much part of the foundations of inclusive teaching. Humans are highly distractible, and we need time and peace to be able to really focus on something for long enough to learn something effectively or produce creative work. Constant interruptions break our concentration, and as adults we can recognise that repeatedly switching tasks is inefficient and impacts on our ability to focus in depth. Our classrooms are full of distractions and pupils also bring their own emotional baggage into class, which can infiltrate their thoughts and get in the way of processing content. Communication is reciprocal and when pupils talk, others respond. For pupils who already struggle with memory and processing, refocussing after a distraction will be extra tricky. Classroom routines and classroom management are vital in an inclusive classroom. Classes will always benefit from the teacher's investment in good organisation, calm starts to lessons and effective strategies to get silence when delivering explanation or instructions.

Inclusive teaching should be about **connections**. Teachers can be forensic in observing and seeking to understand their pupils. Inclusive teaching is a shared approach and involves the expertise of colleagues, external professionals, parents and carers, and the voices of the pupils themselves. Knowing the starting points of pupils can enable teachers to make links with their prior knowledge, and revisiting these connections builds the learning for pupils who need frequent overteaching. Making connections in the wider community offers opportunities to make learning relevant and concrete.

Inclusive teaching is **caring**. Vulnerable pupils do not have equity of opportunity, so there is a strong moral purpose in creating an inclusive ethos and going the extra mile for pupils who are struggling the most. Caring is about being responsive and nonjudgemental. It's about fostering a sense of belonging for pupils on the social fringes, and using restorative approaches so that we model

Setting the scene

and teach pupils that everyone deserves the chance to learn, despite occasionally making poor choices. 'Consistency' is a word we hear a lot in schools. Caring teachers are fair and predictable, but not necessarily consistent in their use of classroom management strategies. We need to think about equity and justice. Pupils are not all on a level playing field, so it is fair to adjust our practice for some pupils in order to meet their needs or to teach them skills that other pupils may already be competent in. Caring classes will show empathy to peers if the teacher's boundaries are transparent and consequences are communicated in a neutral and non-shaming way.

Inclusive teaching is **creative**. Individual pupils will stretch our ingenuity. It's about occasionally shaking things up and providing variation. Engagement is key to learning. Working out how we are going to help pupils engage with the curriculum is a challenge. Problem solving for how we are going to deliver content in an accessible and interesting way keeps lessons fresh. Every class is different, and even when we know a scheme of work inside out, we still need to modify it, adapt, scaffold it or substitute different ideas in order for it to engage everyone.

Inclusive teaching is simple enough in theory, but difficult in practice within a system stretched for time and resources. There will always be compromises in any school structure. If a school leadership prioritises inclusion, the ethos and culture make it easier for staff to collaborate and share concerns openly. Pupils in mainstream schools are presenting with many more challenges than in previous years. Schools are expected to deal with and cater to a range of medical and social needs and maintain strong safeguarding systems. Many teachers have had little training on how to teach pupils with special needs, complex or otherwise.

Luckily, the good news is that small things can make a huge difference. We need teachers who are willing to do some research, observe their vulnerable pupils, try out different approaches and reflect on their own practice. We need school systems that support teachers to be inclusive – with resources, time and, most importantly, a culture and philosophy that welcomes diversity, however obstructive the financial and accountability systems might be. An inclusive approach to teaching using simple classroom strategies will go a long way towards breaking down some of the most common hurdles to learning:

- **Relationships** – Knowing each pupil's starting points is essential. Know your pupils' interests and triggers. Pre-empt difficulties.
- **Language** – The language used with pupils is important for helping them see themselves as successful learners, and introducing new vocabulary early builds confidence.
- **Relevant and real** – All pupils learn best when tasks are designed to be accessible, challenging enough, but also relevant and authentic.

Setting the scene

Instructions – The inclusive teacher delivers instructions with clarity and brevity to minimise impact on working memory.

Level – Teachers need to consider the curriculum content and pitch the level appropriately, so that pupils can work as independently as possible to achieve their next steps. Teachers can adapt tasks and provide a choice of ways in which pupils can participate.

Keep it simple. Nudge pupils out of their comfort zone. Scaffold and support learning but focus on independent steps in understanding and skills, rather than task completion. Pitch content upwards but know when to track back to consolidate. Try something out, refine it, review it and either embed it or discard it. Usually persistence pays off, and some things start to work at the point when you were thinking of giving that idea up! Value and celebrate diversity. Share resources, ideas and worries with colleagues. Be reassured that the inclusive teaching approach is a way of changing **some** of the things you do, rather than adding things on top of what you already do. Your pupils will be the evidence that it is working.

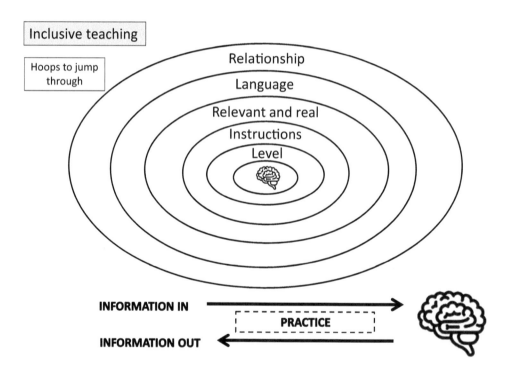

Inclusive teaching hoop model

Setting the scene

Teacher expectation

Context

Every teacher can make a difference to pupils who struggle to make progress at school. All teachers have high expectations for their pupils. Expectations can be about standards; quality of teaching; behaviour and culture; or an ethos which embodies the idea that every child can fulfil their potential. Teachers will have high aspirations for their pupils in that they will absolutely want the best for them, but expectations are about belief: believing pupils can improve and achieve.

In Greek mythology, there is a story about a sculptor who fell in love with a statue he had made that was turned into a real human. This is known as the Pygmalion effect, and is the idea that high expectations can have a positive effect on performance. Sports psychologists use this effect with athletes for visualising success. Conversely, the Golem effect describes the idea that negative expectations lead to poor performance. We see this played out sometimes in schools; when teachers lack belief that some pupils will make progress, expectations are then lowered.

When pupils are labelled with additional needs or challenging behaviours, teachers may make allowances for poor performance, adjust the lesson content to a lower challenge and cut potential opportunities for pupils to perform at higher levels. Staff may do these things with the best intentions, but there is a danger that the result is a self-fulfilling prophesy where pupils are primed to lower their own expectations, and subsequently lose motivation. There may be pupils for instance, in lower sets, who would have the potential to reach a much higher level **if** they were given access to curriculum content at the top of their cognitive capacity. Pupils with additional needs vary widely in their capacity to achieve academically, and it is important that we do not impose any kind of ceiling on where we think the pupil can get to.

Consider

We need to take a leap of faith into inclusive teaching and become more self-aware as teachers, recognising *when* we are influenced by external stereotypes. We need to establish high expectations in our pupils by using optimistic language with them and giving detailed feedback about how they could achieve their next steps, whilst encouraging pupils to challenge themselves, be confused, ask questions and enjoy solving problems. Once we see that a pupil has secured their knowledge or skills at the level first pitched, we can then push their boundaries to the next level and see how they fare. It's a trial and error cycle, because pupils may be ready for

Setting the scene

some concepts but not others. Sometimes you may need to go back to basics and reinforce the topic foundations before attempting higher-level work. Learning is open ended, so setting low long-term targets may limit expectations.

Success means different things to different people. In schools we generally measure success by performance in exams. If a pupil is making great steps in learning – such as improved social skills, managing their emotions, attending school, participating in extracurricular activities, enjoying friendships, becoming interested in topics and knowing facts about things, learning about the wider world and being able to talk about it, having the confidence to do practical tasks or just simply becoming more independent – these are all amazing achievements that we need to celebrate and record. If we can lift the quality of teaching that we provide to the pupils most in need of support, we can influence life chances.

 Reflect

Are you aware of your own prejudices and beliefs?

Setting the scene

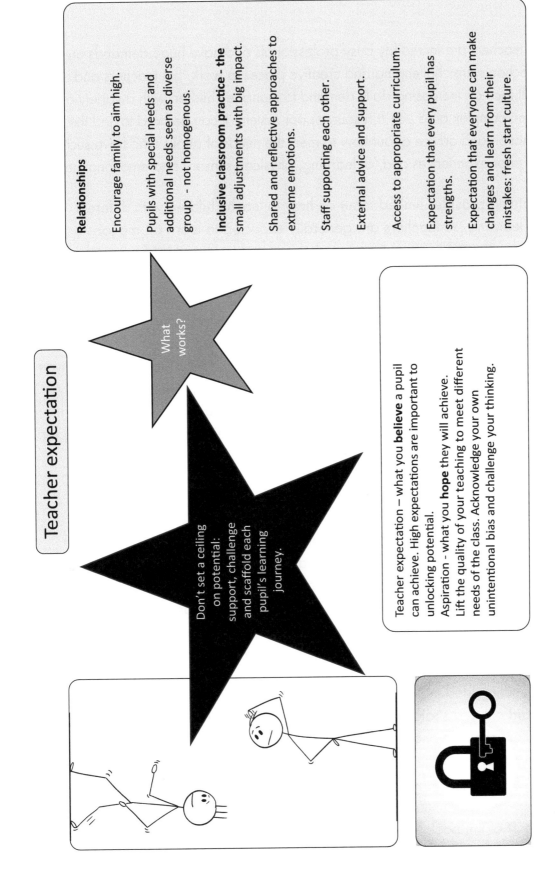

Teacher expectation

Relationships

Encourage family to aim high.

Pupils with special needs and additional needs seen as diverse group - not homogenous.

Inclusive classroom practice - the small adjustments with big impact.

Shared and reflective approaches to extreme emotions.

Staff supporting each other.

External advice and support.

Access to appropriate curriculum.

Expectation that every pupil has strengths.

Expectation that everyone can make changes and learn from their mistakes: fresh start culture.

What works?

Don't set a ceiling on potential: support, challenge and scaffold each pupil's learning journey.

Teacher expectation – what you **believe** a pupil can achieve. High expectations are important to unlocking potential.
Aspiration - what you **hope** they will achieve.
Lift the quality of your teaching to meet different needs of the class. Acknowledge your own unintentional bias and challenge your thinking.

Teacher expectation

Setting the scene

How to use this book

Classroom teachers are incredibly busy professionals and have huge demands on their time. Schools are challenging and creative places to work, but teachers and support staff face an increasing daily demand to manage children with a variety of needs – often complex ones – in a resource-poor system. It can be hard to find the right information and advice about how to meet the needs of pupils who have such a diversity of prior experiences and/or learning, physical, sensory and emotional needs.

Teacher training provides limited input on how to teach children with different barriers to learning, so teachers are generally expected to learn on the job. Teachers are expected to be able to tweak their teaching to adapt for a wide range of needs but often lack the support or guidance about how best to do this. Pupils with additional needs are not a homogenous group, but they are vulnerable to underachievement. Schools need to think differently about inclusive approaches; a more generic approach to differentiation is required. Many schools have skilled and proactive SEN and pastoral leads to help advise and train staff, but time given for specific professional development is often limited and expertise varies widely between schools. Teachers are highly motivated to engage pupils who struggle in school, and reflective teachers are constantly refining their practice and looking for useful strategies they can use in class to improve the progress of their pupils.

How does the book work?

This book is designed to be a handy, visual guide for teachers and support staff. This book is filled with tangible strategies that can be trialed and embedded in everyday classroom practice. All the strategies are tried and tested, and work in a range of settings and across age groups. I am hoping that many strategies will be very familiar and that many teachers will read through and feel heartened that they already possess a lot of knowledge and skills which are inherently inclusive.

The book is subdivided into short, bite-size sections, each with a clear focus. Each section is laid out in a straightforward, digestible format; the context, the strategies, a question for reflection and a visual guide. The context provides background information about the strategy or the barrier to learning. The 'consider' section lists a range of useful approaches. The text is accompanied by a visual page which either acts as an 'aide memoir' of the key strategies or provides specific examples. The early part of the book focuses on general practices such as lesson planning and how to create an inclusive classroom. Later chapters include several common barriers and how to adapt classroom practice to support specific needs. There are

Setting the scene

some useful appendices with an inclusive teaching checklist and an ideas menu, jam-packed with adaptable lesson activities to choose from, for those moments when you have run out of inspiration. In order to be accessible for teachers at all stages of their careers or experience, the book attempts to cut through the jargon and use language that every teacher is familiar with. Many pupil needs overlap, so instead of highlighting specific diagnoses, the barriers included are the broader and more common 'what you might see in class' behaviours and difficulties.

The visual pages have been fun to design, and my idea is that you could use the spiral-binding format to easily find and leave pages open for reference, share with colleagues or use pages as visual reminders. It is so easy to forget strategies learned on courses, so using this book 'little and often' will reinforce the ideas over time so that you can naturally embed them in your day-to-day teaching. The images of pupils and staff are represented by stick figures which have been chosen to represent any age, gender, race, need, etc. I refer to children as pupils throughout the text to avoid pigeonholing different age groups. Although the book is about how to ensure teaching includes pupils with additional and different needs, I am very much of the view that each class includes such a diversity of strengths and weaknesses that it is not helpful to get stuck on labelling. What is good for one specific individual pupil, will work well for other pupils for whom you hadn't necessarily intended to adapt for. In terms of the language I use to describe pupils, when I talk about additional needs, special needs, vulnerable pupils or pupils with challenging backgrounds, I am including any pupil who struggles to access learning in school – whether their barrier is a learning need, a medical need, a mental health or emotional need, a physical or sensory need or because they have experienced poverty, trauma, family breakdown or other external factors which impact on their wellbeing. You will notice that several strategies are repeated throughout the book, as they work so well for many types of barriers.

I have chosen not to include specific referencing within the text because all the strategies included have been gleaned from a long career of teaching in different settings; professional development; a lifetime of reading; hours of discussions with external professionals and parents; and years observing pupils and colleagues. I wanted to keep the text concise and write it from the view of a practitioner. The idea is that this guide will be your 'go-to' reference for everyday planning and can act as a springboard from which to build or refine your specific expertise. This is a guidebook for classroom teachers who need quick and easy strategies and guidance, and is not meant to be a substitute for specialist guidance. Whether you are just starting out in your career or are an old hand, I hope everyone will find some useful ideas in the book.

There is a bibliography for further reading suggestions.

Glossary of strategies

Most inclusive strategies I have used are explained within the sections of the book, but the strategies in the glossary that follows come up regularly; I have included a bit more detail about how they work so that when you see them referred to, they will make more sense.

Strategy	What is it?
Chunking	Dividing a task into sections. Explaining, modelling or giving instructions at each stage rather than all at once. Circulating materials or resources bit by bit. Cutting content up and delivering it in portions. For example, cut a long piece of text into sections and circulate one strip at a time to discuss or work from.
Repeat without rephrasing	When giving an instruction or explaining a point. Repeat the phrase either to whole class or to individuals to help them process the language. If you change the wording, it's like hearing an additional piece of information. Explain clearly and then repeat.
Wait time	Teachers often don't wait long enough for a pupil to process a question and formulate an answer. Between 8 and 10 seconds is needed for pupils who take longer to think about the question. Avoid rushing or letting other pupils jump in.
Sequencing	Sequencing is when pupils are given some content that could be ordered in some way. Pupils read the text or look at the images and discuss how to order them. They can reorder cards or strips of text or pictures, number a list or hold a card and get into a line of pupils. Ranking is a higher-order skill but can be used to help pupils engage with text or understand a concept.
Matching	Match words with definition, picture, person, colours, numbers. Great way to get pupils involved with content without having to write. Good for memorising and vocabulary teaching.
Scaffolding	Providing levels of support to a pupil – giving cues, choices, visuals, sentence starters, writing frames, model answers, etc.

Setting the scene

Reduce demand	Think about working memory and cognitive capacity. If the content level is high, keep the task simple. If the concept is simple or familiar, the task can be more complex. For example, if a complex concept has been explained, the task could be labelling diagrams or answering fact questions. If the content is revisiting familiar information, the task could be more analytical or evaluative.
Positive instructions	Using do, can, will, please, thanks, rather than don't; when redirecting, diverting, reinforcing which behaviours you want to see.
Proximity prompting	Roving the room and standing, hovering or sitting near pupils you want to redirect. Avoids using verbal prompts, lets pupils know you are on to them, less disruptive to rest of class and more likely to reduce escalation than trying to reprimand across the class.
Pre-teaching vocabulary	A very useful strategy where vocabulary is introduced at start of lesson and revisited frequently throughout sequence of lessons. Share vocabulary in various ways according to class needs. Ideas – show single word with image, show word with definition, use think, pair share to discuss possible definitions, share words in sentences and discuss meanings, make word maps with word, image, spelling, example in a sentence, sounds like, similar words that mean the same, etc.

Chapter 2
It's all in the planning

LESSON PLANNING – THE HOUSE MODEL   18

It's all in the planning

Lesson planning – the house model

Lesson planning is an inclusion cornerstone: the better your lesson planning is, the easier it is to know how you are going to cater to the variety of pupils in your class. The lesson plan itself doesn't have to be a lengthy, detailed tome; it's more about the process you go through as a teacher when you are thinking about how you are going to teach a certain piece of content. It's not about creating the perfect lesson plan or scheme of work, and it's certainly not about writing all your lesson plans in the holidays ready for the start of term. I have always thought of lesson planning as a bit of an organic process. You may start with the scheme of work or long-term plan as an outline – a template showing where you might go – but the lesson planning is about adapting and adjusting the journey according to the aptitude and engagement of your pupils. The process involves a trial-and-error cycle alongside having the confidence to deviate from your original plan if the scheme isn't working as well as you'd hoped for a particular group of pupils.

The best place to start is with the pupils. What do you know about their knowledge and skills in relation to the topics you are intending to teach them? Have you looked at their data? This might include previous test data in your subject or year group; data in different subjects; reading and spelling ages; behaviour and attendance logs and/or individual pupil profiles. This should give you some idea about the sort of level at which to pitch your starting lessons. Is the class set by ability or mixed? Can you see how broadly you need to go in terms of scaffold and challenge? It's a good idea to map out a possible path through the scheme of work to begin with but to be flexible in terms of the pace and depth once you get into the lesson delivery. There will always be a conflict between how much content to cover and how thorough to be. Teachers will always have to make decisions about when to move on and when to slow down. All classes, even if grouped by ability, will have a range of strengths and weaknesses: it is unrealistic to think that every single pupil can be reached at their exact level in every lesson. The best we can all hope for is that over a series of lessons, we can plan tasks which extend and consolidate learning, so that at different stages individual pupils are making good progress and that overall at the end of a scheme or term, each pupil will have moved forward in some areas, some making small steps and some racing ahead. And that is fine.

What can we do in 15 minutes? This is the length of time, on average, that any of us can maintain attention and concentration. Teachers tend to talk too much,

It's all in the planning

and when we are passionate about our subject, it is easy to get carried away and cram in too much new content in a lesson. In general, about **15 minutes** or less of teacher talk is enough. If the talk is chunked into other activities like pair discussion, a game or a sticky-note task, then the teacher talk session can be extended.

It's all about quality rather than quantity!

We want pupils to remain focussed, and we need to consider their working memory capacity. If the new content is familiar and low demand – for example, straightforward facts about something they have seen before – you can extend a little because they are not having to process complex content. If, however, the new information is conceptual – for example, a new calculating method, a scientific theory or a comparison activity – then you will need to allow plenty of processing time and repetition.

You can vary the levels of difficulty in lessons by having different pathways in terms of where you are hoping the pupils will end up. They may all be studying the same topic, but the differentiation will be in the way you scaffold the tasks; the format used to complete the tasks; the pace and intellectual demand of the task or the amount of support you provide. If you have a pupil in your class who is at a *very* different ability level from the rest, you may need to work with the SEN team to plan a separate pathway. If you are creative, you can usually find parallel tasks at a simpler level that a pupil may work on that are in keeping with the class task. For instance, in a class doing a science experiment, the main objective may be to understand chemical reactions, whereas your key pupil may be participating in the experiment but working on describing what they see or naming and using the equipment.

Once you have sketched out your sequence of lessons and possible activities that will provide opportunities to learn the content, the exciting bit is to think about engagement. How are you going to hook pupils into the topic? Do you know the interests of the pupils you teach and how they work together as a group? Do you have areas of interest that excite you and that you could bring into the lessons? Pupils will be inspired if you are motivated and enthusiastic about the subject.

There are several lesson-planning models and templates which teachers could use to make planning easier. Your school may have a set template to work to. To ensure that you plan with inclusion in mind, it is helpful to have a visual structure to remind you of how learning is constructed. The house model described below is a way to think about your planning. It's inclusive because it can be adapted for whoever you are teaching – at whatever level. It considers prior learning and helps you think about the steps needed to prepare the class for new content.

It's all in the planning

Foundations

It is so often the case that teachers breeze ahead with new content with interesting activities and at a pace, to keep the learning moving, only to find that many pupils have not made the expected steps in understanding and seem to have forgotten what they appeared to be grasping during a previous lesson. Many pupils with additional needs struggle with recall, and this is probably because they didn't have secure understanding in the first place. We can usually only remember something at a later stage if we have a reasonable understanding of it. Many pupils with additional needs don't make expected progress because the teaching is pitched at the wrong level and new content is added before prior skills and knowledge are secure.

If the foundations are shaky, the house will fall down.

To secure the foundations, you need to know where the pupils are starting from. In my experience, it's best not to make assumptions, even if you know they have studied certain topics before. There is nothing that destroys confidence more than teachers telling pupils that they 'should know this'.

Finding out what pupils know is a bit of an art, but could entail looking at previous data or work as a starting point. Your school may use subject baseline assessments at the start of a year or new topic and if so, these will be useful if they are appropriately levelled for your set of pupils. If not, you won't get a realistic level, and you may instead have to adapt the assessment to make it more useful. You could include some open-ended questions which would help to ascertain what pupils do know, or redesign the wording of the assessment to make it more accessible. If you have support staff, you can use them to help a pupil with the test and get feedback from them about the areas the pupil could have a go at, along with corresponding gaps and misconceptions.

Here are some other ideas to gather information about starting points:

- Provide some key words or images and ask pupils to define them, rank them, sort them into groups and discuss.

- Get pupils to draw what they think something means – for example, I once asked a class to draw an atom at the start of a topic, and many of my science set remembered the electron shells, but some just drew a dot. I could see from this that they knew atoms were small and that some of them knew they had a structure. They had at least all heard of the word 'atom', so I wasn't starting from scratch.

It's all in the planning

- Set a question.

- Show a picture or set of images to describe or spot links/mistakes.

- Do a general Q & A and get feedback from round the room – could work in pairs and feedback to class or do a mini whiteboard exercise.

- Give pupils a grid to complete with activities related to topic – key words, images, making links, questions.

- Quiz or multiple-choice test.

- Self checklist for pupils to mark red, green and amber to traffic light their confidence or knowledge – teacher reads it out to make sure everyone can access (smiley faces, thumbs up or ticks and crosses can also be used for pupils to show what they can do independently and what they need support with).

- Set a short practical task and observe.

- Set a prediction question – what if X?

Once you have gauged where you think the pupils are in terms of foundation knowledge, you may have found out that all or some of the class need to secure some skills or knowledge **before** you can deliver the topic content. The foundations will vary but will usually be factual, contextual or skill based.

Background knowledge – It may be that pupils have gaps in knowledge that they will need to draw on in order to assimilate new content.

For example, if you are doing a project on rivers in the United Kingdom (UK), do the pupils all know which countries are in the UK, and where they are? If you are asking pupils to write a persuasive letter, do they remember the format of a general letter?

Contextual information – It may be that you need to fill in the broader context to help the new content make sense. If your topic is about a story set in Victorian times, do the pupils have a visual image of what life was like then, how many years ago it was, what the buildings were like, what people did for a living, etc.?

Skills – Sometimes pupils will be lacking the underlying skills needed to secure a new topic, and you may need to spend some time revisiting these. For example, in a maths topic about calculating areas, some pupils may need to practise measuring with a ruler to make sure they read the scale from the right end and can understand the centimetre markings.

It's all in the planning

Similar concepts – It is always worth connecting new content to other work pupils have covered but may not automatically make links to. Spending time refamiliarising a previous topic or skill prior to a new comparable topic will help pupils practise skills and generalise this to the new topic.

Decisions about how much time to spend making sure the foundations are secure are tricky, as you will be keen to make progress. Be aware that some pupils need more time. You may find out that the foundations of the whole class are shaky and that they are not ready to move on at all. This is where important decisions about curriculum coverage and pupil learning take place. It will be up to you to determine whether it is worth introducing the new content. It may be that you 'dip your toe' into new concepts or skills with the class and see how the pupils manage.

It's all about having an awareness that foundations are important for the solidity of the learning. So many teachers say that some pupils don't seem to be *able* to retain knowledge; often this is because they were adding new content onto a shaky foundation – meaning, it didn't stick.

Bricks

The bricks are the important facts and skills needed to master the **new** content. Bricks can be part of the general teaching or they can form part of any pre-teaching. Bricks will include new vocabulary, new practical skills, key numeracy skills, a new format or layout, key facts or maybe a certain routine that pupils need to learn for a task.

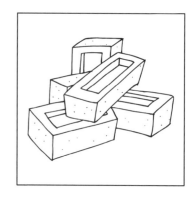

Vocabulary – Pre-teaching important vocabulary is a great inclusive routine to get into; it's simple, effective and can be used at any level of ability. You can use images, definitions, example sentences, film clips, drama or real objects to illustrate meanings of new words. You can adjust the complexity or number of words according to individual pupils or cohorts. Having the words defined, visually displayed and frequently referred to helps pupils use the language of the new topic straight away. Remember to include some of the non-subject words in your pre-teaching. Sometimes the command words confuse pupils, e.g., what's the difference between 'describe' and 'explain'? Providing exemplars will help.

Numeracy – Sometimes key numeracy concepts need to be introduced explicitly. For example, you may need to pre-teach the class or individual pupils how to complete a tally chart if you are working on an environmental topic and they are going to be doing a survey.

It's all in the planning

Formats – If pupils are writing a letter, the bricks might involve looking at layouts of different kinds of letters and explaining why the details, such as addresses, need to be included. It may be that some pupils need to learn to write their own address in the correct format first. It may be that you need to revise capital letters for names. If writing a science report, you will need to teach pupils how to construct a report and show them how to use the template before they work on their own.

Key facts – The bricks of a more complex task such as writing an argument or solving a problem may include the key facts embedded in the topic. These can be introduced in any way but for some pupils, they may need to be visual and concrete or repeated several times so that they are secure enough in pupils' memories and don't take up thinking time from the task itself. It may be helpful to display the key facts during the task.

Practical skills – Many activities include specific practical skills that need to be explicitly taught and modelled, such as measuring out chemicals for an experiment, using a tool, cross hatching in art, using a piece of software, etc. Often pupils with additional needs may not have picked up these skills alongside their peers and need further direct teaching rather than quick demos. Physical education teachers teach the component parts of a game using drills and mini-games before going into a full game, and it's this idea that will work well for pupils in other subjects. It is worth building in time or adult support to make sure the component practical skills are practised before being used in a wider context. Not only is the learning going to be more successful, but the confidence of vulnerable pupils will improve because they will have rehearsed first. An example of this in action was a science lesson where I wanted the pupils to carry out a chemical reaction accurately. The equipment was new to the class, as they had used measuring cylinders before but not a special piece of glassware called a burette. We spent a whole lesson modelling, practising and recording measurements with the new equipment, using only coloured water rather than the actual chemicals. The stakes were low; therefore everyone was happy to make mistakes and discuss ways to pour the liquid without spilling, how to crouch to eye level to read the measurement and how to work as a pair to get the recordings down. The time taken paid off when it came to the real experiment because they all (mostly!) were competent and confident by then.

Routines – Sometimes a lesson involves pupils working in groups, in a carousel or in a whole class debate. These types of lessons require pupils to work in a slightly different way and can cause stress, conflict and time wasting if pupils are not used to the new routine. Practising routines will save time at a later stage, and benefits pupils who find it hard to adapt to change or who struggle socially with others. You can teach pupils how to move into groups before getting bogged down with the intellectual demands of the task. Have some practice sessions where they move into groups, work in groups to do an easy task, rehearse a class debate or practise a routine such as tidying or collecting materials. Some pupils need lots of practice and peer modelling to become familiar with the new expectations, but once the class knows how you want them, it will be a much smoother transition when you need them to work in this way.

Construction

Once the foundations are in place and you have prepared the pupils with the prerequisite skills and knowledge, it's time to deliver the main content.

Everyone will do this differently, but to scaffold your struggling learners, the basic principles are as follows:

- Get their attention and make it personally engaging.

- Repeat and model routines and content.

- Teach in chunks to allow time for processing.

- Make it as visual and concrete as appropriate.

- Make links to what they already know.

- Constantly assess and refine your lesson plan.

At any point you can return to foundations if required, or steam ahead with more new content if they are progressing well. At this stage, planning for **everyone in mind** is easiest to do, and remember that visual and concrete prompts will not be wasted on more able pupils, as these strategies help reinforce learning for all abilities. My philosophy is to make sure everyone knows something new at this point, however small a step it is. For some pupils, being able to recognise one new key word is progress, whilst for others, understanding a whole concept is appropriate. You can use strategies such as targeted questioning or pair discussion to advance those who need more challenge. It's in the mortar section that you can really differentiate the activities to an individual level.

It's all in the planning

Mortar

The mortar is the activity that hopefully cements the learning. Pupils need to engage in activities that reinforce the content or skill through practise and application. This is where adapting and adjusting is key, and where you can be really creative in thinking about how to help certain learners access an activity at their own level.

There are several ideas in this book about how to adapt your teaching to meet the needs of your various learners.

Modelling is an important part of the process.

Levels – The activities can be planned to be open ended so that everyone can start a task, but different pupils can achieve and complete it to varying levels of complexity or depth. At this point you can make decisions about the kind of challenge and choice you set. Some pupils will be working at a key word level; others will be using the concept to answer and ask questions, reorganise the concept and produce it another format or embedding the concept in different ways. Other pupils may be secure with the concept and use higher-order thinking to produce work around the concept.

Scaffolding level – You can also scaffold the amount of support for different pupils' access. You may use differential peer or adult support across the class. You could provide writing frames, sentence starters or worked examples for specific pupils whilst allowing other pupils to work totally independently. Some pupils may need to do more or less of a task. You may use aids such as scribes, computer assisted technology or concrete props to support some pupils.

The mortar part of the lesson can be chunked. It can be carried over a series of lessons or it can be reinforced as homework. Be mindful that when setting homework to consolidate learning, some pupils will need very clear instructions and guidance, such as a grid with key words to match.

Décor

We get to the décor once the learning has been constructed and stuck together, and when you think pupils will be able to use what they have learned to extend their thinking and apply the new content in a different way. Many pupils with additional needs find this very hard, but if the foundations are secure and they seem confident with some of the new content, you will want to test whether they can think *around*

It's all in the planning

a subject. Teachers can set activities that use the content in a different genre or format. For example, after studying energy sources in science, pupils write a letter to the head teacher about which renewable energy the school could invest in.

If pupils have struggled with the main concept, they may need more opportunities to practise the original work rather than move on at this point, but if you think laterally it may be that other skills can be incorporated into a task which enable the pupil to be included with others. For example, you might have groups planning a piece of drama around a 'what if' question related to the topic. Some pupils may be discussing a complex concept, while others may be preparing the props or acting a scene with peer support. In this way they are generalising other parallel skills whilst being part of the group, and in addition, you are giving them the opportunity to listen to others and therefore be exposed to rich subject vocabulary and different perspectives. Often, pupils may pick up some of the extended thinking. These extension activities can provide a great opportunity to rove the class and gain feedback from your pupils which will help you plan the next steps.

Snagging

Talking of next steps, *snagging* is the part of the building process that involves completing all the little jobs that were left undone – the skirting boards, the unfinished tile grouting, the door handles, the plug sockets. If snagging is not done, the house cannot work efficiently! (My explanation of snagging is an example of pre-teaching vocabulary, as described in the glossary of strategies!)

In teaching, the snagging is all about the gaps. If you don't plan in enough time to revisit gaps, pupils will move forward with gaping holes in their knowledge or at worst, continue with misconceptions. In the learning cycle, you need to build in time for assessment and testing but also time to revisit and reinforce the missing knowledge and understanding. It may be that in your subject or year group, you know that you will be going back to the concepts later in the scheme of work or that the topics are not vital for subsequent learning.

Current thinking about retrieval is that we should be revisiting learning little and often as part of the memorising process. If pupils are struggling to retain information, I have found that starting each lesson with a revision of previous learning is a good way to drip-feed pupils your key words and facts. With more able learners, you can leave time gaps between retrieval, but some pupils need much more frequent reminders, otherwise they cannot hold onto the new content. Building in quizzes where you combine new facts with some of the previous content is a good way to consistently build knowledge.

It's all in the planning

Testing and assessment form part of this cycle and allow you to ascertain where the gaps are. Some pupils may need more extensive time to revise or may benefit from overteaching to try and backfill gaps. It may be that you can use support staff to withdraw a pupil or group to go over some previous learning, while you have the rest of the class, or vice versa. It is important for the teacher to work directly with struggling learners and not rely on support staff, if you are lucky enough to have additional adults in the classroom. Struggling learners need the specific teaching skills of a specialist, more so than other pupils.

Snagging is not particularly fun, as most pupils don't like going back over previous work; hence, a bit of creativity may be needed. If you praise and encourage pupils when they gradually start to recall key knowledge, it can become a reassuring and satisfying process for vulnerable learners. As they start to realise they can be successful, they may enjoy repetitive content. Introducing games or some choice, challenge or competition may engage pupils. There are lots of ideas in further sections of this book to help give you some inspiration. Working collaboratively and using peer tutoring can be a nice way to help close gaps and has the advantage of reinforcing the work in the memories of the peer tutors.

The house model is a way of thinking about inclusion. The visual image of a house helps us fit the concept into the schema of buildings, so we can conceptualise the idea of a shaky foundation and the importance of building the learning from a secure base. I hope you find it useful, and you will find plenty of ideas about the individual components in the rest of this book.

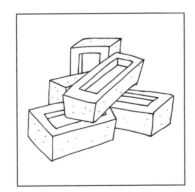

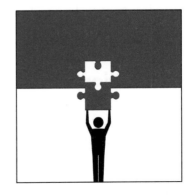

It's all in the planning

House model in action – lesson planning

Secondary school example

Elements and compounds	Timing
Elements and compounds	1–3 hours

- All substances are made of atoms. An <u>atom</u> is the smallest part of an <u>element</u> that can exist.
- Atoms of each element are represented by a <u>chemical symbol</u>, e.g., 'O' represents an atom of oxygen.
- There are about 100 different elements.
- Elements are shown in the <u>periodic table</u>.
- <u>Compounds</u> are formed from elements by <u>chemical reactions</u>.
- A <u>mixture</u> consists of two or more elements or compounds not <u>chemically combined</u> together.

Learning objectives

- **Describe elements, compounds and mixtures**

Foundations – what do they already know?

Are they able to describe how categories can be grouped? Practise categorising other things and discussing the process. Games. Show them the periodic table. What do they know? Do elements quiz with pictures? Match chemical symbols with words. Can they describe chemical reaction signs?

Bricks – the building blocks needed

The underlined words will probably need pre-teaching – using images and concrete examples. Revisit chemical reactions concept using some simple reactions in class where they describe what they see. Show pictures of atoms. Define element and tell story of atom.

Construction – the new content

Look at lots of different elements, mixtures and compounds. Describe features. Record similarities and differences. Group them. Provide definitions. Teach chemical symbols. Demo chemical reactions and symbol equations. Video of history of periodic table.

It's all in the planning

Mortar – activities

Look at actual compounds and elements. Carry out reactions. Record features – differences, similarities. Observe demo reactions. Matching activities. Practise chemical symbols. Quizzes. Practise finding elements using periodic table. Highlight, colour, cut and stick. Pupils try to categorise elements and compounds using periodic table. Practise chemical questions using cards with symbols. Research features of chosen element. Presentations.

Décor – using the content in different ways

Use formulae to categorise chemicals. Work out formulae from names. Predict position of element according to description and reactions. Retell story of chemical reaction. Research new elements.

Snagging – gaps

Revisit key words. Quick quiz starters. Teaching assistant overteaching key pupils.

Primary school example

English KS2 News Report Writing – to find the features of a news report	
Starter	In groups, look at the cuttings of different articles for newspapers on tables. On sticky notes, write down what features the articles have in common.
Class learning	Teach and explain key features. Discuss and annotate news article on whiteboard with class.
Independent activities; example news report sheets – pupils annotate	
Pair work to highlight basic features using checklist. Annotate news article.	Annotate features on worksheet individually. Discuss findings.
Share news articles with peers. Reading and discussing.	
Show exemplar news article about school.	
Self-marking/peer marking.	
Next steps – editing/typing up on computer.	
Research topic from outside school.	

It's all in the planning

Foundations – what do they already know?

Newspapers, magazines; name some newspapers. Look at daily papers, local papers, Sunday papers. Experience in families? What do newspapers write about?

Bricks – the building blocks needed

Teach definitions of key words such as headings, subheadings, captions, image or photograph, first person narrative. Text, bold, article, journalist.

Construction – the new content

Read out loud to class, explain article, model on whiteboard, teaching assistant has copy for key pupils to share. Directed levelled questions with choices. Peer modelling. Choose article about topic of pupil interests.

Mortar – activities

News article annotated as model. Range of articles of different text levels and more or less images. Adult support to help find features. Pair buddies to support reading.

Décor – using the content in different ways

Writing their own articles, writing frames partially completed, cloze, choice of recording ideas on tablet in place of writing. Pupils could interview staff to get content for article. Different roles, e.g., photographer for article. Level of independence varied.

Snagging – gaps

Revisit key words in next topic. Use newspapers for reading time. Teaching assistant supported reading using newspaper and targeted questioning. Provide model answers and model articles.

It's all in the planning

Lesson planning – the house model

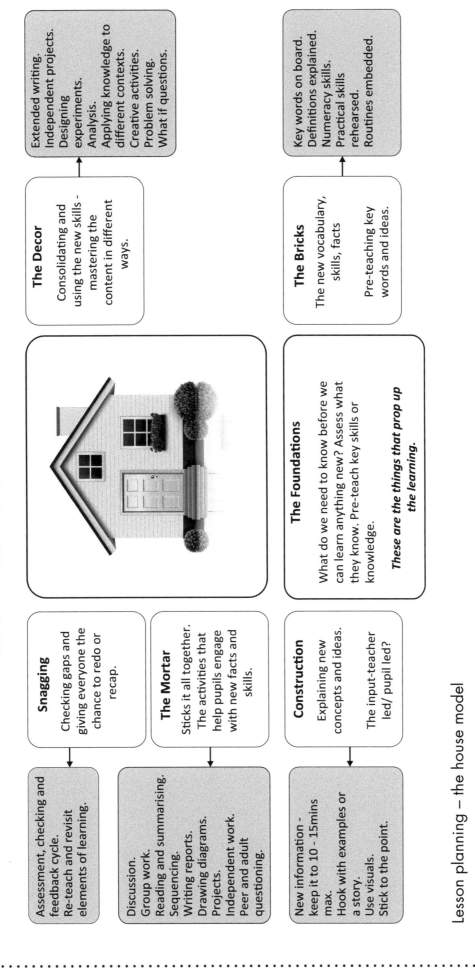

The Decor
Consolidating and using the new skills – mastering the content in different ways.

- Extended writing.
- Independent projects.
- Designing experiments.
- Analysis.
- Applying knowledge to different contexts.
- Creative activities.
- Problem solving.
- What if questions.

The Bricks
The new vocabulary, skills, facts

Pre-teaching key words and ideas.

- Key words on board.
- Definitions explained.
- Numeracy skills.
- Practical skills rehearsed.
- Routines embedded.

The Foundations
What do we need to know before we can learn anything new? Assess what they know. Pre-teach key skills or knowledge.

These are the things that prop up the learning.

Snagging
Checking gaps and giving everyone the chance to redo or recap.

- Assessment, checking and feedback cycle.
- Re-teach and revisit elements of learning.

The Mortar
Sticks it all together. The activities that help pupils engage with new facts and skills.

- Discussion.
- Group work.
- Reading and summarising.
- Sequencing.
- Writing reports.
- Drawing diagrams.
- Projects.
- Independent work.
- Peer and adult questioning.

Construction
Explaining new concepts and ideas.

The input-teacher led/ pupil led?

- New information - keep it to 10 - 15mins max.
- Hook with examples or a story.
- Use visuals.
- Stick to the point.

Lesson planning – the house model

Chapter 3
It's all in the classroom

THE CLASSROOM ENVIRONMENT	35
CLASSROOM COHESION	38
NEW CLASS	41
THE SENSORY ENVIRONMENT	44
THE PHYSICAL ENVIRONMENT	47
RELATIONSHIPS AND BEHAVIOUR	50
LANGUAGE AND BEHAVIOUR	53
USING SUPPORT STAFF EFFECTIVELY	56

USING PEER SUPPORT	59
CHOICE, CHALLENGE AND COMPETITION	62
LEARNING STATIONS	65
PRACTICAL WORK	68
VOCABULARY	71
TALKING	74
MODELLING	77
ACCESSIBLE QUESTIONING	80
GIVING INSTRUCTIONS	83
SIGNPOSTING TRANSITIONS	86
WHITEBOARDS OF ALL SORTS	89
MANAGING TEXT	92
NUMERACY	95
ACCESSIBLE ICT	98
PROPS – CONCRETE AND VISUAL	101
READING	104
WRITING	107
ALTERNATIVES TO WRITING	110
WRITING FRAMES	113
MIND MAPS	116
STORIES	119
GAMES	122

It's all in the classroom

The classroom environment

Context

Vulnerable pupils are very sensitive to the teacher's mood and can feel very unsettled if they think the teacher is feeling sad or angry. The welcome the teacher offers can be key to setting the tone for the lesson. It helps to plan the classroom environment as much as you plan the lesson. Pupils like to know what to expect. They like to know where they sit and how the lesson is going to pan out. Pupils are also affected by sensory and physical needs. Before pupils of any age can learn, it is useful to think about how you are going to meet their basic needs such as comfort and safety.

If you are lucky enough to have your own teaching space, you can control the layout and setup. If you are a roving teacher, it is still worth tweaking the room when you get there. Basics like light, temperature and sound will affect pupils, especially if they are distractible or hungry. All pupils should have a visible line to the teacher, so look out for blind spots and seats where pupils can 'hide'. Have a variety of layouts for different classes or activities, and train the pupils to move the furniture efficiently. A few minutes putting the room in the layout you want is time well spent. Classroom routines are important to pupils as they set up expectations that feel safe. Reinforce your routines and practise them until the pupils know them. Display the lesson structure by writing it up on the whiteboard or using a slide. Many pupils feel reassured knowing the sequence of the lesson in that they can prepare themselves for what's going to happen, and this consequently reduces anxiety. For vulnerable groups, have set places for equipment and books to create a sense of belonging.

Consider

- Displays should be linked to curriculum and contain useful props like key words, exemplars and sentence starters to increase pupil independence. Busy displays can overwhelm pupils with sensory processing needs, so keep things simple and use hook-and-loop fasteners or washing lines to vary the resources rather than cover every wall. Inspirational prop tables are great to provide concrete hands-on exploration.

Copyright material from Rachel Cosgrove (2020), Inclusive Teaching in a Nutshell, Routledge

It's all in the classroom

- Carousel activities need prior planning for pupils who struggle with instructions and literacy. Some individual pupils may need their own workstation with some activities of choice, headphones and/or a computer and some diversion materials – sensory toys, calm box or art materials.

- Vary where in the class you teach from. To get a class really focussed, gather them round close or try a boardroom setup. Lighting and sound can make a difference; to calm a class down, dim the lights, play soft music and lower your voice.

- If you move to a different classroom for every lesson, set up a calming task for the first 5 minutes to enable you to get the register done and arrange things as you want. Low-demand tasks work best – revising key words, card matching or reading, copying definitions from a slide or board. Creating a working atmosphere will pay off in more focussed time later.

 ## Reflect

Do some classes work better in certain rooms? Why is this? Is it the size or sound quality of the room? Is it where the teacher's desk is? If you know you have a class that needs a certain room because of their needs, ask your timetable lead.

It's all in the classroom

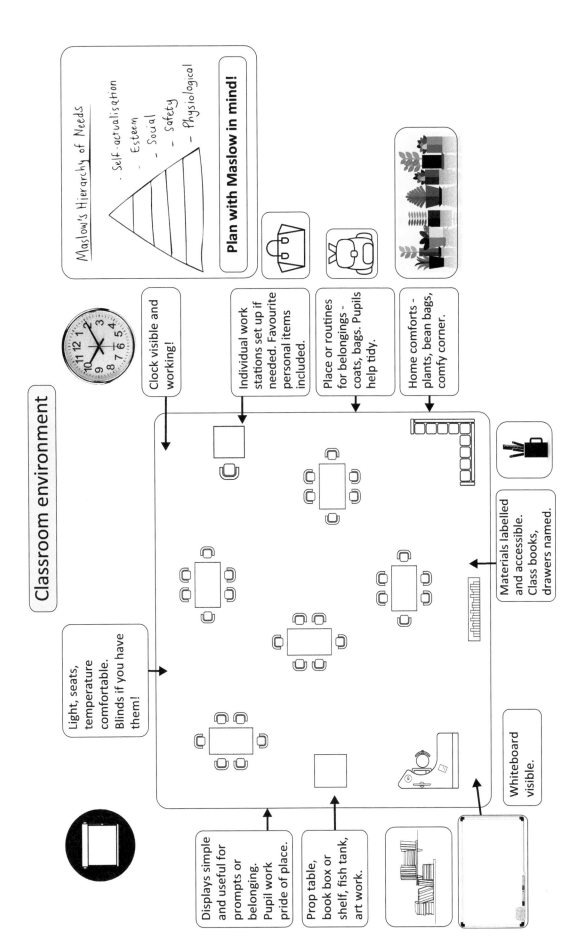

It's all in the classroom

Classroom cohesion

 **Context**

Classroom cohesion is about generating a positive atmosphere in class where all pupils accept a level of challenge and have the confidence to contribute. Learning is a social activity, and teamwork benefits all pupils. Vulnerable pupils especially gain from increased collaboration in class, as peer-to-peer learning can act as additional support. Many pupils with special needs and/or disabilities and differences encounter peer issues at school. They may have experienced bullying and social isolation, or they may be developing awareness about their differences and feel that they don't fit in. Low self-esteem, poor self-image and low confidence can have a massive influence over a pupil's attitude towards learning. The teacher sets the tone, and the classroom culture you develop will make all the difference in how pupils respond to each other. Be explicit about the culture you are aiming for, both in terms of learning and socially. Teachers who celebrate and nurture successes and mistakes will have the kind of classrooms where all pupils feel safe and valued. An inclusive classroom is a place where it is recognised that everyone is unique and that the only way to be fair is to consider individual needs. There is a difference between equal and fair, and you will need to explain this ethos to pupils.

The culture you want may take time to develop, so plan to gradually share responsibility within class. Praise specific actions that pupils take that are in line with your classroom ethos. For some classes it may take a long time to embed exactly what you want, and there may be setbacks on the way. Keep your body language open and stay optimistic.

 Consider

Teaching style is unique and individual, but there are some general approaches that are worth trying.

- Get to know the class and help them learn about each other using personal and social development activities, but be sensitive about pupils with difficult home circumstances, as sharing information may not be easy or appropriate.

- Using a growth mindset approach – celebrate struggle.

- Teamwork – Vary groups and pairs and set up activities that depend on teams or partners working together to achieve.

It's all in the classroom

- ◆ Roles and responsibilities – Share leadership in class and delegate roles for vulnerable pupils that will suit their skills/interests or raise their status.

- ◆ Social interaction opportunities will help bonds in class – make opportunities to be social together, both in and outside the class.

- ◆ Community – Invite visitors to class who can share history or a skill, or do something as a class for the community.

- ◆ Starting the day or lesson with an anchoring activity can create a safe routine that helps pupils feel settled in your class.

- ◆ Recognition – Celebrate successes, e.g., have a recognition board in class. Make it inclusive by monitoring *who* is recognised and highlighting small successes as well as significant ones, display everyone's work (however well presented) and maybe let pupils put it up!

- ◆ Feedback – Let pupils have a voice in class but frame it as feedback on routines or activities, rather than person (teacher or peer) related.

- ◆ Laugh – a lot. Bring jokes into learning, laugh at yourself, tell stories, share mistakes with humour and show pupils we can laugh **with**, not at, one another.

Reflect

How far are you willing to delegate responsibility to pupils? It isn't about losing control but about developing leadership in your pupils, whatever their age or ability. Start small and adapt according to the needs of the class.

It's all in the classroom

Classroom cohesion

Pupil ownership through chances to contribute such as class blog, suggestions box, pupils choose rewards, digital surveys, class discussion of rules and expectations, class council, table or group leaders as spokespeople. Make sure reluctant pupils are asked directly or method of contribution adapted.

Groups doing things that scaffold social interaction such as field trips, cooperative tasks, creating art in groups, doing a problem-solving challenge, games, tidying the class, gardening, looking after a class pet, fundraising for charity, doing a school assembly, golden time choices. Support if needed.

Design personal and class shields, 'find someone who' questions, life story comic strips, birthday wishes. Interview teacher and pupils. Show and tell. Stories. Relate topics to people to develop a caring culture. Table of interesting objects. Share and display accomplishments. Pupils present topics of interest.

Vary roles and responsibilities so everyone gets a go. Buddy up some roles so peers can support. Use peer marking but adapt to include everyone. Label resources in room to support day to day jobs. Use visuals to support jobs e.g. prompt cards, tick lists.

Vulnerable pupils need careful groupings. Be aware of pupils who prefer working alone. Use support staff to observe rather than intervene. Set team task and train pupils in group work skills. Work alongside vulnerable pupils to encourage participation. Class motto.

Classroom cohesion

It's all in the classroom

New class

Context

For many pupils, going into a new class with a teacher they haven't met before is incredibly daunting. Teachers, too, may have some anxieties about meeting a new class for the first time. Many pupils with special needs and/or unpredictable home circumstances will be wary of change. What will it be like? Will the teacher be relaxed or strict? Will the teacher make lessons okay? Pupils want to feel safe in the knowledge that you will have boundaries, will make learning accessible and support them so that they can feel comfortable in class. We don't want to pre-judge pupils, but preparation is important, so read any information available or ask colleagues to put you in the picture. Progress and attainment data are also a good place to start, but it is worth checking other sources of information to get a more rounded picture of pupils. Make sure you get access to any pupil profiles to find out what works for individual pupils and how best to plan for them. Support staff may know the vulnerable pupils well, and previous class teachers often have great insight about individual pupils who will benefit from you knowing their needs and potential emotional or sensory triggers.

Planning the first few lessons to include 'getting to know you' activities will help you get a feel for a group. Organise the room how it might work for the group and for individual pupils. If any pupils need physical adaptations, plan for them from the start. Pupils will feel welcomed and valued if little adjustments have been made for them.

Consider

- Meet and greet the class at the door and chat to individual pupils who may need a quiet word to settle them.

- In the first few meetings with the new class, get to know names quickly, as this is a powerful tool for relationships and classroom management.

- Pupils like to know routines and some pupils struggle with getting them right, so explain and display your expectations and refer to them frequently to reinforce the learning.

- Class teachers and form tutors often use icebreakers to learn about their pupils. As a subject teacher it is also worth investing time in relationship building, because many pupils will engage with a task if the teacher can link it to an interest they have.

- Body language and gestures will make a big impression on pupils. Humans have a mirror neurone system which activates when we see or do something. They allow us to tune in to others' emotions. Having a positive attitude, even with tricky classes, will influence the emotions of the pupils positively. Smiling is a great tool to use.

- Be flexible with the seating plan and formalise it when you get to know the class chemistry.

- If a teaching assistant works in your class, ask them to observe and give feedback on the dynamics of the class and the interactions early on.

- If you have anxious pupils, or pupils who appear angry or disengaged, spend additional time building a relationship with them.

- For pupils with big barriers to classroom learning, arrange to meet them before the first lesson to provide reassurance.

Reflect

Do you have school dreams (or nightmares) before a new term? Most of us have new-year wobbles about new classes, so reflect on how this feels for pupils, too.

If you have a potentially challenging class to meet, are there strategies you can use to give yourself confidence?

It's all in the classroom

New class

- Pupils like routines
- Pupils like to know where they sit, how the teacher is going to be and who is in their class.
- Pupils need to know whether the work will be OK or too hard/easy.
- Pupils need to know if the room is light, has a smell, is cramped or spacious and if the route to the class is hard to negotiate.
- Pupils need to know if the teacher is kind, strict, flexible or scary.

All these things can make kids nervous, wary or anxious about change…

CHANGE: can be very difficult for many pupils.

Be prepared - know the needs and strengths of the pupils and think ahead about *small adjustments* that would make a difference to individuals.

How staff can help settle vulnerable pupils into a new year…

Expectations - tell them you have heard great things and that you know they will be brilliant-target the pupils needing support for an extra positive quiet word.

Explain your routines and have them displayed - let the pupils develop the class rules.

Give a short overview of the topic and timelines and what sort of work will be expected. Put the lesson plan on the board.

Plan the seating plan and meet pupils at the door.

New class

It's all in the classroom

The sensory environment

 ### Context

We all use our senses to literally 'make sense' of the world around us. Our nervous system receives messages from the environment via our senses and responds to stimuli. This is what we call sensory processing or sensory integration. We have the five basic senses – touch, smell, sight, hearing and taste – but we also have three other senses: vestibular (balance and spatial awareness), proprioception (being aware of where our body is) and interoception (internal bodily sensations). Our senses are taking in numerous stimuli all the time so we have to choose which sensation to pay attention to at any moment, process this sensation and choose a response. We tune into sensory inputs by their volume, i.e., how strong an input is, and by discrimination, i.e., the type of input.

Some of us are oversensitive to certain stimuli, and some of us are underresponsive to certain stimuli. We are all 'tuned in' differently. Some children have great difficulties with this tuning and can be sensory seeking or sensory avoiding. Some pupils in school may have significant difficulties with sensory processing and need support managing in class. You may notice that some pupils seem to be drawn to loud noises and constantly tap or hum. Others may dislike sticky activities like painting, cooking or using glue. Some pupils may want to chew all the time or put things in their mouths. Pupils who get stomachaches may be responding to the sensations in their gut that may be triggered by anxiety, excitement or sadness. Underresponsive pupils need energising, and other pupils need calming. Observing pupils and seeing what their behaviours are showing is the first step in working out how their senses are feeding back to them. Teachers can be alert to sensory processing needs by using different approaches in the classroom including low lighting, soft or energising music, different voice tone, movement breaks and calming activities such as breathing and stretching. Some pupils may need specific activities as part of a 'sensory diet' to help them learn to integrate sensory information.

 ### Consider

- Structure and routines support pupils with sensory processing difficulties.

- Think about reducing the information coming **at** pupils by limiting how many senses are having to work at the same time, e.g., model a practical activity visually but don't talk, or explain a concept with a simple visual image to back up the oral explanation, rather than a lot of text on the board.

It's all in the classroom

- It is a good idea to have a sensory toolkit to hand that might include some sensory toys or materials for pupils who are fidgeting or chewing their pens, etc.

- Most classes will benefit from movement breaks, but some pupils will need them frequently as part of their routine.

- Cleaning tables or the whiteboard is a great calming activity for energised children.

- Allow headphones for pupils who need to block out sound in order to focus.

- If the activities in class do involve sensory experiences that some pupils don't enjoy, don't force the issue. It is often the anticipation of an uncomfortable experience that will raise anxiety levels. It may be that you can get around the issue by thinking creatively about ways to participate.

 ## Reflect

Put yourself in the pupil's shoes. Which sensory experiences would you avoid? Do you hate certain foods or sounds? Would you avoid a laser light show or a stadium concert?

It's all in the classroom

The sensory environment

Light reflections, glare and bright sunlight can be distracting. Pupils may be sensitive to artificial lights - neon strip lighting can buzz. Consider window blinds, filters, turning down brightness on screens. Coloured paper or acetate filters can cut the glare from white paper. Busy displays can overwhelm. Less is more on walls.

Tactile sensory experiences vary. Some pupils hate uniform because they can't bear the texture and fit of clothes. Be aware of ties and shirt collars as some pupils may find these really uncomfortable. Have alternatives for activities involving touching unusual materials like using gloves, working in a pair, observing.

Smell is incredibly evocative and can trigger emotional memories. Try to keep classrooms fragrance free. If using smell in activities pre-warn sensitive pupils and dilute the smell.

Some pupils may need a 'getting away from it all' space. Bean bags, teachers chair, blankets and even a pop-up tent can provide comforting sensory experiences in class.

Noises have complexity of pitch, volume and pattern. Plan for pupils who are uncomfortable with loud noises. Think voice clarity. For potentially noisy activities, give pupils a choice by pre-warning, offering ear defenders or standing outside the class.

It can be hard to filter out background noise. Think about the acoustics - soften hard surfaces with material or carpet or 3D displays. For pupils who are stimulated by noise; tapping can be irritating to others so build in movement breaks, drama games or planned clapping.

Introduce new **tastes** gradually - never force a pupil to taste anything. Pre-warn pupils and use other senses to explore the food or drink first. Build up to tasting over a period of time.

Balance and coordination activities will support vestibular and proprioceptive skills. Practice describing movement. Use props to help teach right/left. Build in movement activities on the carpet or at tables – 'Simon says' games, warm up exercises.

The sensory environment

The physical environment

Context

Physical difficulties can impact some or all activities in school. Pupils with physical difficulties will have individual and varied needs, but the general areas in which they will need support relate to coordination; balance, posture and mobility; grasping and manipulating objects; and perceptual and spatial skills. Just getting around the school site may present challenges. Pupils may get tired as they use a lot of energy throughout the day to do the things that other pupils do without a problem. Alongside the specific physical barrier, pupils may have missed periods of school, and may also be managing the emotional load of their specific challenges. Day-to-day tasks in school such as carrying supplies around, getting to and from classrooms, using the washroom and accessing class activities will need to be thought out so that pupils are not disadvantaged. Some pupils will also be battling with people's assumptions about what they can and can't do. There is real risk that confidence has taken a battering, and dependency on adult support can lead to social and academic isolation. Older school buildings are often not set up well for accessibility, so it is important that staff plan for adaptions and adjustments in good time, so that pupils are not facing last-minute or awkward situations where their access needs have not been well considered.

There are obvious adjustments that are needed such as ramps, adjustable tables, lever taps, special equipment for practical work and support for mobility; however, it is often the day-to-day adjustments that are overlooked. For example, not all classrooms are tidy and well organised. Cluttered classes with bags and paraphernalia on the floor or in corridors can be a risk for pupils with coordination or mobility issues. Timetabling can cause problems when subjects are timetabled in rooms upstairs or classes are swapped. Think about how it must feel if as a pupil you are sent to work elsewhere with a teaching assistant because they cannot get to the room.

Consider

- If pupils are arriving late or leaving early, plan the activity timing and homework so they don't miss out, or set up a buddy system so peers can be primed to explain the task.

It's all in the classroom

- Think about the layout of the classroom so the pupil can get access both to you, the teacher, and to their peers. If teaching assistant support is available, think about where the adult sits, so they don't act as an obstacle to peer interaction.

- Train the class to put bags well under desks and keep routes clear.

- If the pupil needs certain equipment – ergonomic seat, cushion, writing slope – think about how it is going to be stored or carried between classes. In larger schools, equipment can often be mislaid or tampered with by other pupils if not stored carefully.

- The pupil may need prepared notes or alternative ways to record work. Prepare resources and share lesson planning prior to the lesson with adults who are supporting the pupil.

- Any offsite trips should be planned with accessibility in mind. It may be a challenge to find appropriate transport, so plan this early on.

 Reflect

Think about how the pupil sees the world and walk the class or school with their abilities in mind. Is there equipment or software that you could learn to use so you can work more effectively with the pupil? How can you include diverse role models and materials in lessons to challenge the stereotypes of physical difficulties?

It's all in the classroom

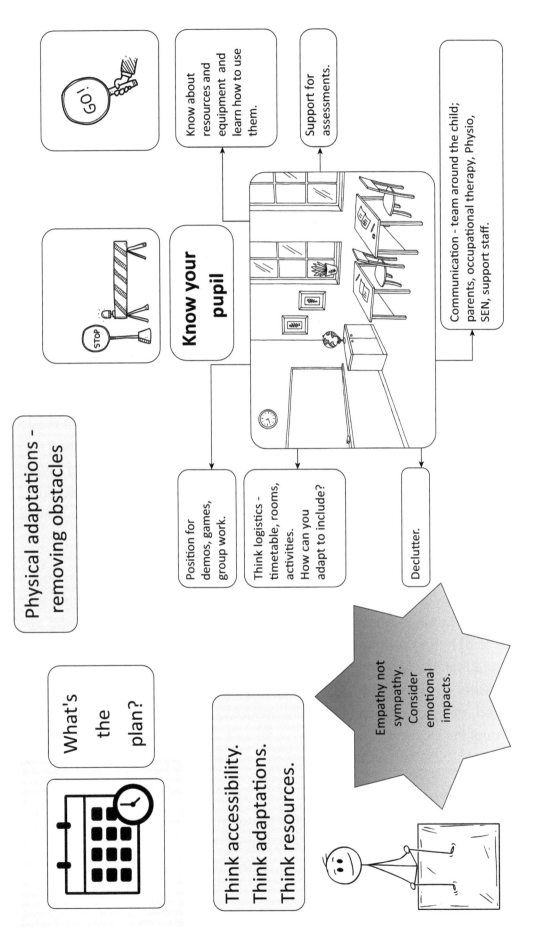

- Know about resources and equipment and learn how to use them.
- Support for assessments.
- Communication - team around the child; parents, occupational therapy, Physio, SEN, support staff.
- Position for demos, games, group work.
- Think logistics - timetable, rooms, activities. How can you adapt to include?
- Declutter.

Know your pupil

Physical adaptations - removing obstacles

What's the plan?

Think accessibility.
Think adaptations.
Think resources.

Empathy not sympathy. Consider emotional impacts.

The physical environment

It's all in the classroom

Relationships and behaviour

Context

Pupils will be more receptive to learning well when classrooms are calm and skilfully managed. Behaviour is one of the ways through which pupils communicate unmet needs. Behaviour is contextual and interactive. The developmental stage of a pupil will have a huge bearing on the emotional regulation skills they have acquired. Most behaviour issues in class will be masking a need; emotional or social, or linked to comprehension or literacy needs. The behaviour may be telling us that the pupil is feeling ashamed, threatened, or embarrassed or is seeking reassurance or power through attention. Pupils' sense of belonging can be nurtured or unravelled by the nature of their relationship with the teacher. The teacher sets the tone of the lesson, and inclusive teaching goes far beyond adapting the curriculum. The most effective teachers can be consistent and predictable whilst sensitively adapting their classroom management to adjust to the chronological and emotional age of pupils. Most pupils need to feel that the teacher cares and can keep them safe: spending time understanding individual pupils will pay off in terms of being able to influence their responses.

Underpinning the development of relationships is preparation – lesson planning, knowledge of pupils' needs and setting up expectations clearly while allowing for the fact that some pupils may need a more flexible approach to succeed. Read pupil profiles, talk to SEN and pastoral staff and look at the scheme of work to see how you can ensure that any obvious triggers are avoided. Pupils like it when they can see that a teacher has taken their needs and interests into account. When lessons are well paced, deftly organised and scaffolded well, there is less wiggle room for pupils to disrupt the learning.

Consider

- Learn names early and glean information about pupils' interests, strengths and weaknesses. It is helpful to greet pupils by name at the door or as they come in. Try to talk to pupils outside of lesson time, especially the pupils you need most to get on your side.

It's all in the classroom

- Try and find out potential triggers. Scan and observe. Being vigilant about things that you know will cause issues will help nip things in the bud before possible conflict can spark.

- Shouting can be uncomfortable for many pupils; avoiding this will create a more respectful and safer environment. At times you may lose your cool, but if you can acknowledge with the class when this happens, you can model how to manage emotions.

- Try and learn empathic listening; this is good for clarifying and solving problems collaboratively without blame.

- Use non-verbal body language well – The teachers' handy toolkit of gestures and glances includes the raised eyebrow and sustained stern look which often goes by the name the 'Paddington' stare, after the eponymous bear from Michael Bond's books.

- Humour – Avoid sarcasm, but well-timed laughs are a great energiser and fantastic at defusing stressful situations.

- Fresh-start approach – Every lesson or every task, try to always expect the best and give pupils opportunities to do the right thing at every chance; some pupils may need a lot of chances.

- Restorative approaches – Protect the relationship and give the pupil and adult a way to repair and rebuild.

- Tag with another colleague – If things are going awry, step away before the relationship is compromised.

Reflect

Do you find yourself taking pupil behaviour personally? Behaviour can stem from complex unmet needs and may take its toll on teachers' emotional energy. Remember that the pupil may be bringing all sorts of issues into school that you cannot control. Elicit support from your team.

It's all in the classroom

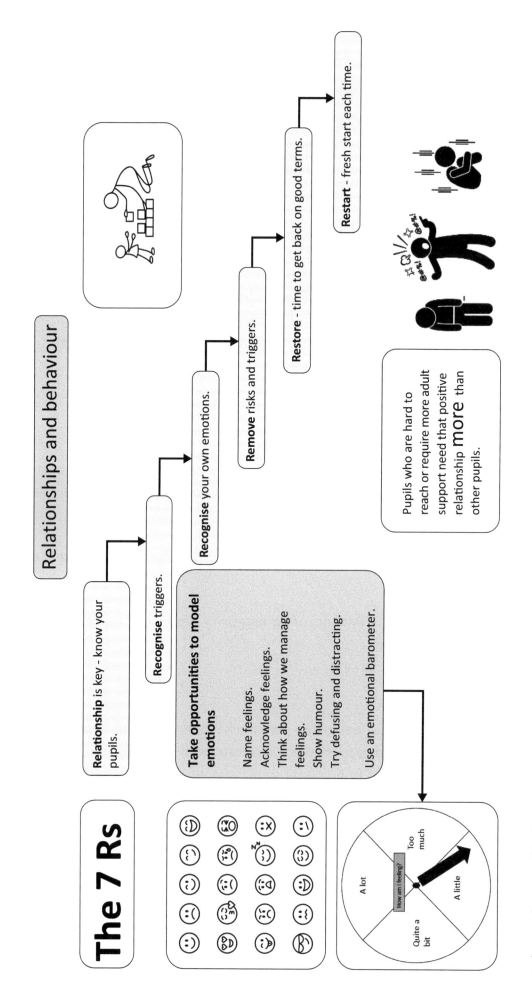

Relationships and behaviour

The 7 Rs

- **Relationship** is key - know your pupils.
- **Recognise** triggers.
- **Recognise** your own emotions.
- **Remove** risks and triggers.
- **Restore** - time to get back on good terms.
- **Restart** - fresh start each time.

Take opportunities to model emotions
- Name feelings.
- Acknowledge feelings.
- Think about how we manage feelings.
- Show humour.
- Try defusing and distracting.
- Use an emotional barometer.

Pupils who are hard to reach or require more adult support need that positive relationship MORE than other pupils.

Relationships and behaviour

It's all in the classroom

Language and behaviour

Context

Language is a powerful priming tool. Language can be positive and optimistic. Language can be emotive and misunderstood. What we say in class has a direct bearing on the emotional responses of our pupils and the likelihood of cooperation. Many pupils who struggle to manage school expectations probably have low self-esteem and will have experienced negativity at school and home. Negative language reinforces their already fragile self-image, and language that is unclear or ambiguous can be confusing and can unsettle pupils who need boundaries to help them feel safe and secure in school. Using negative language primes pupils into a conflict situation. Language that implies that you don't expect compliance can also be a problem, as it can weaken assertiveness and set up a power struggle between pupil and teacher. Avoid asking a pupil why they are doing a behaviour – the chances are that they will have no idea. Frame your language around the behaviour you **want to see**. Actions such as a smile, a thumbs-up and a 'thanks' will redirect pupils towards positive choices – hopefully!

When giving directions in class, it is important to think about how clear and specific the instructions are. Literal thinkers will need unambiguous language, without idioms or colloquialisms. For some pupils, such as those on the autistic spectrum, requests will need to be cued in by name. Stand still to allow pupils to focus, and be specific, **positive** and clear about what you **want** pupils to do (not what you don't want them to do). Allow take-up time so the direction can be processed. When teachers expect compliance and promote good choices through clear directions, they are creating an environment where behaviour is part of the learning process and mistakes are an opportunity to reflect and reset.

Consider

There are three useful strategies that can be amazingly effective when used well:

◆ For helping to steer resistant pupils in the right direction, try the 'broken record' technique. State positively what you want a pupil to do and wait; repeat the instruction and expect compliance, adding a 'thanks' and repeat again if needed. When you repeat the same words, **the pattern-recognition ability of the brain** eventually notices that something is being repeated. The key to this technique is to be calmly persistent but not to show irritation!

It's all in the classroom

- ◆ Language of choice. Provide the pupil with two or three choices, all of which are appropriate and on your terms in that whichever option is chosen results in on-task behaviour. This gives pupils back a sense of control and an opportunity **not** to go into battle. It places the responsibility for the behaviour choice with the pupil. It takes the wind out of a potential emotive standoff.

- ◆ Catching pupils making good choices and specifically praising them works well for all ages and can be used to teach self-regulation. Most pupils seek affirmation, so praising on-task behaviours has a ripple effect, because pupils see what is required to receive praise and follow suit. It works because it reinforces your expectations and gives attention to the pupils living up to your expectations.

 Reflect

Do you hear yourself coming out with phrases that escalate behaviour or that pupils ignore? Ask a colleague to observe the language you use with specific pupils. If you notice you overuse negative or less assertive phrases, it may be helpful to write some 'scripts' to use to reinforce phrases you think will work best.

It's all in the classroom

Language and behaviour scripts

Broken record

'Adam, you're talking. Adam, you're talking. Thanks. Listening, good.'

'Coats off please. Coat off Gibby. Coat off Gibby. Gibby, coat please. Thanks'.

'I need you to leave the room. Yes, I know that, and I need you to leave the room.
Off you go. Thanks'.

'Jed, you're sitting here. Sitting here. Over you come, sitting here. Thanks. Great stuff.'

Language of choice

'James, you can either work quietly by yourself or you can come up and sit with me.'

'You can settle and do the task, or you can work next door with Mr Hollies.'

'Great idea Ali, how are you going to type this; in different colours or in bullet points?'

'Shall I write the title for you and you do the opening sentence, or do you want to do both yourself?'

Positive acknowledgement

'Luke - thanks for listening - thank you.'

'Harry, Jodie and Seth have all started the task already. Brilliant. Well done you lot.'

'Tom - you have waited to be asked, excellent- what would you like to say?'

'Louis is ready to start, well done. Sam, also ready, thank you.'

'Aiysha has done 2 questions already - fantastic.'

Language and behaviour scripts

It's all in the classroom

Using support staff effectively

 Context

A well-trained, effectively deployed teaching assistant (TA) is a great support for teachers who are developing their inclusive practice. TAs are used in a variety of ways by schools and differ in the way they are deployed across different pupil age ranges. We know that teachers lack training in knowing how to use TAs effectively, and that TAs are often spending a lot of their time with the most vulnerable learners – those learners who need access to good teaching the most. TAs often have a great deal of knowledge about pupils they work with, and in collaboration with teachers can help adapt the curriculum and improve access to learning.

TAs are most effective when they have time to discuss pupils and tasks with the teacher, when they know what the learning intentions are and when they are trained in pedagogical approaches such as open questioning. When TAs are mainly focussed on task completion, pupils experience shallow learning and often show learned helplessness because they wait until the TA steps in. If teachers have TA support with their classes, it is important to plan for the work the TA does. Making time to collaborate can be tricky in busy schools but if you can make any time to communicate, the effort will pay off in the classroom as the TA will come prepared and with a good idea of how to help scaffold the lesson.

TA styles of working tend to be either like a helicopter, roving the class and prompting several pupils; or like glue, sticking to one or two pupils and sitting alongside. Neither of these approaches is as effective as the **scaffolder** style. Scaffolders facilitate learning by liaising with the teacher; helping the pupils make connections with their peers, the teacher and the task; and by removing obstacles to learning while probing and questioning to deepen understanding.

 Consider

- Learn the names of TAs and find out who is supporting your classes, and what the plans are for cover if TAs are away. Don't be embarrassed if you can't remember names – ask again. Develop a relationship with your TA. If they are more experienced than you, get them on your side and use their knowledge.

It's all in the classroom

- Share learning plans with TAs ahead of time. Discuss how you might differentiate content and resources for pupils.

- If possible, give the TA time to prepare additional resources.

- If your TA is running an intervention, make sure you are kept fully informed about progress and that you regularly review and plan next steps.

- In class, direct TAs; the teacher could work with high-needs pupils while the TA roves the class. Try to avoid TAs being glued to one place in class.

- Share pupil plans with the TA – perhaps note down key questions for them to use, annotate the lesson plan or model how you want them to work.

- If TAs talk during whole-class explanation, understand why they might feel they need to talk to pupils who are unfocused, but clearly insist on total quiet.

- Ask your TA for feedback about pupil progress during or after the lesson. TAs are sometimes uncomfortable giving feedback because they are worried that teachers will think it's not their place – keep feedback focussed on pupil progress and how this will inform next steps.

Reflect

Are you relying on the TA to differentiate by outcome – i.e., if you have a TA, do you hope that **they** will adapt the task? Use their expertise, but remember that the teacher is responsible for the curriculum content.

It's all in the classroom

Using support staff effectively

TOP 10 TA Strategies!

What can support staff do to scaffold learning?

Emotional readiness
TAs build relationships with pupils and offer reassurance, safety and encouragement in class.

Provide pupil with learning strategies
TAs can suggest ways for the pupil to tackle a task - helping pupils start and build their confidence.

Providing props
TAs can help make something visual or concrete by providing visuals or by introducing real examples to aid conceptual understanding.

Testing
TAs can test understanding through questions, observing the pupil and by setting challenges.

Support literacy
TAs can read, scribe, explain text and provide spellings to help pupils access text.

Scaffolding
A key strategy TAs can use is to scaffold a task by providing starter sentences, grids, lines on the page, key sentences or words, or talking through with the pupil.

Questioning
Asking varied questions helps pupils verbalise what they know. Questioning to break down the task into learning steps can deepen understanding and clarify meaning.

Feedback
TAs provide relevant feedback to pupils on how they are progressing - correcting errors, encouraging and helping pupils extend what they can do and know.

Repetition
Repeating the task, rewording or re-explaining an idea can help the pupil remember/ focus or understand better.

Modelling
TAs show the pupil how to do something by doing the task themselves - modelling what the expectations are for the pupil. Pupils can see what they are being asked to do explicitly and practically.

Using support staff effectively

It's all in the classroom

Using peer support

Context

There are so many reasons to embrace peer support in the classroom. We learn by observing others and engaging in reciprocal interactions. Watching others do a task fires up our mirror neurones and enables us to mimic and build our own repertoire of skills. Learning from more competent peers is great for pupils, as their peers can often pitch the task at the right level, give more relevant examples and use age-appropriate language. When pupils explain tasks or concepts to each other, they are using higher-order thinking skills such as synthesis and evaluation; memories are reinforced and consequently, the learning is more meaningful. An additional benefit is that peer teaching allows pupils to learn others' varied perspectives and incorporate these into the way they see themselves. Both the 'tutee' and the 'tutor' benefit.

To make peer support work, planning should provide structure so that the 'tutor' has a framework. Peer support works best when it is used as a consolidation of material; revision of previously taught material; working on facts and core skills the class has learned; or as reading support. Vulnerable learners gain specifically from this type of support. When pupils are supporting each other, **they** are doing the work, rather than the adults, and peers are likely to hold their classmates to account. Paired seating becomes a form of differentiation, because pupils have an immediate source of support.

It is valuable for pupils to look at peer work. Providing exemplars from the class; displaying work live to the class; getting pupils to work on the teacher's computer, live on the board or using pupils to plan parts of lessons; are all opportunities for peers to learn from each other. If you have developed a caring culture in class, pupils will value contributions by all abilities of learners and be willing to support each other.

An inclusive idea is to develop peer leaders in class – e.g., maths experts, spelling ambassadors, dinosaur specialists, space connoisseurs. These peers can impart specific knowledge or lead group work. Many pupils with additional needs may have a great capacity for facts, so this would be a lovely way to enable them to contribute.

Consider

- ◆ Train pupils to use peer support strategies – expect that it may take time to develop and it may go wrong at times. Be flexible with pair dynamics to see what works.

It's all in the classroom

- The 'expert' in a group is another idea, where you give some pupils time to learn something and they teach the rest of the class by rotating round the groups. If you vary the topic, you can include pupils working at a lower level as leaders, because repeating the same topic is fantastic for memorising content and boosts confidence if successful.

- Be very explicit about what you are asking peers to teach.

- Make sure you provide easy and clear resources.

- Reward the efforts peer tutors make – praising cooperation and teamwork recognises and reinforces social skills.

- Be sensitive about pairs; look out for any bullying behaviours. Some pupils may not want to work this way so either use adult support, give the pupil a whole-class role or set up an independent task.

 Reflect

Are you worried about peer tutoring not stretching some pupils at the expense of others? Try it out and evaluate it in your class. Greater engagement is a winner for everyone, and teaching is the best way to learn something!

It's all in the classroom

Using peer support

Pairs and groups

Ideas for setting up peer support include:

- Investigate older pupils as peer mentors/tutors.
- Choose pairs carefully (friendships work well) and train pupils to get into pairings quickly.
- **Swap pairs for different tasks.**
- Use 'think, pair, share' and 'tell your partner' 'talk partners'.
- **Vary groupings - mixed, ability, interest, random.**
- Vary the level of tasks for different groups.
- **Be sensitive to pupils who struggle to work with others.**
- Group leaders -jigsaw, snowball, fishbowl and expert group ideas.
- **Peer modelling of answers, writing on board.**
- Peer support for practical tasks -give roles.
- Peers as experts/leaders in curriculum or social skills.

Resources

Ideas for props include:

- **Flash cards with key facts.**
- A mini script with questions and answers.
- **Materials pupils are using are written in clear and easy to read language.**
- Pupil friendly mark schemes.
- **Visual cues.**
- If you use learning checklists for revision they need to be easily understood.
- **Give time signals.**
- Traffic light cards.
- **Posters, pen pots per group, ready cut images or key words.**
- Camera, access to ICT to record and present.

Using peer support

It's all in the classroom

Choice, challenge and competition

 Context

In order to achieve in school, pupils need to participate and engage. You will probably have observed pupils who have low academic aspirations, who rely heavily on adult coaxing or extrinsic rewards to complete tasks. These pupils may have previously struggled to access learning and subsequently feel they cannot achieve. This can result in gradual withdrawal of effort and eroding of self-belief. Praising pupils who then make half-hearted efforts to do a task can backfire, as well-meaning encouragement can inadvertently convey low expectations. All pupils seek acceptance, self-advocacy and recognition in some form. We need to think of ways to encourage pupils and try to generate a bit of excitement to increase engagement.

Three possible strategies are to use choice, challenge and competition. Pupils are motivated by doing something better and experiencing small successes, and it is less about tangible rewards and more about their experiences of overcoming a challenge. We need to show them *how* to achieve and narrate their success, so they can see their own improvements.

 Consider

- ◆ Trusting pupils to make choices gives them agency and helps develop their self-advocacy. You can provide choice around many aspects of learning, and you can set tasks so that whatever the pupil chooses still results in on-task engagement. It's about selling the task to convince pupils that they have some control over how they work. Choice can be about who to work with, which task to do first, choice of texts, format of a task, ways to complete a task, colours of pen, type and timing of rewards, etc.

- ◆ Challenges and goals motivate our brains; problem solving, puzzles and mysteries are good ways to deliver a task to pupils who need a higher level of engagement. The task itself could be a challenge, or you can sneak in challenges in any task. Set a time to achieve a task – e.g., 2 minutes to find 10 items, words, complete sums, etc. The other handy technique is to contrive a limit in a task – such as explain something in a tweet, make a mnemonic, in a set space on the page or using only certain materials. This is effective in many ways because it contracts the task into what appears to be a more manageable chunk, helping pupils perceive that they *can* do it. The limits force pupils to think outside the box, which galvanises their higher-order skills. It is a differentiated task by outcome, due to the fact that everyone can achieve at their own level, and it focusses and reduces the key learning points. Goals should be achievable and linked to content. You can vary the tasks according to ability.

- Any kind of competition can generate excitement and teamwork. Group challenges, team quizzes and buddy pair challenges can all be used to increase enthusiasm and bring out the competitive spirit in class. Prizes tend to heighten anxiety about winning, so try to either give small prizes/stickers to winning teams or just congratulate successes verbally and specifically praise achievement and team ethos or collaboration.

Sometimes an approach will work well but then the next time you try it, it won't! Monitor the mood of the class. Whatever you are trying out, present it with great enthusiasm, because the 'selling' of the task is very much part of engaging your pupils with the promise and anticipation of the activity.

Reflect

How can you personalise these approaches to the classes and age groups you work with?

It's all in the classroom

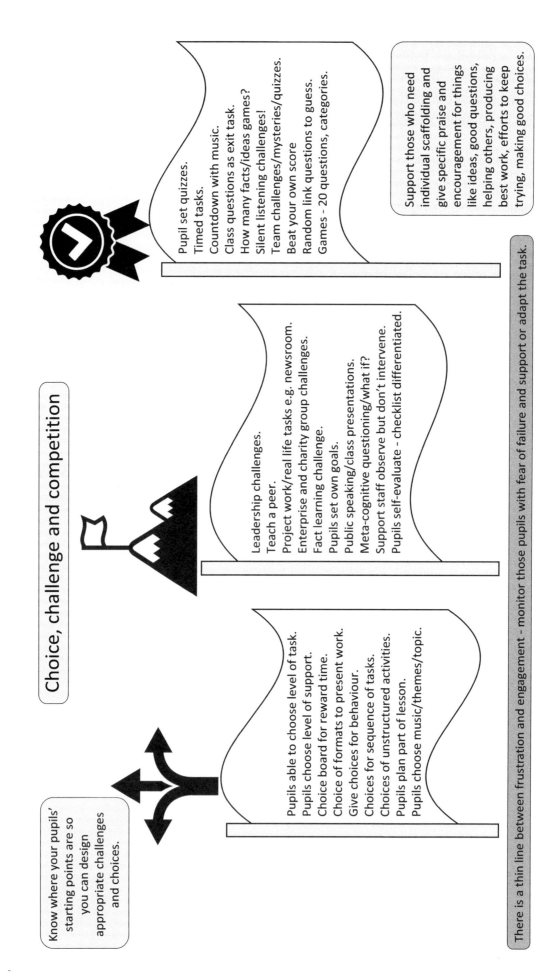

Choice, challenge and competition

Choice:
- Pupils able to choose level of task.
- Pupils choose level of support.
- Choice board for reward time.
- Choice of formats to present work.
- Give choices for behaviour.
- Choices for sequence of tasks.
- Choices of unstructured activities.
- Pupils plan part of lesson.
- Pupils choose music/themes/topic.

Know where your pupils' starting points are so you can design appropriate challenges and choices.

Challenge:
- Leadership challenges.
- Teach a peer.
- Project work/real life tasks e.g. newsroom.
- Enterprise and charity group challenges.
- Fact learning challenge.
- Pupils set own goals.
- Public speaking/class presentations.
- Meta-cognitive questioning/what if?
- Support staff observe but don't intervene.
- Pupils self-evaluate - checklist differentiated.

Competition:
- Pupil set quizzes.
- Timed tasks.
- Countdown with music.
- Class questions as exit task.
- How many facts/ideas games?
- Silent listening challenges!
- Team challenges/mysteries/quizzes.
- Beat your own score
- Random link questions to guess.
- Games - 20 questions, categories.

Support those who need individual scaffolding and give specific praise and encouragement for things like ideas, good questions, helping others, producing best work, efforts to keep trying, making good choices.

There is a thin line between frustration and engagement - monitor those pupils with fear of failure and support or adapt the task.

Choice, challenge and competition

It's all in the classroom

Learning stations

Context

You may occasionally have pupils who find it impossible to maintain concentration for long periods of time within a busy classroom. These pupils may have significant learning or social difficulties and require a more bespoke curriculum at times, or respite from the hustle and bustle of whole-class activities. Having some space set up and ready for a pupil is a great way to enable them to withdraw when they need time on their own or away from peers. The space can be set up either outside the classroom, if you have a suitable safe and supervised area, or can be within the classroom itself in the form of a learning station or 'workstation'.

A learning station is an individual pupil space – it could be a cosy corner or a desk which is set up with a key pupil in mind. It could be slightly screened from other pupils or facing a wall or window. The space should have equipment and resources adapted to an individual pupil – this might include headphones, art materials or colouring activities, puzzles or learning games for chillout time, books or computer access, folders of worksheets/activities, sensory toys or personal items that the pupil has chosen to bring in. You may want to use a learning station as an extension activity, and have it set up with higher-thinking tasks. The notion is that the pupil can use the learning station to work quietly or independently away from peers. A teaching assistant may support the use of the station, or the pupil may be able to use it effectively on their own. A visual timetable or task management board can help the pupil choose activities. If the pupil needs to use the space for calming down or de-stressing, a 'cool down box' could be incorporated. This is a box of any kind that holds chosen 'calm down' activities such as modelling clay, favourite books or fidget toys or anything that the pupil can use to help them self-regulate. Learning stations can support the inclusion of pupils with high levels of anxiety who benefit from class input, but struggle to work alongside peers all the time.

Learning stations can also be used in whole-class lessons in the form of a carousel of activities. I would advise modelling the task physically by demonstrating how each station works before starting, otherwise time will be wasted in explaining the task repeatedly to pupils who can't recall verbal instructions.

Consider

- For older pupils, a temporary learning station way of working could be incorporated into a subject classroom by using a seating plan strategically and by keeping a folder or box of key resources. A small whiteboard could then

Copyright material from Rachel Cosgrove (2020), Inclusive Teaching in a Nutshell, Routledge

It's all in the classroom

act as a task management board. A laptop set up with a propped box file as a screener would provide a useful quiet space. Headphones could be used to block out classroom sounds.

- ◆ Logistical planning of carousel activities is worth investing time in – especially if your pupils are not good at organising themselves or have poor literacy skills. If using a rotation of activities, set the stations up prior to starting, have clear instructions or labels, have the materials and props out and ready and group pupils carefully so that those needing support are with steady peers. If you have support, share the stations between you and your TA.

Reflect

Could you focus in a busy classroom? Maybe learning stations could be helpful for deep-thinking work.

It's all in the classroom

How to use a task management board

Bespoke board - paper, cards, sticky notes, laminated or whiteboard - 2-3 tasks listed.
Could be visual.
Could be choices.
'First-Then' cards.
Tasks could have times and limits.
Could be a checklist for routines.
Colour coded.
Rewards or stickers space or tick boxes.

Learning stations

- Position in room to minimise distraction and help pupil feel safe?
- How to store resources and activities?
- Adapting to sensory needs? Headphones? Soft material? Sensory toys?
- Access to ICT for adapted resources/extension/individual project work?
- How to manage chill out versus productive work? Timer? Check list? Adult support?
- Could set up as individual programme space. 1-1 work.
- Strategies for moving pupil on from learning station to another activity? Clear information about timing, 'when' and 'then' statements.

Learning stations

It's all in the classroom

Practical work

Context

Practical work provides concrete learning experiences for pupils. Pupils with additional needs can be very successful in practical work. Pupils with sensory, emotional or physical difficulties may need specific adjustments. Planning for specific pupils is important for practical subjects; likewise, practical activities within non-practical lessons will need a bit of thought. Anyone who has set up a cut-and-stick task with a class will have noticed the time it can take for some pupils to use scissors and glue correctly – or not! Pupils may have difficulties in carrying out practical tasks due to physical issues such as dexterity, strength, mobility or balance. Some pupils struggle with spatial skills – both moving around in space and conceptualising objects in space. You may need to think about sensory needs if you are doing a noisy activity or using different textures, smells or media. Practical tasks often prove challenging for pupils who don't get on with peers or who struggle to manage their attention or emotions. You will also need to think about the developmental age of your pupils, as practical work may involve a managed degree of risk. If some pupils can't follow directions or have a limited sense of danger, you will need to plan accordingly.

Consider

- Preparing ahead is the key to successful practical work. Think about the pupils in your class and visualise how they will manage the proposed task. Rewind to see which steps you need to take to remove any potential barriers or pitfalls.

- Pre-cut any worksheets that pupils need to cut and stick. You don't need to do this for everyone, but it will help the pace of the lesson. Support staff are a great help with this and can be cutting things up whilst you introduce the lesson if needed.

- Other things that may be helpful include weighing chemicals or ingredients out – if time is limited and the measuring techniques are not the main lesson objective.

- If you are using resources, having them laid out in the room or in sets for each table is a visual prompt and helps start the activity smoothly.

- Think about adapted equipment that might be needed and make sure it is available in the lesson – things like clamps for holding items to tables, high

It's all in the classroom

stools, adjustable tables, adapted tools or cooking implements, adapted PE items, chunky pens or brushes, wide grip scissors, etc.

- If the lesson is going to include sensory experiences, check that you have headphones, workstations set up; or if using tactile materials, you might need gloves or alternative ways to interact with items such as tongs or stirrers if pupils don't like to touch things with their hands.

- The task needs to be planned with strengths and needs in mind, and scaffolding may be needed in terms of adapting the task, providing adult or peer support, alternative strategies such as use of information and communication technology (ICT) and providing additional modelling or physical prompts.

- Make sure support staff or peer buddies are aiming for as much independence as possible.

- Plan in peer support and monitor any adult support so this doesn't become a barrier to peer interaction.

- Model the task and provide visual instructions.

- Make sure any practical work is started when the class is calm and you are sure that any reasonable risks are controlled. Know that you can stop the class if anyone is working unsafely.

Reflect

Would you consider changing a practical lesson to be truly inclusive – i.e., everyone plays seated volleyball?

It's all in the classroom

Practical work

Art
Choice of media.
Position - adjustable table, easel, slope, backed stool, access to materials.
Adapted materials - lightbox, larger pens, brushes.
Size and type of paper/board.
3D activities as alternatives - clay, modelling.
Support with outlines, trace, photocopy.

Music
Choice of media, genre, instruments.
Use electronic instruments.
Careful group support for composition activities.
Sensory needs - headphones, practice space, give notice when noise is to start.
Encourage participation and listening and be sensitive of pupils not wanting to perform.

Physical Education
Equipment adapted - softer balls, large bats, goals, nets, benches.
Consolidate basic skills.
Pupil medical plans in place.
Adapt court space.
Buddy/group support.
Change rules so everyone plays adapted game.
Have alternatives ready - pupils could referee, score, coach.

Technology
Adapted tools and workspace - adjustable benches, clamps.
Pre-cut materials.
Sensory needs - headphones, warning when machines on.
Risk assessment. Support for safety, but independence for making.
Physical prompts, physical support to ground the materials or provide guidance or extra force.

(Centre)
Have additional equipment and resources ready.
Plan groups and buddies.
Assess risks and adapt task if needed.
Direct support staff clearly.

Cooking
Equipment prepared and labelled or laid out ready.
Adaptable furniture used.
Ingredients could be weighed or pre-cut. Adapted equipment ready - clamps, tongs, gloves.
Adult support for safety - independence encouraged.
Recipe adapted re smell, taste, restricted diets.

Drama
How to make space feel safe-create boundaries/sensory spaces with furniture or material.
Sensitive groupings.
Build in characters accessible to all pupils-be sensitive about bullying.
Structure needed - timed activity, clear rules, noise levels.
Have clear prompts for transitions.

Science
Equipment prepared and labelled or laid out ready.
Pre-prepared recording sheets.
Clear instructions and rules for experiments.
Adult support for safety.
Model task more than once.
Chunk instructions.
Roles for buddy pairs.

It's all in the classroom

Vocabulary

Context

Receptive language is what we hear and read. Expressive language is what we say and write. A language-rich environment with discussion, play, books and experiences gives children a good start in their vocabulary development. The vocabulary we acquire is important to our ability to progress in school. Children with a smaller vocabulary will be limited in how they construct sentences – which in turn diminishes the opportunity for practising and developing spoken language. Children from socially disadvantaged backgrounds may start school with a language delay; speech and language difficulties represent the most common form of special need in children. Poor vocabulary development affects thinking and writing. Word-poor pupils find it hard to talk and write fluently. Some pupils can understand words but struggle to retrieve them from their memory. Vocabulary knowledge is tested in exams. Being articulate is an advantage in social situations.

All the new words we learn are hooked into what we already have stored in our memories. We build schema (linked webs of knowledge) from what we have experienced. The richer the schema, the easier it is to assimilate new learning. For children with a vocabulary gap starting school, the gap widens unless teachers can help build up their vocabulary. To learn new words, pupils need to hear them and then use them frequently. Teachers can explicitly teach new vocabulary at the beginning of a lesson or topic and then provide repeated exposure to the new words. Topic and subject words are a good place to start, but often some general terms will not be secure. Never assume that pupils are understanding what you are saying. Always spend time developing the language and vocabulary in any lesson, whatever the age of the pupils. A nice way to check understanding is to simply stop on a word and ask pupils to talk to their partner about what they think it means. You can then vary who you ask to contribute ideas and share the definitions, or tell the class yourself. Pupils are usually fascinated by the origin of words. You can look at word families or break down words to see where the word comes from. Most words in English have Greek or Latin derivations. Children love to hunt for patterns, and researching words is fun. For example, I found out that the word vocabulary comes from 'vocare' meaning *to name*, and 'ary' meaning *belonging to*.

Consider

- Pre-teaching vocabulary is a great starter activity and useful for introducing a variety of words which are needed for a task. There are many ways to

Copyright material from Rachel Cosgrove (2020), Inclusive Teaching in a Nutshell, Routledge

It's all in the classroom

do this – using images, examples of sentences, definitions, looking for links, categorising and grouping words and looking for roots.

- Plan talking activities such as visits, role plays, discussion, games, exploring actual objects or representations of concepts.

- Ways to consolidate the new vocabulary would include writing, making key word lists, glossaries, matching activities, debates, quick quizzes, listening and drawing, comprehension questions and basic Q & A.

- Pupils need to be exposed to new words several times before they are secure in their memory banks.

- Some pupils will need frequent revisits to vocabulary lists.

- With pupils struggling to recall words, provide choices or give them the starting sound.

- Word games – alphabet, Pictionary, odd one out, find a link.

 ## Reflect

Have you ever tried to learn a new language at an evening class and struggled to retain the vocabulary? Which strategies did you try, and would these help in your teaching?

It's all in the classroom

Vocabulary

Revisit words little and often in subsequent lessons.
Quick quiz.
Matching games.
Drawing games.
Homework revision tasks.

Practice pronouncing the words.
Provide definitions.
Sentences with examples.
Ask pupils for examples.
Questioning with the words.
Match word to meaning.
Illustrate words.

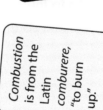

Provide images to illustrate new words.
Explore roots of words.

Combustion is from the Latin comburere, "to burn up."

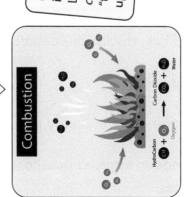

Vocabulary

It's all in the classroom

Talking

 ## Context

Talk sometimes gets bad press in schools, because we seem to spend too much time telling pupils to stop talking! Nevertheless, being able to verbalise is an important foundation for literacy skills. Talking enables us to express our feelings, develop relationships and social skills and stick up for ourselves. Pupils who struggle to verbalise their feelings may externalise in other ways or bury their feelings. Oracy is important in the workplace and in our personal lives; being able to express our point of view is important for self-advocacy. Many pupils with additional needs miss out on opportunities to develop their talking skills because they struggle to access language in the first place. Consider how you make space for good talking opportunities in your classroom. Talk, as part of routine lesson planning, needs as much scaffolding as other tasks.

Many pupils with learning difficulties or English as an additional language have fewer opportunities to practise task-related talk, as they may be overshadowed by more confident speakers. They may lack vocabulary or be masking their difficulties with off-task chat or daydreaming diversions. Many pupils do not initiate conversations and seldom volunteer answers, which means they have fewer interactions with teachers throughout the school day. Some pupils will literally appear to hide in lessons, and usually there are plenty of vocal peers to keep teachers occupied. How can we build productive talk into lessons in order to develop subject-specific vocabulary and improve the oral fluency of pupils? Can we harness talk, so it links to the content we want pupils to learn? Can we scaffold talk for less confident speakers so they can be more motivated to contribute?

 ## Consider

Talking time can be part of the lesson plan. The key strategies to support talk are teacher-led talk, discussion, debate and listening techniques.

Teacher-led talk:

- ◆ Think, pair share in buddy pairs.

- ◆ No hands-up targeted questioning with prompts such as choices, starter sentences.

- ◆ Use of signing, symbols and gestures to encourage talk.

It's all in the classroom

- Prompts such as real objects, stories, playscripts, drama, pictures.

- Collaborative telling – i.e., teacher retells an event, leaves gaps for pupil to chip in, rehearse with pupil adding more.

- Make story books together and retell.

Discussion and debate:

- Provide information and prompt cards/roles for groups and consider groupings so that confident speakers don't dominate.

- Provide clear topics or question for discussion – you can vary this according to ability of group.

- Rove around groups and steer discussion if needed.

- To increase participation, have times when everyone gives an opinion or constructs a sentence to summarise as feedback.

- For debates, characters can work well and can be chosen to work for individual pupils, especially if you plan in time for pupil to research and practise what they are going to say – you can provide written prompts for specific pupils.

- Don't let discussion drift into non-productive talk – time and chunk periods of talk.

Listening:

- Make time for 1-to-1 listening.

- Don't finish sentences for pupils.

- Look like you have plenty of time to listen.

- Use non-verbal responses to encourage more talk.

- Use open-ended starter sentences to encourage pupil talk.

- Allow reasonable wait time before you jump in, so pupils have time to think.

 Reflect

Are you comfortable with a classroom that is busy with 'on-task' talk? Try developing the skill of getting total silence in contrast, to enable quiet, focussed thinking **after** the productive talk.

It's all in the classroom

Talking

Teachers do a lot of talking.
To support vulnerable pupils' verbal communication development, it is worth practicing **listening** techniques.

Reflective listening
Good for helping pupils share their feelings and to feel understood.

Don't ask any questions but...
get them to tell you what is happening and then....

Label the feeling - 'you look/sound/seem sad/angry'.
'I can hear that you are frustrated'.

Reflect back - clarify or summarise what the pupil has said to you using their words e.g. 'So I am hearing that you are worried about...'.
'You didn't like it when he said that to you'.

Normalise - 'You are feeling...I guess I would feel....too'.
'Can you think of what you could do next?'

Meta-cognitive prompts
Good for helping pupils say and see how they are learning.

Open questions to prompt more talk
- Tell me what you are doing.
- Have you seen something like this before?
- What did you do first?
- How did you do that?
- How did you know what to do?
- What questions did you need to ask?
- How does this work?
- What would help?
- What are you going to do next?
- Tell me about....
- What might happen if?
- Could you do this differently?
- What could you do to make it easier?

Non-verbal gestures
Good for encouraging pupils to speak more.

No talking - prompt with gestures!
- Eye contact (or if this is uncomfortable; focus near pupil or on their work).
- Nod.
- Tone of voice - soft, calm.
- Facial expression - interest.
- Thumbs up.
- Wave hand to show go on.
- Smile.
- Thinking stance.
- Hands up to show slow down.
- Lean to one side to show listening.
- Posture - relaxed, open hands.
- Think personal space.

Talking

Modelling

Context

Modelling is a commonly referred to teaching strategy and is a brilliant way to explicitly show pupils exactly how a process works or what the final product should look like. Many struggling learners don't pick up implicit cues from classroom teaching. They may not be able to read between the lines or take hints. They may lack a mental representation of what a piece of writing or drawing should contain. They lack the confidence to leap in and experiment. Peer or teacher modelling can provide a framework on which a pupil can build.

Modelling is important across all areas of the curriculum. Children learn by observing and copying. We pick up physical and thinking skills through watching others. We learn how to behave by seeing what others do and noticing how their behaviours are responded to. Some pupils need to have more opportunities to overlearn skills that others may pick up quickly. Behaviour is learned, and teachers can use modelling of appropriate behaviours to explicitly teach social and emotional skills.

Teachers can model a process and narrate alongside – thinking aloud while working on a task shows pupils the way you make choices, correct mistakes and expand or edit the work. You can write on the whiteboard to show a task, type at the computer and display or work alongside pupils. Narration is useful because you can show pupils that first ideas are often rejected, and that even adults are unsure of what to do sometimes. You can ask pupils to give feedback on the task you have done to get them thinking about how to improve it. You can adapt the level of the work you produce according to the pupil audience. How about recording your narration over your slides as an additional explanation?

Consider

- Narration can also be used to verbalise behaviour expectations – point out which pupils are doing the right thing by stating the behaviour, e.g., 'Table 4 has their hands up, thank you. X is listening, brilliant!'

- Exemplars and marked examples are a good way to show pupils what they are aiming for; provide different levels and in different formats.

- Chunking the exemplar into manageable pieces and talking through a model answer helps pupils see what is needed to get specific marks.

It's all in the classroom

- Demonstrations – Any practical task will have a better chance of success if the process is modelled. You can narrate a demonstration or use a diagram or instruction sheet to go alongside.

- If the task has many steps, model each step at a time and give the class a chance to follow before you give them the next part.

- If the class is doing a carousel, demo each station. Getting pupils to repeat back or demo will reinforce.

- Silent demonstration – Sometimes language distracts focus because pupils are processing the words instead of observing the steps. Gather class to watch a demo in total silence. You can then repeat and get pupils to narrate back. I find this technique surprisingly useful for pupils with language and attention difficulties. They seem to really enjoy the novelty of the teacher not speaking, and focus so well that they can often start the task without support!

- Once some pupils have got the gist, you can send them to start the task and repeat the process for those needing extra modelling time.

 Reflect

Do you ever practise your modelled task to other adults to see if your explanation is clear?

It's all in the classroom

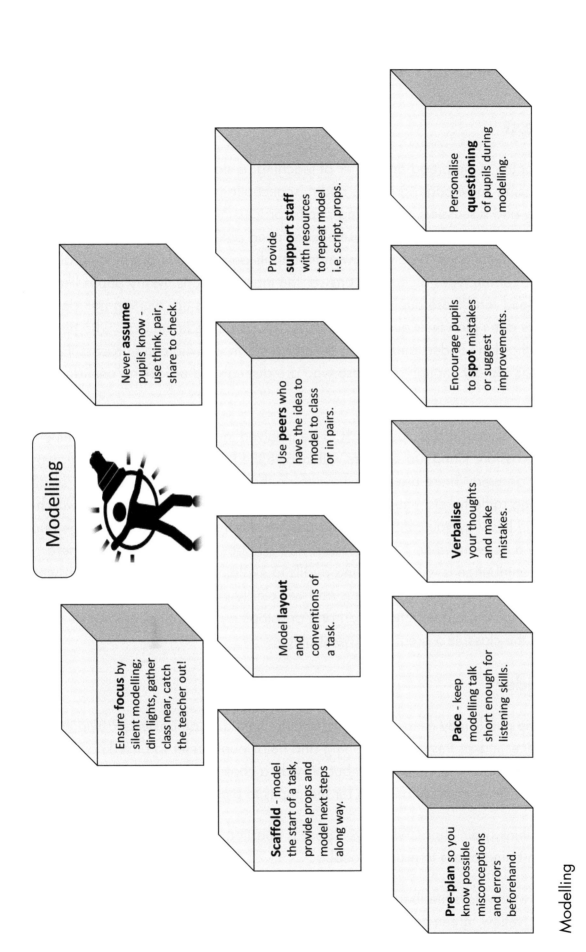

It's all in the classroom

Accessible questioning

Context

Questioning is the bread and butter of teaching: a staple! Questioning is important in assessing knowledge, progress and misconceptions. Questioning generates thinking and discussion, scaffolding pupils' processing of new ideas. Observing teachers questioning pupils is a useful continuing professional development activity. It can be illuminating to notice how many pupils participate in questioning and whether certain types of learners answer the most questions. Many pupils like to think aloud, and these pupils will be the ones with hands up, blurting out ideas. If teachers don't plan their questioning, there will be pupils in the class who miss out: those who don't understand what is being asked, those who can't process the questions rapidly enough and those who are disengaged or lacking confidence to answer.

Ideally, everyone in the class needs to be involved in the process of questioning and discussion. Hands-up answers will involve the keen few, so choose other ways to elicit answers. There are many ways to do this – random name generators, lolly sticks and raffle tickets – but it is beneficial to level your questions and know **who** to target. In this way you can take varied answers from the class. To encourage pupils to have a go even when they are unsure, it's all about creating a culture where every contribution is valued. Getting pupils to explain how they found an answer is an insight into their thought process and will clarify misconceptions. Snowballing – i.e., asking simple questions to start and developing the depth of answer as you ask around the class, is a great inclusive strategy.

Consider

- Some pupils may need scaffolding to help them give an answer. Providing choices makes this less threatening and helps pupils refer to prior knowledge. For example, ask the question but provide a choice of images as cues or provide two or three possible answers for the pupils to pick.

- Try think, pair, share, where you pose a question and pupils talk in pairs before then being asked to provide feedback.

- For whole-class feedback and engagement: thumbs up/down, true/false cards, red, yellow, green cards and mini whiteboards work well and allow pupils to be included at their own level.

It's all in the classroom

- Try continuum questions, where everyone moves to a spot in the room. Unsure learners can follow the lead of others.

- Questioning is impactful at an individual or pair level, so make time to move around the class, sitting with pupils and listening and observing.

- Meta-cognitive questions can be used to assess progress. You can provide support staff with question scripts or learning prompts. Support staff can also be particularly useful as stooges in the classroom and can prompt teachers to clarify or pitch questions appropriately if pupils are struggling.

- Repeating questions is helpful for many pupils. Make sure your question is clear and don't rephrase the question, as this adds new language to process.

- Wait time should be slightly longer than you think it should be to enable pupils to process the language and retrieve an answer.

- Repeating back an answer to a pupil is useful in enabling you to reframe the sentence and insert technical vocabulary.

- Pre-teaching vocabulary to be used in questioning sessions is always a good idea.

Reflect

How many open questions do you use? Asking closed 'right answer' questions is sometimes reassuring to teachers, as we can feel the class are 'getting it', but it's usually not a good indicator of deep learning. Try 'questions with questions' and provide scaffolding to include everyone.

It's all in the classroom

Accessible questioning

Here is the answer, what is the question?
Pupil generated questions

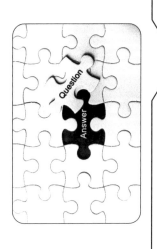

Processing
- Wait time of between 5 - 10 secs.
- Listen to whole answer – don't interrupt
- Keep language clear and don't rephrase
- Use question words on board.
- Pre-teach question words.
- Model questions and answers using subject vocabulary.
- Praise effort to answer.
- Pupils ask peers – 'three before me'.
- Open book questions - pupils can check work or resources to find answer.

Target your questions

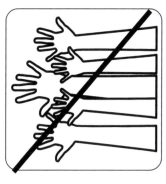

Question Grids

	Is?	Was?	Can?	Should?	Would?	Will?	Might?
What?							
Where?							
When?							
Which?							
Who?							
Why?							
How?							

Increasing complexity of question

Scaffolding questions
- Write questions up.
- Limit the length of question.
- Sticky notes for answers/draw answers.
- Tell your neighbour.
- Give choices of answer.
- Give images as clues.
- Teach the answer and then ask.
- Give a sentence starter as prompt.
- Give examples of possible answers.
- Use open ended questions.
- Match question with answer.

Accessible questioning

Giving instructions

Context

Giving instructions is one of the most common things we do as teachers, and we should be experts at it! However, I expect that all of us have turned to colleagues during staff meetings because we have missed a point! Either our minds wandered, or we have forgotten the steps in a direction. Instructions depend on working memory capacity and attention skills.

Giving instructions can be a hurdle for pupils receiving them because they need to do numerous things **before** they can respond. Firstly, they need to focus and listen to the teacher. Then they need to recognise the language the teacher is using and store the words in their working memory in order to process them. They then need to retrieve the words and work out the actions being demanded. Most of us can store approximately four items in our working memory, so any instructions containing more than four steps are unlikely to be followed accurately, and most instructions of three steps are going to be missed by several pupils. Many teachers don't stand still when giving instructions. They may be demonstrating something, writing on the board or moving around the room giving out worksheets or books and gesturing to pupils to get settled. This all adds to pupils' working memory load, as they will be distracted by watching the teacher or peers. Sometimes teachers give instructions in the middle of explaining a task. Often the instructions will be lengthy and elaborate, with specific details about how a task should be done or who pupils are going to be working with.

All these examples lead to the instructions being missed or half missed by several pupils. Pupils may then do the wrong thing, or talk, or do nothing. It is very important to think about cognitive overload when giving instructions. There will be a variety of processing speeds and working memory capacity in the class. Some pupils will have difficulties processing complex language. Some pupils will have attention difficulties or may be involved in social or emotional thoughts that are absorbing their focus. Pupils with additional support may simply not bother to listen, as they are relying on their supportive adult to relay instructions to them!

Consider

- ◆ To manage the attention of the class, insist on silence and stand still.

- ◆ Keep instructions short and clear.

It's all in the classroom

- Avoid ambiguous language and break down the instructions into chunks, with time in between to carry out each step or steps.

- Back up instructions with steps on the board or model the instructions by demonstrating the routine or choosing a pupil to do so.

- Getting pupils to repeat back the steps is a good way to check whether what you have said is understood.

- Having resources set up in the right position and ready to distribute gives pupils a visual cue.

- If the instruction is about grouping, always wait for the groups to be ready before giving the instructions about the work.

- If the task is set up and pupils have the resources in front of them, that is the time to give instructions about the task itself.

- Think about how you can label resources or store things in the room so you can use gestures more than talking.

- Silent demos are surprisingly effective at removing language from the instruction.

 Reflect

Are you a talkative teacher? Be aware of the fillers you use around your explanations: stories and anecdotes have their place but get in the way of clear instructions.

It's all in the classroom

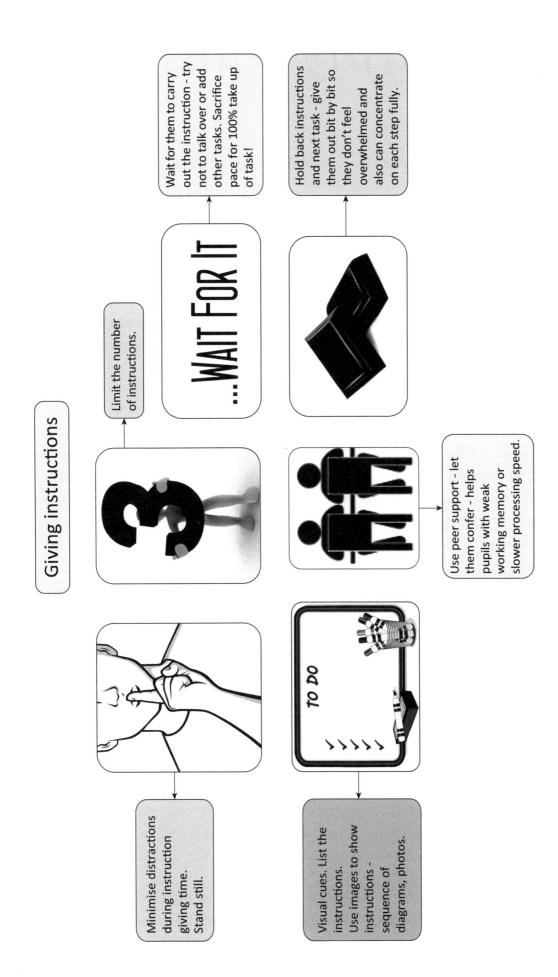

Giving instructions

It's all in the classroom

Signposting transitions

Context

Transitions happen throughout the school day, and pupils get used to constantly changing classrooms, teachers, activities and peer groups. Many pupils handle the numerous changes with ease, but for some pupils this can be confusing and disorientating. You will spot the pupils who struggle with these transitions, as they may be daydreaming, late to lessons, slow to start a new task, wandering around the room, fooling around with resources or generally not doing what the rest of the class is doing. Some of these pupils may have slow processing speed, attention difficulties or social interaction difficulties and miss instructions because they are otherwise distracted. Pupils on the autistic spectrum can miss cues from teachers because they don't pick up on whole-class instructions.

If the transitions are well planned and signposted by teachers, it is much easier for pupils to track the different episodes of learning and follow the lesson pathway. By signposting transitions, I am referring to flagging any changes explicitly to the class. This could be done by writing up the lesson tasks on the board and ticking them off when completed. To get the class ready for instructions about the next task, it is useful to have general 'stop and listen' routines. For any changes involving a different room or space, seating plan or unusual activities, prepare the class by explaining beforehand what is going to happen. For some pupils who find change very hard to manage, you might talk to parents and/or support staff to help you with preparing a pupil, as some pupils will need a longer time to anticipate and get ready for a transition. The same goes for any planned trips and visits, both in and around the school or to an outside venue. Early preparation will go a long way to allay anxieties and encourage pupils to participate. Springing changes without warning may cause total nonparticipation for your most rigid or anxious pupils.

Consider

- In lesson routines, try out some signposting ideas to see what works for your subject or age groups. Counting down, hand signals, call and response, hand claps, praising pupils who are not talking and standing and waiting will all work for when you need the class totally quiet to listen to the next instruction.

- Making the instructions unambiguous works for those pupils who don't pick up on implied instructions. So, spell it out by referring to the task as **the next task** or give a time reference with a visual prompt, such as 'at 20 past we are going to go over the questions in groups'.

It's all in the classroom

- Some pupils will have little concept of passing time, so you can be creative in explaining how long tasks should take by using visual cues such as sand timers, countdown clocks or providing regular time checks to the class.

- Give an overview of a week's activities or a term's outline of topics, including any assessments or outside the usual activities.

- Help pupils settle, e.g., social story script, sensory toy, sitting near an adult.

- Practise routines for fire drills, etc., with key pupils several times.

Reflect

It can be hard to balance spontaneous and exciting learning activities with the need for routines and pre-planned changes. Spur-of-the-moment teaching can be fantastic if you have a great idea during a lesson – how could you help pupils cope with these times?

It's all in the classroom

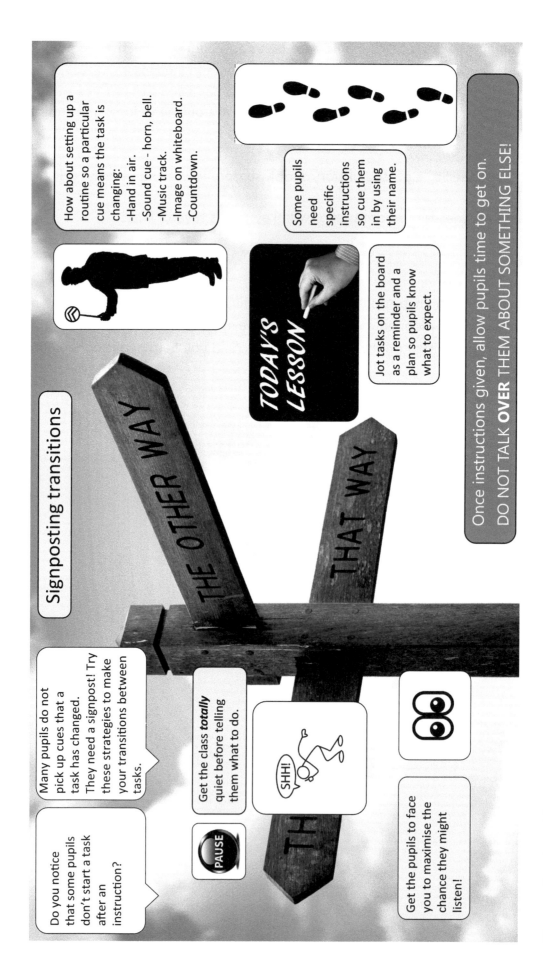

Signposting transitions

It's all in the classroom

Whiteboards of all sorts

Context

Whiteboards are a fantastic inclusive teaching resource. Whiteboards used well can help pupils access lesson material, engage their senses and scaffold many barriers to learning.

Wall mounted boards are commonly used to display instructions, explanations and day-to-day routines. Don't overlook the potential impact of your board; to make your board accessible to learners with sensory, attention or literacy difficulties, planning is required. Pupils work well with routines and like to know what is going to happen in the lesson, often asking repeatedly when they enter the class. Keep your whiteboard simple and uncluttered to provide visual prompts for your lesson procedures. The board should be in a position on the wall where everyone can see it easily, with no distracting display work around it. If your board is old or badly positioned, get it changed or it will undermine clarity of visual prompts. Have your own standardised format – display instruction, outline of lesson, and homework if appropriate. Tick or rub away tasks once completed. You can mark off zones on the board using insulating tape, lines or boxes around text. Writing needs to be appropriately sized and neat; well-inked blue and black pens are clearer. Adapt lighting for glare and reflections; it's worth standing in different places in your room to see what the board looks like at different angles. If using the board for class notes, photograph it as a record for pupils.

Pupils love writing on whiteboards on the wall. Using several smaller wall-mounted boards around the room is engaging, motivating and accessible for group and pair work in any subject. The ability to rub out makes the task editable and engaging for reluctant writers.

Interactive whiteboards add visuals, sounds, moving images and direct interaction through touch to lessons. These multisensory elements can bring content alive and improve focus. You can face the class and make use of numerous resources such as animations, film clips, interactive games with immediate feedback and live data streaming. Using a linked-up camera or visualiser facilitates demonstrations and modelling of work. Image and font size and colour can be manipulated for pupils with visual needs. You can close off parts of the screen to 'reveal and spotlight'.

Mini whiteboards provide an easy, wipeable way of recording answers; planning and supporting writing; assessing knowledge; practising spelling and handwriting; drawing and problem solving. They work well for pupils who need scaffolding or

It's all in the classroom

who are reluctant to write on paper, and for small group work, pair activities and carpet activities.

Consider

- You can personalise boards for pupils by drawing grids, binding the edge to provide contrast or trying different sizes of pen.

- Get movement breaks in by using the board for sticky notes, notes, scores, etc.

- You could bring groups up to the board for discussion or targeted explanation.

- Modelling using the board – get pupils typing, solving a problem, drawing and talking.

- Avoid any extensive copying from the board. Pupils with literacy issues find it uncomfortable to track from board to paper repeatedly and will miss the meaning.

- Whiteboards for true/false questions, continuums and quick quizzes are useful for assessing knowledge.

- Encourage use of whiteboards for spellings or for scribing ideas before writing.

- Download visual and sound alternatives for pupils with hearing or visual impairments.

Reflect

Have you observed colleagues' use of boards? Can you share some of the strategies to make boards more accessible?

It's all in the classroom

Whiteboards of all sorts

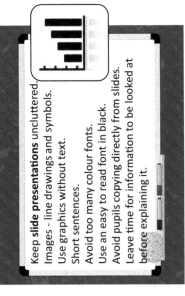

Working whiteboards around room - good for calculations, lists, silent debates, post it ideas, planning stories and writing, practicing spellings, games, group idea recording, scribing in pairs before writing. Good for movement breaks and collaborative work.

Coloured tape round border of board to help spatial skills.
Grids for spacing work.
Tape lines for writing.
Different pressure pens, angle board on slope.

Support staff can scribe.
Low stakes writing practice/planning.
Provide key spellings.
Alternatives to writing-i.e. drawing ideas, storyboarding.

Keep slide presentations uncluttered.
Images - line drawings and symbols.
Use graphics without text.
Short sentences.
Avoid too many colour fonts.
Use an easy to read font in black.
Avoid pupils copying directly from slides.
Leave time for information to be looked at before explaining it.

Flexible groupings at the board - teach from the board while demonstrating visuals.
Support staff use board as prompts.
Individual tuition.
Record lesson for pupils not attending.
Pupil presentations/talks at the board.

Date...
Tasks
-
-
-

h/w
Key words

Props for literacy - during the lesson.
Key words.
Use interactive board to finger trace or write - converts writing to text.
Sentence starters for those who need.
Sharing pupil ideas as scaffolds for others.
Mind maps.
Template for writing, e.g., draw flow diagram on board as guidance.

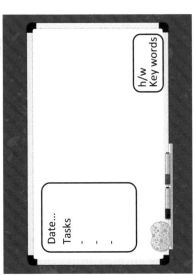

Whiteboards of all sorts

Managing text

Context

There are several things that classroom teachers need to understand and do to help weak or novice readers in lessons. Pupils may struggle with different aspects of text. Pupils may have trouble decoding (breaking down individual sounds in words), pronunciation, comprehension (understanding of vocabulary and meaning) and fluency (speed of processing from written word to reading out loud or in head). Pupils who read at a slow rate are often trying to rely on decoding each word, and this takes so much effort that there is limited capacity left for concentrating on meaning.

Because reading is at the core of many activities, text can be a real barrier to learning. It is useful to have an idea of reading ages – both of pupils and of the texts you are using. You can work out the reading age of texts using readability calculators, which you can find online. Subject-specific textbooks often have surprisingly high reading ages. Knowing this will help you to judge the appropriateness of text and how much support might be needed.

There are several things you can do as a teacher to build confidence in your pupils. Explicit teaching of reading skills such as skimming for clues, summarising the main gist and asking for clarification can help develop comprehension. When introducing text in any subject, sharing the big picture with the class first will support weaker readers. For example, point out the images associated with the text; introduce key words by pre-teaching vocabulary or reading more complex words out loud; and read aloud short extracts. Analysing the text by making a timeline, mind map or a grid of key facts or features will break down the text nicely and give weaker readers the themes and key words in advance, before they try to tackle the text independently. Novice readers struggle with many subject-specific words. Vocabulary teaching is very important at all age groups, so think about which words to introduce first and use images, sentence examples and discussion of meanings to build the understanding of weaker readers. This will help them when they come to trying to decode, as they will already know some of the meanings and so will comprehend more of the text.

Consider

- Provide parts of the text at a time rather than overwhelm the pupils with several pages crammed with words. Simply cutting the text up into strips and introducing a bit at a time can make the task much more accessible.

It's all in the classroom

- A useful strategy is to use a buddy system where weaker readers are paired with stronger readers; it is important that the pairs get on well enough for reciprocity to work.

- Often, we forget that talking about a text in depth is a fantastic way to develop comprehension and share knowledge across the class. Using pair, share type strategies and small group reading can lower the text demand for targeted pupils and help them participate.

- If your school uses silent reading time, consider your weaker readers and think about choice of text, reading out loud to these pupils or group reading to ensure that these readers benefit from the activity.

- Computer readers – Text to speech is a good way for struggling readers to highlight and read with headphones on, at their own pace.

Reflect

Are you worried about having to simplify text? It's all about the pre-teaching and breaking down of the text – don't shy away from challenging text as long as the meaning is explained, and pupils can enjoy the ideas.

It's all in the classroom

Managing text

The history of humankind
The Victorians started to think that all the questions about how the world began might be explained by studying science. This philosophy was supported by explorers who brought back strange animals and plants from foreign countries, both alive and dead, to exhibit in museums and zoos.

Around reading age 13

The football game
There was a boy who did not like to get out of his bed and go to school. His Mum and Dad made him go. He was not happy, but he went.

Around reading age 7

5 ideas to try

1 Talk about the text - before, during and after. Discuss word meanings, sum up, encourage pupils to visualise and ask questions.

2 Back up text with visual cues and chunk it into shorter pieces of reading.

3 Adult reads text out loud. Buddy up pairs. Buddy reads.

4 Have fun with vocabulary and idioms - look at etymology of words. Key words on board. Word banks.

5 Plan structured questions to help pupils predict, clarify, infer and summarise. Teach skimming and scanning to pull out text.

Managing text

94

It's all in the classroom

Numeracy

Context

Unfortunately, when pupils have difficulties with numbers early on in school life, misconceptions or gaps in knowledge and skills can be compounded as they get older. Pupils who have not grasped basic numeracy concepts struggle not only in maths but will also struggle in activities such as graph work, measuring and life skills. Pupils who struggle to recall number facts often lose track in any procedures that have two or three steps. Pupils with numeracy difficulties will often have poor knowledge of maths vocabulary and will struggle with everyday tasks, such as telling the time and dealing with money. When pupils have experienced early struggles in maths, they may develop anxieties around numeracy and develop a resistance to believing they can improve. Pupils may have learned some routines by rote or rely on using their fingers or counting in steps – but the conceptual understanding is lacking, so all their effort gets used up recalling the procedures. When test questions are set with unfamiliar examples or wording, pupils don't know where to start.

Pupils with these types of difficulties need to be supported to go back to basics and will need practical and concrete experiences to help them build solid cognitive models. Teachers need to be aware that pupils struggling with numeracy will need support in many areas of the curriculum. Providing manipulatives in class such as number rods and tiles; tangrams, bricks and counters; plane and solid objects; fraction bars and number lines will help pupils learn procedures by physically moving the materials and visualising the concept. Making number tasks close to real-life situations can build confidence and help move the pupil from concrete to abstract. Approaches using stories, games, projects and everyday examples will be much more accessible and motivating for some pupils. Modelling is a great way to illustrate the thinking steps of a problem. Abstract thinking develops in children on average between 12 and 19 years of age, so even older pupils will benefit from using concrete and visual props, especially when learning new topics.

Consider

- Maths language can be confusing when so many different words may mean the same process. Vocabulary can be explicitly taught, and meanings displayed or provided in key word lists or numeracy mats. Learn root meanings of words such as 'poly'.

It's all in the classroom

- Check numeracy skills before teaching topics needing maths – scaffold learning using worked examples, drawing items in the questions, pre-teach the calculation steps to key pupils, provide part worked answers.

- Store manipulatives in an easily accessible place, so any pupils can help themselves.

- Groups and pair work may be helpful to build confidence for pupils with numeracy weaknesses. Pupils are often good at explaining how something works, as they tend to use more 'pupil-friendly' language and examples than adults do.

- Use online programmes that can provide visual cues and interactive tasks – these can be a good way to set individual levelled work.

- In subjects using maths skills, the same ideas apply; provide concrete and visual props, model the processes and explicitly teach the vocabulary.

- Pupils with numeracy difficulties will need extra thinking time in class and longer lesson sequence time to master new skills.

- Pupils are notoriously bad at generalising skills from maths lessons to other curriculum areas. Explicitly signpost that this is a **maths/numeracy** skill!

Reflect

Are you confident in teaching calculation or graph skills in your subject area? Talk to the maths leads to check the methods that pupils have been taught, so you can be consistent.

It's all in the classroom

Numeracy

Visual props

Numeracy vocabulary

plus → + → add
+ → sum
+ → total
+ → in all

Model

Narrate the process. Get pupils to model and explain their method. Make mistakes and rework answer.

Visualisers can be used to demo processes in action so pupils can see all the steps.

Pair work

Detective

Work out where the misconceptions and gaps are by observing and listening to pupils describing how they solve problems. Share ideas with colleagues from other year groups and subjects. Try and track back to their error and work out what their understanding is.

Concrete props

Numeracy

It's all in the classroom

Accessible ICT

Context

Information and communication technology (ICT) can be a great equaliser for learners. It can also be a time waster if not used properly! Pupils with literacy and handwriting difficulties benefit from having access to word processing; pupils with physical difficulties can access the curriculum via personalised ICT support; and English as an additional language (EAL) learners can use translation sites to support writing. There are some key tools which can support pupils to be more engaged and independent in lessons, such as speech to text dictation or text to speech; symbol processing and concept keyboards; screen resolution or size/colour; predictive text; mind-mapping software; real-time data collection, audiobooks and quizzes; photo editing and animation and interactive whiteboard activities. Touch screens, alternative keyboards/mice and head switches will support pupils with reduced motor skills. Peer support at the computer is also great for pupils who are anxious about speaking or who don't like eye contact.

Access to ICT provides pupils with a range of visual cues and literacy support; being able to edit or spellcheck and include images and graphics improves the quality of work and motivates pupils who struggle to present work. For pupils who prefer working on their own, ICT gives choices and, with headphones, blocks distractions. Think about how you make it okay in class for pupils to be working in a different way from their peers. You may need to be creative about assessing work produced using a laptop, because printing out work can be an organisational barrier for some pupils. If pupils have exam access arrangements using ICT, ensure they are used in lessons on a regular basis and for any assessment. Booking a computer suite for a class in the hope that having access to ICT will improve output, is hopeful at best! Pupils are adept at task avoidance and having the internet available will potentially derail task completion. The key to success is tight lesson planning. Pupils forget logins or can avoid logging in to delay working. Pre-empt this by having logins to hand. Consider the seating arrangements and whose screens you need eyes on. Seat those needing more support **within your reach**.

Consider

- For laptop or tablet access, you may need to rearrange the seating plan to improve access to plugs.

- Make time to help pupils file, print or upload their work.

It's all in the classroom

- If you have teaching assistant support, you can give them time out of lessons to upload resources or set up templates for pupils.

- Buddy proficient computer users with less confident pupils.

- Do your research and look at resources and links prior to lessons.

- Pre-teach specific skills to targeted pupils. Instructions need to be short and steps modelled.

- Display easy step-by-step guides with screen shots.

- Produce templates for tasks so that pupils have a structure to work from.

- Track what pupils are doing by roving the room or by using monitoring software.

- Work in short bursts and get feedback at stages throughout the lesson so you can keep the pace appropriate and redirect as needed.

- Turn off screens and insist on eyes to the front, headphones off, when giving any instructions.

- Teaching content in a regular classroom and then moving to computers later might work for classes who need more direct delivery.

 Reflect

Do you know when to abandon a task if the ICT is getting in the way? Are you up to date with resources in your age or subject range? Who can support with this?

It's all in the classroom

Accessible ICT

Planning Ahead
- Pre-teach language and skills.
- Prepare templates.
- Prepare key word/skill banks.
- Instruction aids clear and uncluttered.
- Make an exemplar.
- Prepare differentiated resources, e.g., sentence starters, gap fill, shorter step task, adapted task.
- Brief support staff.
- Do you need headphones?
- Plan seating and pair work.

In the Lesson
- Check environment is safe - cables, wires, glare, ventilation.
- Seating accessible and supportive - adjustable seats, height of screen etc.
- Everyone can see and hear the teacher.
- Individual equipment accessible.
- Build in breaks.
- Low arousal workstation as required.
- Monitor internet use for risks.

The Task
- Templates at different levels.
- Upload resources for individuals.
- Model task.
- Monitor delay tactics such as font and image hunting!
- Encourage peer collaboration.
- Show how to use text to speech.
- Teach how to use synonyms, spell checker.
- Use peer explanation to support those needing more instructions.

End of the Lesson
- Ensure pupils know how to save as *before* they start.
- Support with labelling and organising files, otherwise work will be 'lost'.
- Build in time for printing if needed and stagger access to printer!
- If setting homework tasks using ICT, check home access and build in time for pupils to use school facilities.
- Have a routine for lesson finish - saving work, logging out, screens off, chairs under, checking equipment.

Accessible ICT

Props – concrete and visual

 Context

When we learn new things, we do so in the context of what we already know. Our experiences of activities are held in our memories and connect to mental maps of previous learning. Most of our memories develop from concrete, hands-on experiences. Even adult minds struggle with abstraction and prefer concrete knowledge. If we can see it, it's easier to understand it! Children generally develop the ability to form abstract thoughts anytime between the ages of 12 and 19 years. For pupils who have delayed development, concrete thinking will continue very much into secondary school and beyond. Every pupil will be at a different stage in their abstract thought processes. What this means is that when we are teaching new concepts, we need to provide concrete and visual resources and activities first, before we lead onto abstract ideas. We can use analogies and everyday familiar examples to help pupils link the new idea to what they already know.

Once a pupil has grasped a concept in class in a concrete way, using familiar examples and practising the skill in different ways, you can provide unfamiliar examples to introduce a slightly more abstract way of thinking. For many lower-attaining pupils this is hard, and this is when you see them struggle. For example, they can carry out a measurement in a science experiment accurately as modelled by the teacher, but when asked to design their own experiment measuring a different aspect of an experiment, they come unstuck because they may struggle to imagine the different variables. They may learn key facts in one scenario but can't use them in another scenario. Concrete, hands-on props and activities are vital for supporting pupils who are new to a concept or who have yet to master a skill.

Visual representation represents the next stage from concrete learning. Images of a concrete experience will help bridge the gap between concrete and abstract. You can use diagrams, photos or drawings to represent a concept. Symbols are abstract. Visual representation is a great tool for helping pupils who struggle with language recall or understanding an idea. Over time, we can try gradually fading the props when pupils are confident in a new concept. Pupils will vary in their need to flip from concrete to abstract in different subjects and tasks – dependent on prior experience and cognitive capacity.

It's all in the classroom

Some pupils may not be ready for abstract thinking at school because they are still developing their concrete and visual understanding. If introducing some abstract ideas, provide examples, use stories to link ideas and encourage peer discussion so pupils can pick up perspectives from other pupils.

Consider

- Bring in in props for learning such as objects, outfits, artefacts and visitors. Any concrete experience will target the learners in your class who lack prior knowledge of the topic.

- Use life skills topics with pupils to ground ideas in real life.

- Model making is a great way to make an abstract concept real and tangible.

- Visual props – drawings, art, photos, cartoons, film clips and diagrams.

- Try abstract thinking out using very familiar topics – provide question stems and narrate model ideas to frame the process.

- Try using design activities to get pupils having fun drawing their abstract ideas.

- Play 'what if' or odd one out games to encourage abstract thought.

Reflect

How can you bring concrete and visual props into your subject or age group? Think about how the media hooks us with visuals.

It's all in the classroom

Act it out
Hot seat.
Role play.
Make a drama.
Write a script.
Use costumes/hats.
Teacher plays a character.
Use puppets.

Visual
Draw ideas.
Use images.
Animations.
Storyboards.
Picture games.
Film and video.
Create art to represent.
Illustrate words.
Dual coding – words with visuals.
Infographics.
Timelines.
Graphs.
Use camera.

Models
Make a model.
Modelling clay.
Bricks/counters/sticks.
Craft.
Junk models.
Virtual models – computer aided.

Experiences from Real Life
Stories.
Journal entries.
Video clips/media extracts/news.
Photos.
Narratives.
Newspaper articles.
Invite a speaker.
Pupils interview others.

Props – concrete and visual

Props – real objects

Props – pictures and photos

Real Life Experiences
Use school facilities – library, canteen, gardens.
Problem solving.
Trips.
Practical activities.
Homework that is experiential.

Props – concrete and visual

It's all in the classroom

Reading

Context

Reading is a complex process which develops in stages from emergent reading in early childhood to adult expertise. If reading engages us emotionally, we are influenced to read more, and practice is what makes us experts over time. When we read, we are employing five key competencies which interleave patterns, sounds and meaning, allowing us to comprehend the text. **Orthographic** skill is the recognition of shapes and patterns of letters in words and is important in sight reading and fluency. **Phonological** processing involves mapping the letters to the 44 sounds in the English language; individual speech sounds are known as phonemes. **Semantics** is the meaning of words and developing vocabulary. Being able to understand sentences using grammatical structure is known as **syntax**. Lastly, **context** is all about being able to communicate language and information through our knowledge of how text works – for example, 'they were too close to the door to close it'.

Some pupils struggle to grasp the complexities of reading and the reasons can be varied – poor working memory, difficulties with visual tracking, poor phonological processing, vocabulary or language difficulties leading to poor comprehension, lack of reading opportunities and, influencing all of these, is prior experience of reading. To complicate things further, English has an inconsistent orthographic system and has sounds with distinctly different spellings and words originating from several languages. If pupils struggle to gain reading skills, they will lose confidence and reading will not be enjoyable, meaning that access to further learning may be compromised.

All teachers can support the development of reading by providing interesting texts and modelling fluency by reading out loud. It is useful to know that at the start of secondary school, about one in five pupils may not yet be fluent readers and listening comprehension skills tend to be higher than reading ability. Many pupils may mask their lack of reading ability by relying on peers, distracting others or delaying getting on with a task, or creating a diversion to get told off for a less embarrassing reason.

Consider

- ◆ To improve the confidence of weaker readers, teachers need to structure reading activities by pre-teaching vocabulary, practising dictionary skills, breaking up text with visual cues and encouraging discussion.

It's all in the classroom

- Generate excitement about reading, being creative with topics and bringing characters' stories into lessons wherever possible to provide emotional connection.

- Reading out loud, along with pupils, helps pupils familiarise themselves with the context so that when asked to read independently, they are less anxious.

- Think about how your classroom space is promoting reading. Do you have appealing examples of books for your age group or subject and at an appropriate level for your readers? Pupils love funny books, graphic and visual books and books relevant to their experiences.

- Silent reading is a regular activity in many schools, but it needs planning for those developing readers in your classes. Are these pupils *really* reading in these sessions? Do you know the reading ages of your class? For weaker readers, shared reading, audiobooks and podcasts are great alternatives to silent reading.

- To support comprehension in any subject, pre-teaching vocabulary is a must, followed by thorough questioning to fully dissect the text. Ask questions to predict, describe, clarify, summarise, infer and make links with prior knowledge. You can do this as a whole class, in groups or working alongside a pupil.

 Reflect

Do you read for pleasure? How can you find reading material which will motivate your pupils to enjoy text?

It's all in the classroom

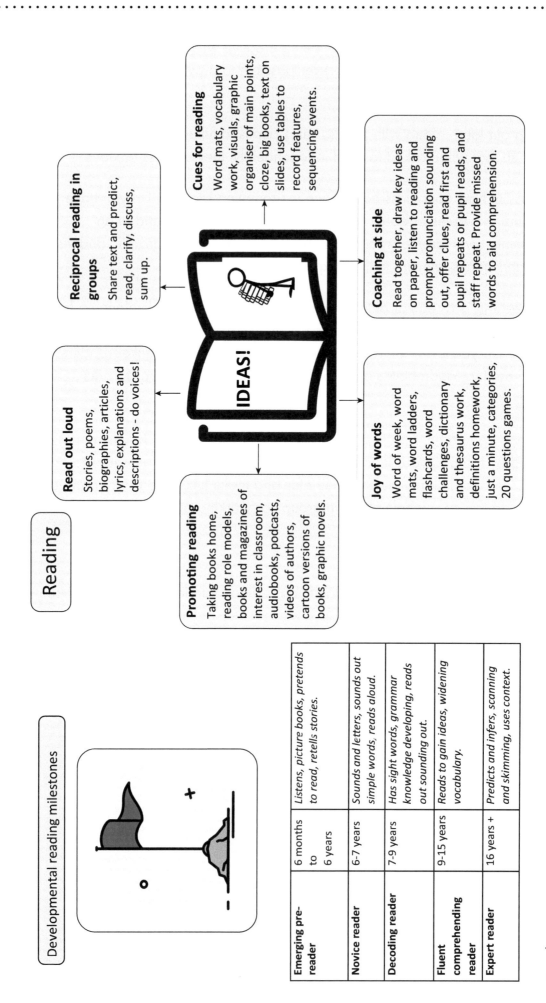

Reading

Reciprocal reading in groups
Share text and predict, read, clarify, discuss, sum up.

Cues for reading
Word mats, vocabulary work, visuals, graphic organiser of main points, cloze, big books, text on slides, use tables to record features, sequencing events.

Coaching at side
Read together, draw key ideas on paper, listen to reading and prompt pronunciation sounding out, offer clues, read first and pupil repeats or pupil reads, and staff repeat. Provide missed words to aid comprehension.

Read out loud
Stories, poems, biographies, articles, lyrics, explanations and descriptions - do voices!

IDEAS!

Joy of words
Word of week, word mats, word ladders, flashcards, word challenges, dictionary and thesaurus work, definitions homework, just a minute, categories, 20 questions games.

Promoting reading
Taking books home, reading role models, books and magazines of interest in classroom, audiobooks, podcasts, videos of authors, cartoon versions of books, graphic novels.

Developmental reading milestones

Emerging pre-reader	6 months to 6 years	Listens, picture books, pretends to read, retells stories.
Novice reader	6-7 years	Sounds and letters, sounds out simple words, reads aloud.
Decoding reader	7-9 years	Has sight words, grammar knowledge developing, reads out sounding out.
Fluent comprehending reader	9-15 years	Reads to gain ideas, widening vocabulary.
Expert reader	16 years +	Predicts and infers, scanning and skimming, uses context.

Reading

It's all in the classroom

Writing

Context

Writing is a complex process and is important for demonstrating knowledge and thinking. To write about what they know, pupils need to have grasped some key skills: spelling, grammatical structure and letter formation. Pupils then need to think about what to write, choose vocabulary, formulate sentences, process and organise the sentences and write it all down legibly before they forget. Writing is a common barrier for many pupils. If your literacy and/or handwriting skills are poor or undeveloped, vocabulary and life experience is poor, or if you struggle with sensory, processing or attentional issues, writing is going to a challenge. Some pupils are reluctant to put thoughts on paper because they fear failure.

Teachers can create an inclusive approach to writing by looking at two key strategies – talking for writing and scaffolding support for writing.

Having opportunities to talk is the key to any sort of writing, and it is not always prioritised in lesson time. Pupils need to be able to speak in sentences before they can write them. This is hard for many pupils who may use phrases but not full sentences. Pupils need to think aloud in order to generate ideas, which is why asking pupils to begin writing in silence doesn't always work. Pupils need to listen to the ideas of others and hear modelled sentences to learn how sentences are structured. Verbalising before writing needs to be planned into writing tasks.

Teachers can scaffold writing for struggling writers in a variety of ways. Anything that can support executive functioning by chunking ideas, helping with layout or organisation and removing literacy barriers will help. Templates, writing frames, models, sentence starters and literacy lists are key resources to have ready. Teach writing as a series of steps – ideas generation, drafting, editing and proofreading.

Consider

- Choose topics that pupils can relate to so they can bring prior experiences into their writing.

- Pre-teach key vocabulary and provide example sentence starters and phrases.

- Visual prompts help pupils describe what they see with further questioning developing the details.

Copyright material from Rachel Cosgrove (2020), Inclusive Teaching in a Nutshell, Routledge

It's all in the classroom

- ◆ Model good speaking. Use the whiteboard to jot down shared ideas which pupils can refer to later in the lesson. Save ideas as pupils are talking – record on a tablet, scribe or mind map in pairs or groups. Staff can augment talk by rephrasing pupil sentences with corrections or topic-specific vocabulary.

- ◆ Remember that pupils who don't write well will not want to edit their work, so provide laminated sheets, tablet or laptop or scribing to make it less of a nightmare. Focus on a few edits, so pupils are not overwhelmed with rewriting.

- ◆ It is helpful to limit the task by specifying the number of words, sentences or subject words to include, or specific connectives to use.

- ◆ Rove round during writing and coach from the side.

- ◆ Writing buddies can provide peer support with spellings and editing.

- ◆ Praise and mark the content and ideas of struggling or reluctant writers more than technical skills.

- ◆ Make key word and phrase mats for topic areas to have ready in class (for prompts, 5–10 key words, and for spellings, up to 20 words).

- ◆ Use plain paper/whiteboards to generate live writing frames, mind maps.

- ◆ Book computers for extended writing for pupils whose barrier is spelling or handwriting.

 Reflect

Do you prioritise literacy in your teaching area? If you are a subject teacher, talk to primary colleagues or English teachers about support for writing.

It's all in the classroom

Writing

Scaffolding the process

Sentence starters and key word lists, word wall, literacy mats.

Props like dictionaries (although some will find this tricky) or access to laptop.

Gap fill and 'cloze' activities to get writing started.

Storyboards with images and words to link.

Tables - blank or partially filled in.

Sequence cards or photos to sort and write from.

Spinners or dice with sentence starters, connectives etc.

Laminated or paper **writing frame** for pupils to write on.

Images surrounded by questions or sentence starters to complete.

Template on **computer** with key words and questions.

I write, you write - a sentence each: good for encouraging reluctant writers.

Model the writing.
Pupils model writing.
Give a **narrative** to show your thinking.
Provide **exemplars** at different levels.

Remember ~ a blank page is a barrier in itself!

Talk first

To get started

Try a variety of **pens** and pen grips.

Provide different paper and whiteboards.

Mark out grids or lines to put writing in.

Draw **margins** in if needed.

Draw text boxes or outline bubbles on page.

Write part of the sentence for pupil to complete underneath.

Use **sticky notes to write ideas** and then stick and move on page.

Writing

It's all in the classroom

Alternatives to writing

 Context

Writing can be a real problem for some pupils. Pupils with poor literacy skills might be able to talk about their work, but struggle to translate ideas on paper. Pupils with poor expressive speech may not be able to verbalise what they think, let alone write it. Pupils with slow and laboured handwriting may produce poorly presented, hard-to-read script. Some pupils on the autistic spectrum may not see the point in writing down what they have understood. Pupils may be fearful of writing, as they may be judged. There will also be times in lessons when stopping to write may not serve the learning purpose for some pupils. In these situations, it is helpful to have a range of alternatives up your sleeve. We can categorise the alternatives into three general strategies: verbal, pictorial and use of technology.

Talk is a powerful tool in the classroom. How can pupils use verbal skills as an alternative to writing to deepen their own learning? Pair or group discussion can be used to review prior learning, and with prompts, pupils can share ideas and rehearse explanations. You can rove and listen or get feedback from each pupil or a group spokesperson or use an envoy approach, where pupils take turns to teach classroom groups. You could get competent writers to record the main ideas for each group and then photocopy for others. Drama and role play are other ways for pupils to take what they have learned and generalise it into a verbal summary. This can work across subjects and benefits from having structure and time limits, so that pupils focus well. Providing key phrases, resources and defined space for each group will help – they don't have to be moving around necessarily, as you can set up seated role play in the format of a something like a news report.

Pupils can **draw** what they know. Pictures are great for sequencing and for macro thinking, i.e., portraying a whole concept. Graphs, diagrams, charts and graphics can be used. Pictures and symbols can represent words. Comic strips and storyboards can be used with prefilled words. Pictures can be sequenced to retell a story or explain a process. Pupils can work independently or in groups to construct a pictorial representation of a concept.

Computer aided writing can take away the difficulties of producing legible handwriting, can provide spellings and be used to convert speech to text. The process of editing and redrafting can be made less painful by using a computer. Devices to record and film learning can provide a record. If you have a class camera, you can use it to take photos of practical work and print for pupils to record in their books.

It's all in the classroom

Consider

- Use additional adults to listen to pupil talk and help scribe ideas for weaker writers. Practising dictation is a tricky skill, as pupils have to learn to use full sentences, and this helps them to clarify their thinking.

- Model making of any kind is interactive and can be used in association with verbal description to show knowledge; modelling clay can be a quick way to model an idea.

- For pupils working well below their expected age range, using photos to record the learning journey is a lovely way to track small steps.

Reflect

Think about the purpose of writing tasks. Is it always necessary to have pupils writing? Are you nervous about having something to show in pupils' books?

It's all in the classroom

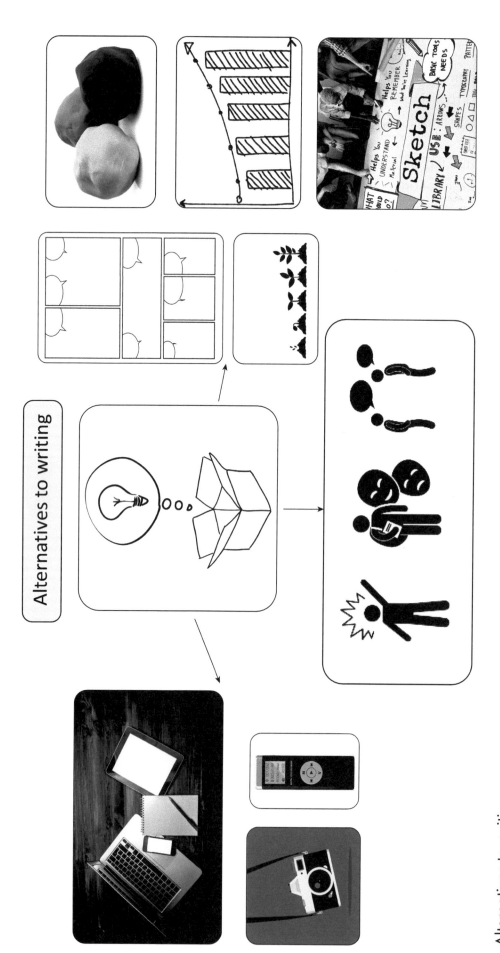

Alternatives to writing

It's all in the classroom

Writing frames

Context

Writing frames are extremely useful as an inclusive strategy for planning, recording ideas and structuring writing. Writing frames are ready formatted outlines which provide a template for writing and can used at any age or in any subject. They provide a framework to help organise information into a logical sequence. The frame sequences the steps, reducing the load on any executive functioning processes. For many pupils, a blank page is a huge hurdle and 'just getting started' is a common issue that teachers will be familiar with. Writing frames can act as a to-do list, a guide for writing, a template for a specific genre and a prompt for use of specific vocabulary, connectives, punctuation and paragraph layout.

Writing frames – or graphic organisers, as they can also be known – are not just planning and scaffolding tools but also help pupils see connections between concepts. They allow pupils to be creative as they reduce the cognitive load involved in writing and enable the pupils to complete some of or all the task, which leads to a growing sense of achievement. Writing frames create natural chunking of the task for pupils, consequently making it more manageable. Writing frames reduce the amount of processing pupils need to do therefore freeing up thinking capacity to focus on the concept being taught. For more able pupils, they can be used to encourage higher-order thinking by structuring the text to remove literacy barriers and structure space for inputting inference and prediction. Writing frames help pupils hook the concept into their mental maps, enhancing their own developing topic schema and helping them see the big picture. They can also be good tools for explaining cause and effect, comparisons and opinions, problem solving, project reports and note taking.

Writing frames can be produced in several formats, e.g., conceptual, big picture, hierarchical, chronological, mind map, sequence of paragraphs or template format, and can be used very creatively across different subjects.

Consider

- ♦ Writing frames can come in any shape and support any ability level. You can scaffold the frame to include vocabulary, spelling, topic phrases, visuals and images to support your targeted pupils.

It's all in the classroom

- Adapt a class writing frame to different levels – it looks similar but has different levels of scaffolding, such as more or less key words, phrases, more complex questions or sentence starters, space for extended writing.

- Writing frames could be printed or laminated to be reused.

- Draw a simple writing frame on a mini whiteboard or the main board. Sometimes something as simple as three boxes with a starter sentence in each is enough to support pupils to make a start.

- Have writing frames on slides in your topic areas to project on the board. Print a few for those pupils needing to write on paper or have it next to them.

- Encourage pupils to make their own writing frames so they get used to a specific format – this can be great for exam preparation.

- Learning a format and tagging a mnemonic to it can reinforce a structure.

- Fade the need for writing frames by rote learning key structures for standard questions.

- For struggling writers, cut out key sentences and provide a bank of ready-made phrases, sentences or key words for pupil to place on the writing frame to construct their own sequence.

 **Reflect**

Do you use writing frames enough? Your own lesson planning tool is in fact a writing frame that teachers use well!

It's all in the classroom

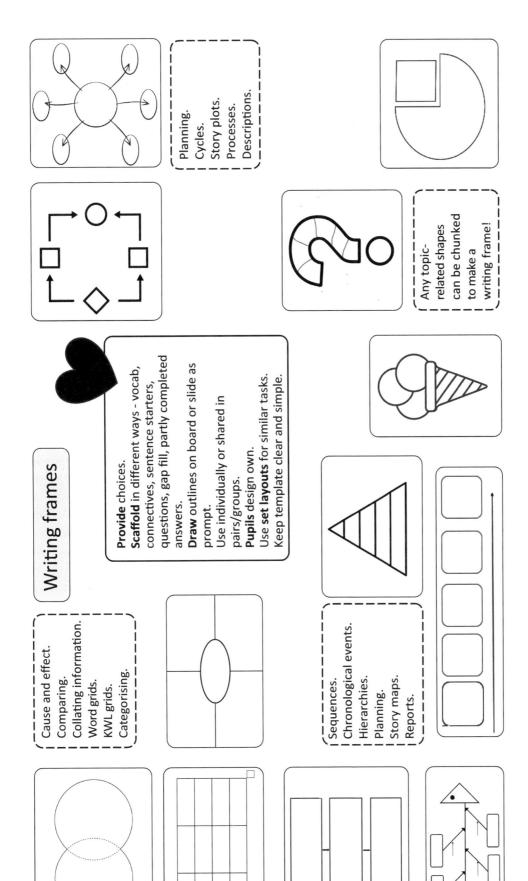

Writing frames

Planning.
Cycles.
Story plots.
Processes.
Descriptions.

Any topic-related shapes can be chunked to make a writing frame!

Provide choices.
Scaffold in different ways – vocab, connectives, sentence starters, questions, gap fill, partly completed answers.
Draw outlines on board or slide as prompt.
Use individually or shared in pairs/groups.
Pupils design own.
Use **set layouts** for similar tasks.
Keep template clear and simple.

Cause and effect.
Comparing.
Collating information.
Word grids.
KWL grids.
Categorising.

Sequences.
Chronological events.
Hierarchies.
Planning.
Story maps.
Reports.

Writing frames

It's all in the classroom

Mind maps

Context

Mind maps are forms of graphic organisers which can be created by pupils, and by teachers *for* pupils. They are specifically useful for struggling learners because they are produced using **single** words or single images. Many pupils find conceptual thinking very difficult or are overwhelmed by a lot of text. Making mind maps allows pupils to pull single ideas from their memory and then build a bigger picture as they think of associative words and images. Because the brain makes links between words, pupils can start with a simple idea and then develop it, literally one word or image after another. This is handy for retrieving stored memories and is very accessible because the mind map can be recorded using just images, or by using single words. The volume of writing is reduced, and pupils can focus on key words rather than getting bogged down with superfluous language.

Mind mapping is great for pupils who find writing difficult and for pupils who struggle with thinking and organising ideas. As mind maps are drawn quickly as we think, they can be helpful for pupils with working memory and processing difficulties. If an adult or buddy can scribe, the pupil can focus on recall. Another beneficial aspect of mind maps is the way you can use them to sequence and order ideas into a hierarchy; the main ideas come first, and the detail can be added in words linked to key themes. The way mind maps branch out, helps pupils to visualise a concept. Linking the words helps pupils connect related facts or regroup ideas. These connections are important for deeper learning.

Consider

- Mind maps can be used in class for any kind of planning. The branches can be numbered to sequence a story, for example.

- Use for assessing depth of knowledge and revision tasks – give key topic words and ask pupils to produce their own mind map showing their wider conceptual understanding.

- Pupils needing help getting started can have a scaffolded map with some branches mapped out, key words listed on the page to put into a map or images included to add words to – or words to illustrate.

- Mind maps work well with buddy pairs and with groups.

It's all in the classroom

- Adult support with writing by scribing ideas – this can be done quickly round the class with several pupils when planning writing.

- Some pupils (and teachers) hate mind maps because they like to record in a linear way, so be sensitive to this!

- Presenting information – When adapting mind maps for pupils, less is more. Keep the mind maps uncluttered and differentiate the words using **bold fonts** rather than underlining. Colour can be helpful but can also be distracting; keep maps simple and add symbols or drawings to illustrate key words. Hierarchies can be shown by changing font size or shape of text box.

- Spotlight parts of mind map using online tools.

- Pupils can highlight or answer questions based on the map. They can add details like word definitions.

- Mind maps can be cut out and reorganised.

- Mind maps produced using computer templates can be converted into lists.

- You can set a mind map task with limits such as using a mnemonic, having a set number of words or links, or using a question as the central stem. This is a very accessible way to encourage lateral thinking.

Reflect

How might mind maps work in your subject or age group? Could you make mind maps physically – out of concrete props?

It's all in the classroom

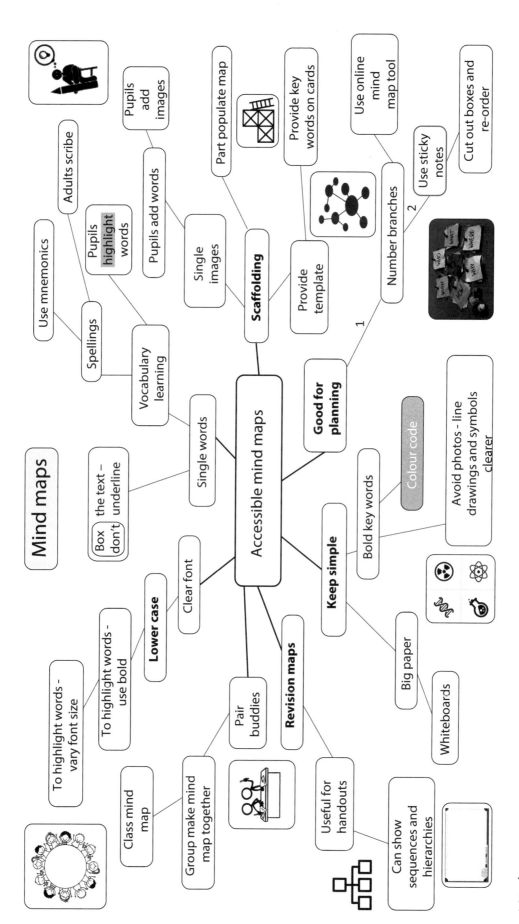

Mind maps

It's all in the classroom

Stories

Context

The brain is a story processor. Through stories we can imagine what others might be thinking and feeling, helping us start to experience the world from different perspectives. Stories activate our sensory experiences and our emotions. Memories are strongly influenced by emotions, and teachers can harness this aspect of stories in lessons to help pupils consolidate and retrieve information. Teachers can choose stories that pupils can relate to or spark their interests, consequently providing a magical hook into curriculum content that interacts with pupils' own experiences. This supports them to make connections and reshapes their thought processes. Stories are engaging and interactive for even the most reluctant or inattentive learners. Literacy and language skills can be explicitly taught through stories in any subject. In addition, stories support executive functioning skills because story structures are sequential, providing useful links to skills involving recounting and planning.

Stories can be used as specific interventions for pupils with additional needs. Teachers can use stories to help pupils who need to develop emotional and social skills. Stories can be therapeutic, in that they bridge between a child's inner world and outer real world. Sometimes stories can be helpful in addressing conflict or worries indirectly. Sharing stories in which the narrative relates to common issues such as grief, family splits or childhood fears can reframe pupils' anxieties and help them externalise their thoughts. Social stories are a format used to teach pupils about social skills and routines. Many pupils struggle to pick up social cues readily and need to learn the rules of social interaction. You can take an everyday experience, such as eating lunch together in school, and create a simple story about how it works and how people behave. Children on the autistic spectrum benefit from these stories and when they are repeated frequently, the child can internalise the new script and learn to adapt their behaviour in context. Social stories also work well with younger children and can be very helpful in dealing with conflict and routines. They can be verbal and/or written/illustrated.

Consider

- Have fun hooking new content into lessons by telling a story – a personal experience, a character's story, a 'how this came into being' story.

- Use film or cartoon clips to bring a story to life and make links to the content.

It's all in the classroom

- Life stories of characters or real people can be used to shape moral or ethical thinking.

- Use stories to sequence events or concepts. For example, the history of the first vaccination could be storyboarded and used as a sequencing task or a matching or annotating task, or could be retold as a writing exercise.

- Get pupils to turn content into a story; use visuals only to retell a story or act it out. This helps them visualise the big picture and sequence the steps.

- Use stories to structure revision of previous learning material.

- Play story games – i.e., charades or retelling a story as a group using one sentence or word per pupil to develop sequencing, listening and collaborative skills.

- There are so many films that can be linked to the curriculum, and films are particularly engaging for reluctant learners. Pupils may know the genre and characters even at a young age, so they are a fruitful resource for literacy and language learning. You can pause, rewind and slow down film clips if you want to use repetition to reinforce learning.

 Reflect

Which parts of your curriculum would stories enhance? Find some social stories to try in your setting.

It's all in the classroom

Stories

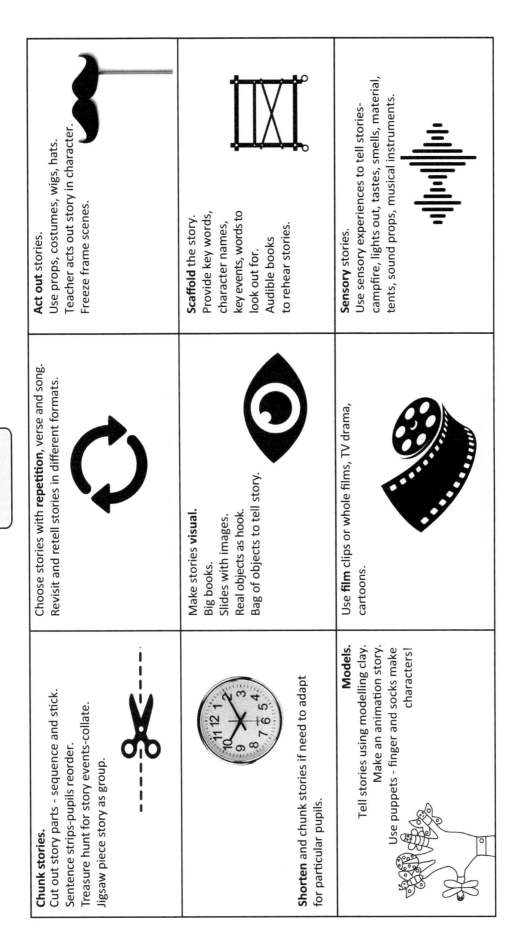

Act out stories.
Use props, costumes, wigs, hats.
Teacher acts out story in character.
Freeze frame scenes.

Scaffold the story.
Provide key words, character names, key events, words to look out for.
Audible books to rehear stories.

Sensory stories.
Use sensory experiences to tell stories - campfire, lights out, tastes, smells, material, tents, sound props, musical instruments.

Choose stories with **repetition**, verse and song.
Revisit and retell stories in different formats.

Make stories **visual**.
Big books.
Slides with images.
Real objects as hook.
Bag of objects to tell story.

Use **film** clips or whole films, TV drama, cartoons.

Chunk stories.
Cut out story parts - sequence and stick.
Sentence strips-pupils reorder.
Treasure hunt for story events-collate.
Jigsaw piece story as group.

Shorten and chunk stories if need to adapt for particular pupils.

Models.
Tell stories using modelling clay.
Make an animation story.
Use puppets - finger and socks make characters!

It's all in the classroom

Games

 ### Context

Introducing games to lessons is a great way to engage and motivate pupils, especially pupils who struggle with more traditional lesson formats. Games are fun. Games are creative. Games can get pupils learning without them realising they are working! Pupils often find games immersing and activating. Games develop links from a child's inner world to reality, helping pupils to express themselves and communicate their emotions. Most of us love the chance to be playful, and laughter benefits classroom cohesion and relationships. Pupils can learn safely through failure in a game, as it's 'only a game' and the stakes are comparatively low. Games involve active processing of information, which allows pupils to rehearse concepts and vocabulary freely. Games facilitate the expression of emotions. Games can be energising; however, they may also be used to settle a class.

Many pupils who struggle in the classroom enjoy learning through games. Games promote many social skills and enable pupils to practise turn taking, listening and cooperation. Early years practitioners understand the importance of play, but playful experiences often get squeezed out as pupils get older. This is such a shame, because games spark interest and make learning motivating and accessible to harder-to-engage pupils. Sometimes it is useful to use playful language to defuse stressful situations. For pupils who are on the cusp of an outburst, distraction or humour can, in the right situation, break a negative cycle and help restore communication and calm.

There are many ways to incorporate games into any age range or subject; vocabulary teaching; maths strategy games; learning set routines or practical work, memorising and revising; critical thinking and role play. To make games accessible to all learners, teachers need to be well prepared with the logistics of the game – seating, timing, grouping, prompts, and instructions. The learning outcome should be directly aligned to the game. Explaining the rules clearly is a must. The success of a game as a learning experience depends on the teacher being vigilant, monitoring progress and participation and stopping just at the right time.

 ### Consider

- ◆ Timing is important. Games are good starter activities and can generate excitement and focus. Have a game set up ready with a visual prompt. Games as frequent starters help pupils learn the routine. Using a starter game as revision of the last lesson's key words is great retrieval practice.

It's all in the classroom

- A quick game in a lesson break could act as a formative assessment, helping to judge whether or not to move the learning on.

- Games as energisers fire up flagging attention.

- At the end of lessons, a game may consolidate key words or concepts, act as reward or close a topic.

- Some pupils are threatened by anything competitive and may either dominate or withdraw. Think about how to lower the potential stress of a game by providing choices in how pupils participate, providing visual cues, allowing pupils to draw or write answers or choosing a role for a pupil such as keeping score.

- Watch out for games drifting on too long, beyond the time when pupils are learning what you had intended.

- Make sure games are not triggering overexcitement because you haven't planned the transition to the next task cleanly.

Reflect

Do you fear the loss of control of introducing a game? Think about how you could introduce games in a structured way. Are there pupils who opt out? How can you encourage some form of safe participation?

It's all in the classroom

Games - top 20 easy-to-prepare games

Alphabet Games	Odd One Out and Why?	Pairs Matching	Here is the Answer, what is the Question?
Key words, adjectives, facts.	Juliet, Malvolio, Lear	Pupil come to board and match a pair. Na, Lithium, Pb, Lead, Li, Silver, Gold, Au	because she ate the three-course gum — calcium
Stand Up if you… Fact questions. Experiences. Things in common.	**20 Questions**	**Categories** Name 5 or 10 items in set category in 30 seconds.	**True or False** T/F?
What's the Link? Images, words, objects- pupils describe and explain the links.	**Guess the Picture** Images magnified, strange angles. Images partially covered. Pupils guess and describe.	**What is Better?** Pick 2 items- character, place, fact, skill - topic related - to generate discussion.	**Charades/Pictionary** Topic - related key words-act or draw in teams.
Taboo Target words- describe without using words on card.	**Hangman** Key words or phrases	**Thumbs Up, Heads Down** Pupils of all ages love this for some reason! Link it to topic by having targeted questions to choose pupils for each round.	**Kim's Game** Memory game - adapt with facts, images- topic related. Pupils memorise items - guess all or which one removed.
Memorising a Diagram or Annotated Picture In groups send one member to picture/diagram- return to group and try to recreate. Others take turns until picture is complete. Timed.	**Who am I?** Pupils describe an item to others. Guess who or what they are.	**Bingo** Facts in the boxes. Questions as clues. Can adapt facts according to ability?	**Team Quiz** Correct answers give chance to remove a block in a stack, take a turn in noughts and crosses or battleships.

Games – top 20 easy-to-prepare games

Chapter 4
Accessible assessment and feedback

ACCESSIBLE ASSESSMENT	126
ACCESSIBLE FEEDBACK	133
ACCESSIBLE FEEDBACK CHECKLIST	135
ACCESSIBLE HOMEWORK	137
TEACHING ASSISTANT/ TEACHER COLLABORATION – PUPIL FEEDBACK	142

Accessible assessment and feedback

Accessible assessment

 ## Context

Whatever your subject or age group, you will be carrying out ongoing formal and informal assessment of all your pupils on a regular basis. What is assessment for? Assessment is a key part of the teaching and learning cycle and is used to review performance during or at the end of a topic or time period, as feedback to pupils about what they need to do next and to provide teachers with useful data on progress that pupils have made and to inform us about missing knowledge, underdeveloped skills and misconceptions. Assessments inform our planning going forward.

For most pupils in class, the assessments used are appropriately pitched so the teacher can find out what they need to know about learning, and pupils can see their own progress. For pupils with any additional needs, this may not be the case. Pupils working well below expected age levels may not be able to show their knowledge at all if the assessment is well above their current attainment level. If their score is very low, you won't learn much about what they **do** know, and you may risk damaging pupils' self-esteem irrevocably so that any further assessment provokes anxiety and feelings of failure. Other pupils may be able to do well in an assessment because they have secured content knowledge and can comprehend well, but they may struggle to access the assessment without scaffolds such as a reader or use of a word processor. For some pupils with emotional needs, the process of being assessed formally can trigger huge anxieties and may result in outbursts, avoidance and even school refusal on days when assessments are planned. Assessments may not be providing you with the full picture of your class's progress.

It is common for teachers to be unsure about how far to differentiate assessments, as there may be a fear that the content is watered down in some way and that the assessment will lose its impact or be unfair. However, if we go back to the point of assessment, we need to find ways to help pupils demonstrate what they have learned, so 'one size fits all' doesn't always work. Teachers planning their teaching and learning cycle for specific cohorts of children will need to think about adapting assessments, doing more informal assessments or removing the barriers preventing a pupil demonstrating their knowledge in the standard assessment.

Baseline assessment is key in knowing the starting levels of each pupil. You may need to adapt a baseline assessment for some pupils to get a true picture; for

Accessible assessment and feedback

example, a dyslexic pupil may be able to do the class baseline assessment with a reader, or a pupil with more complex learning needs may need an assessment pitched at a lower chronological age/content level.

The context of assessment is important as well, in that pupils need to know if a formal assessment is going to take place. They will need to be prepared for it explicitly, and the timing should be planned appropriately so the more vulnerable pupils feel assured that everything is in place for them to do their best. Some pupils find formal testing overwhelming, as they struggle with the expected silence or change of room layout. Some pupils may need adaptions in the classroom such as access to ICT, large print or headphones. Some pupils may have had time out of lessons for different reasons, and so have missed content or assessment planning time. It is helpful to think about your class and check pupil profiles, speak to pupils about what they need and plan with support staff to make any formal testing go as smoothly as possible.

For pupils undergoing any national testing at key times in the school year, staff need to know if special arrangements are required. Special arrangements are exam adaptations made to ensure equality of opportunity, such as having a reader or scribe; a separate space to do the exam; rest breaks or prompts; extra time, etc., that enable appropriate access to the exam for pupils. As a class teacher, you have a role in helping to identify what pupils may need by observing how they get on in assessments and analysing test data with and without support, as evidence of need is required in order to provide exam arrangements. The SEN teams in schools can put in place formal diagnostic testing to verify which considerations might be needed for pupils with disabilities or health needs. If you are aware that certain pupils qualify for additional support or different arrangements for exams, it is vital that the pupils use these for any classroom assessments as well, to ensure equal access, to practise their arrangements in test situations and to ensure they have the chance to do the assessment to the best of their ability.

When feeding back to pupils about their performance in assessments, take care not to compare pupils in front of the class. Reading out scores or ranking pupils by marks is potentially very damaging to vulnerable pupils. Focus on showing pupils the progress they have made compared to their individual starting points. Pupils may compare themselves to each other even at an early age, so it is hard to 'hide' test scores as they may ask their peers anyway. If the class culture is all about personal effort and supporting each other, you can hopefully keep esteem high by pointing out individual progress, effort, teamwork and resilience.

Accessible assessment and feedback

 Consider

Helpful scaffolds for informal or formative ongoing assessment in class include adjusting the materials, timing or depth of answer required:

- Mini whiteboard quizzes where pupils can draw, write or show true/false.
- When checking understanding, scaffold your questions by using levelled questions for different pupils, show pictures to help, provide choices of answers, model answers. Question grids are useful for adapting question level.
- Exit tickets – short answers, open-ended questions for showing what pupils have learned in lesson.
- 'Stand up, sit down if . . .' game to demonstrate factual knowledge, explain to peers, etc.
- Interactive whiteboard games – take turns or change levels.
- Change the media – i.e., handwriting in sand or on large paper or mini whiteboard.
- Line of continuum – pupils choose where to be and explain why.
- Extra thinking time for questions.
- Support staff to read/scribe and prompt.
- Drawing instead of writing to show knowledge.
- Writing frames with differing scaffolding.
- Different key word banks or sentence starters as props.
- Higher degree of modelling provided for specific pupils.
- Verbalising in place of writing.
- Adapt language to help pupils with poor vocabulary – clarify, provide examples.
- For EAL pupils, allow translation strategies, adapt language and try verbal rather than written answers.

Accessible assessment and feedback

Helpful scaffolds in formal or summative assessment include removing barriers to showing knowledge or adapting assessment:

- Designing the test – Make sure language is unambiguous; make sure any boxes to tick line up with the questions; format the test clearly so questions are delineated from each other; don't cram questions together; don't use a separate answer page to the question paper or have a separate multiple choice answer sheet, as this is very confusing for some pupils and uses up processing capacity; check that there are no errors.

- Design assessment with easier questions at the start so pupils will have their confidence buoyed early in the task, reducing the likelihood of them giving up straight away.

- Include labelling and matching task questions so pupils working at the single-word level can achieve.

- Read questions out.

- Use images in test as cues for specific pupils.

- Provide additional time or chunk test into sections with breaks.

- Multiple choice can be adapted with fewer choices.

- Model types of answers in lead up to test.

- Allow pupils to use resources such as textbook or prompt sheets.

- Provide writing frames for long answers.

- Adapt questions for some pupils – provide appropriately levelled tests.

- Use ICT to support – online tests, speech to text, etc.

Before any testing, it is helpful to prepare the pupils so they know where the assessment fits in, what you are using it for and how you will share successes and gaps with them:

- Make the learning linked to the assessment explicit, so they know what is going to be covered.

Accessible assessment and feedback

- Do a practice test – Walk them through it, showing the format and structure of questions and answers, how many questions there will be, how much time they will have and how the marks are allocated.

- Revise or practise with the pupils – Many vulnerable pupils struggle to revise or practise at home.

- Flag the timing ahead of the test by putting it in the homework diary; display the date in class; remind them; email or call parents/carers of specific pupils so they know an assessment is coming up or speak to support staff who can do so; don't spring surprise tests on pupils.

- Check the classroom setup and order the paperwork early so that any adaptions can be made in good time.

- Speak to the SEN team ahead of time if you require support or if it would be beneficial for some pupils to be withdrawn to another room to do the assessment with support.

Alternatives – You may need to be creative about assessing some pupils if they are very young, working significantly below their peers or have missed lots of teaching due to school absence or illness. Here are some ideas that could be adapted according to age and subject:

- Portfolio of work.

- Photographs of pupils demonstrating skill areas and sequences of learning.

- Staff-annotated diary of skill progression.

- Film of pupils demonstrating knowledge/skills.

- Case study by staff.

- Checklist of skills ticked off with dates and level of independence.

- Discussion with pupil – recorded or noted by staff.

- Project.

- Practical task completed.

- Pupil presentations.

Accessible assessment and feedback

 Reflect

Is assessment taking up a lot of time? Can you do more informal and less formal assessment and still know your pupils? Do you have pupils who may demonstrate knowledge or a skill in one lesson only to have seemingly forgotten it the next time you see them? Knowing that any assessment is a snapshot on that day is helpful.

Accessible assessment and feedback

Accessible assessment

- **Space** for answers laid out within assessment.
- **Adapt** assessments or provide appropriately levelled alternative assessments for pupils who are unlikely to score in assessments used for class. Aim for success.
- **Format** uncluttered and clearly defined.
- Provide appropriate **scaffolds** - key words, number lines, images, objects, writing frame, rewording, reassurance of adult etc.
- **Clarity** of language and purpose. Clear mark scheme shared with pupils.
- Provide **support** for barriers; reader, physical prompt, ICT, scribe, extra time etc. Plan ahead.
- Explicit **preparation and practice** of material to be assessed in class.
- Images, objects, media used to help **retrieval** or to prompt pupil.

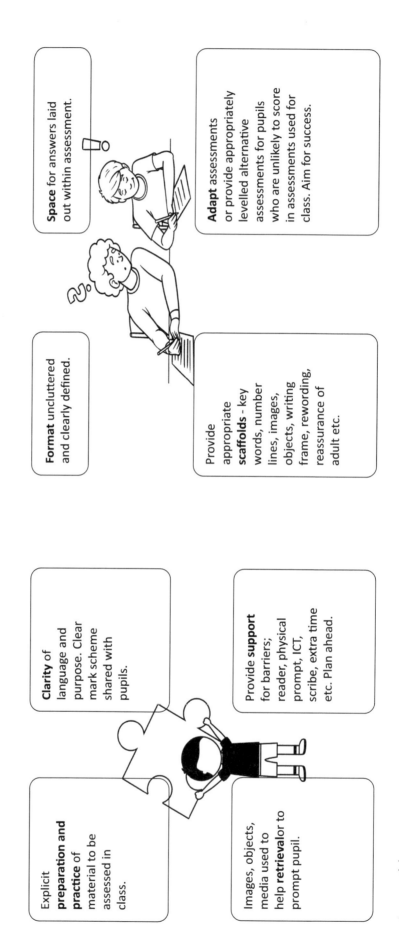

Accessible feedback

Context

Pupils need clear feedback along their learning journey in order to make the appropriate next steps. Feedback policies vary between schools, but many pupils with additional needs benefit from support to access that feedback. This could be because they need support with the literacy or language of the feedback – they struggle to comprehend the meaning of the feedback – or because they struggle emotionally with the concept of feedback. Written feedback can be a big barrier – mainly because pupils can't read the teacher's handwriting or understand the comments. Pupils may not see how feedback fits in with the task.

Marking policies are usually generalised and not personalised. For example, a literacy policy may specify highlighting spelling errors; but for dyslexic pupils, this can be demoralising and unhelpful. If schools use a symbol-based feedback strategy, pupils might not be able to recall the meaning of the symbols. Many pupils with additional needs struggle to skim their work, looking for the most recent marking, and if marking is within their work, pupils fail to notice it. Verbal feedback should be more accessible but works best when carried out *during* tasks, so pupils don't forget it. Pupils may not know what successful work should look like and are not always able to pick up on hints. Pace is always a potential barrier because many pupils need extra processing time to read and act on feedback. If you are spending any time on giving feedback, it's worth planning how you are going to make it accessible to all; otherwise, your efforts will be wasted.

Consider

- Live marking is immediate. Use a visualiser or upload work to display while you mark it, sit next to pupils and mark while narrating what you see, get peers to model marking work.

- Use worked examples.

- Model marking midway through a task, so pupils can edit before finishing.

- Personalise marking for individuals – i.e., mark content, not spelling; mark fewer spellings or only target words; adapt language of feedback for individual pupils who may have comprehension or literacy challenges; be explicit for pupils who need literal guidance; be sensitive with constructive marking for pupils with emotional needs who may have fragile self-esteem.

Accessible assessment and feedback

- When feeding back to pupils with additional needs, it may be appropriate to focus on one assignment or section of a task so as not to overwhelm pupils.

- Try voice recorded feedback – verbal feedback using ICT that pupils can play back.

- If using coded marking or highlighter marking – keep it simple, and display the meanings of the codes. You may need to revisit and re-explain for some pupils.

- If you use a mark scheme or personalised learning checklist for self and peer marking, you may need to simplify, chunk it or talk through.

- If using written feedback, be specific and unambiguous.

- Lists and rubrics can be useful. Many pupils find ratings scales an accessible way to measure their own progress. You could make the progress levels visual in the form of graded ladders of skills, coloured pie charts to complete, etc.

- Use images. Smiley faces and stars may not be providing specific feedback about how to improve, but many pupils of all ages (and their parents/carers) still appreciate efforts tangibly rewarded.

 Reflect

Are you wasting time in class reading out or explaining written feedback to some pupils because they can't access it? If so, you are doubling up your work! Think about what needs to change.

Accessible assessment and feedback

Accessible feedback checklist

Live marking/over-the-shoulder marking – focus on specific sections, chunk and be specific. Check that pupil understands actions needed to improve.	
Live marking – share marking with class and invite suggestions from pupils.	
Exemplars and exemplar actions – provide exemplars and model editing and improving work on the board.	
Coding – keep marking coding simple and display codes in class. Revisit meanings of codes frequently.	
Immediate – for some pupils, feedback needs to be actioned straight away. Support them in making changes while you are still nearby.	
Space – teach some pupils to leave double spaces or pages in their books to add marking in, so they can find it easily.	
Space – some pupils need marking demarcated from their work. Try stickers, overlays, sticky notes, drawing boxes around comments so they can see them.	
Content – differentiate what you feedback on according to needs of pupils.	
Time – build in time to go through feedback in lessons.	

Accessible assessment and feedback

Peers – if using peer feedback, provide a script, checklist or exemplar at different levels, and buddy them carefully so they can appropriately feedback to each other.	
Checklists – use rating scales, differentiate checklists to level, add images, use ICT, colour code, simplify or chunk.	

Accessible assessment and feedback

Accessible homework

Context

Lots of pupils with additional needs find homework really challenging. Homework set in class is often related to lesson content or may involve independent research or skill practice. Pupils may have to record the homework they need to do; they may need to use an online tool to check homework setting, or parents and carers may have to carry out tasks at home such as daily reading. Just getting the correct message from school to home can create issues because of poor organisational skills and lack of capacity at home to support the process. Other reasons why homework can be an issue for many pupils include the following:

- Literacy skills – not being able to fluently read the information or task, or not having the skills to write at an appropriate level for the task.

- Comprehension – not understanding the concept in the first place.

- Comprehension – not being able to understand what the homework task is asking them to do.

- Recall – however successfully pupils may have grasped the idea in class, they may have forgotten it once they get home and are without prompts.

- Recall – not remembering or not being in a routine, so forgetting to look to see if they even have homework.

- Level – the homework is pitched at class level, and some will find it too hard.

- Motivation – **home is home and school is school**!

- Energy – for some pupils, just managing school is exhausting, and they have literally run out of energy for more study when they get home.

- Resources – some pupils don't have access to books, internet, appropriate ICT equipment or space to work.

- Other pulls on a pupil's time – some pupils care for siblings or other family members, work outside or in the home, have medical needs that are time consuming or have extracurricular activities that take place in the evenings or on weekends.

Accessible assessment and feedback

Parents and carers can worry a lot about homework, and some may be spending evenings coaxing, working alongside or battling with their child to get homework done. Remember that parents and carers are **not** in the lesson, so it is hard for them to support at home. Some adults may have had poor experiences of school themselves, and many are not up to date with either the different ways in which schools measure progress or any new curriculum frameworks. Even if they are confident in supporting their children, parents and carers may end up phoning round, researching the topic themselves, doing the homework step by step with their child or in some cases completing the homework *for* the child. This can create huge tensions, stress and worry at home. Worrying about homework, lack of homework, missed or inaccessible homework, the impact of not handing homework in and getting detentions or missing out on grades are all common issues that parents and carers bring to meetings. Many homes have adults who are working long hours or have numerous responsibilities to juggle, and the guilt at not being able to support their vulnerable child can create added tension.

Whatever your setting or age group, consider what the point of homework is before setting it. If it is to instil independent study skills, then giving overly tricky homework defeats the object. If the homework is to reinforce previous learning, remember that it is hard for some pupils to remember what the lesson was about, so extra information may be needed to prompt the pupil or help the parents or carers. Pupils should get benefits from doing homework, such as building self-esteem because they have worked on their own, consolidating learning done in class, practising new skills, finding out new facts and developing interests.

If there is a homework policy in your setting, then it is worth thinking about how you can set appropriate homework for any pupils or groups who struggle to get it done. Just because some pupils may regularly fail to hand homework in, does not mean that other pupils should be denied the opportunity to study at home. Pupils with gaps in their learning may need to have the opportunity to catch up, and homework can be a useful way for motivated pupils to consolidate their lessons. It may be that homework is entirely inappropriate for some groups or pupils, or that the school policy is not to set *any* homework. It is always useful to discuss individual pupils with the SEN or pastoral team in school to agree on the ways forward. It may be that for some pupils, for example, time can be found within the school day to do supported homework in school, rather than at home.

Consider

What kind of homework is more accessible for a range of learners?

- ◆ Learning facts for recall is great for pupils with working memory and processing issues – provide definitions, key facts, key words and get them to match, sort or type.

Accessible assessment and feedback

- Flip learning can be another great idea for older pupils – where the pupils have seen the materials ahead of the lesson so they can prepare, read through and process information before being challenged. Setting topic-related videos for preparing for a topic is very accessible if pupils have access to ICT.

- Can you film part of your explanation in the lesson, or provide a videoed slide presentation?

- For pupils without ICT at home – print out materials for them to take home.

- If the pupil will need support, attach detailed instructions or additional resources so a support teacher or parent/carer can help.

- Give a 'menu' of choices of tasks at different levels and direct pupils to an appropriate task.

- Make explanations **clear and unambiguous.**

- Set very **simple** homework for individual pupils who are working well below their peers – it is good for them to do it independently and feel successful.

- Short deadlines work best – many pupils find project work hard to manage because they cannot organise the steps, and so leave it all until the last minute.

- Be aware of subject-specific words that may be unfamiliar to parents and carers.

- Set 'doing' homework such as interviewing someone, looking things up, learning some words, quiz, do an experiment at home, etc.

- Use quiz or word definitions apps – many pupils enjoy quizzes online, and you can set timings or answer choices according to level of pupils.

- Go through the homework in lesson and model what you want – check to make sure pupils know what is expected.

- For older pupils, if homework is a big issue, invite parents in and explain the syllabus so they have the resources needed.

- For younger pupils, check that reading materials are appropriate and that parents or carers understand what is expected and how to record sessions. Some parents may appreciate coming in and having a reading session modelled so they can build confidence.

Copyright material from Rachel Cosgrove (2020), Inclusive Teaching in a Nutshell, Routledge

Accessible assessment and feedback

 Reflect

Does monitoring homework feel time consuming? What do you do when pupils don't complete homework? Can you pick your battles? Pupils are more likely to do homework tasks if they can see the teacher is taking time to look at it and when they get positive feedback for completion.

Accessible assessment and feedback

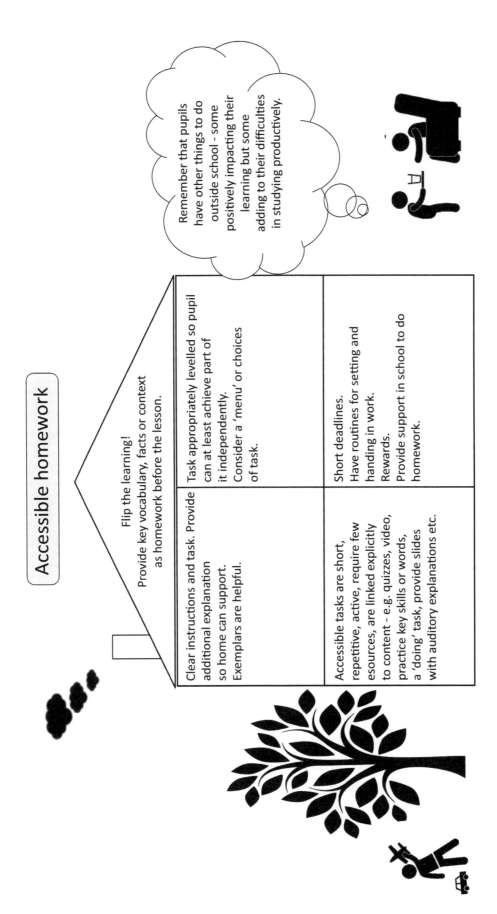

Accessible homework

Flip the learning! Provide key vocabulary, facts or context as homework before the lesson.

- Clear instructions and task. Provide additional explanation so home can support. Exemplars are helpful.
- Task appropriately levelled so pupil can at least achieve part of it independently. Consider a 'menu' or choices of task.
- Accessible tasks are short, repetitive, active, require few resources, are linked explicitly to content - e.g. quizzes, video, practice key skills or words, a 'doing' task, provide slides with auditory explanations etc.
- Short deadlines. Have routines for setting and handing in work. Rewards. Provide support in school to do homework.

Remember that pupils have other things to do outside school - some positively impacting their learning but some adding to their difficulties in studying productively.

Accessible assessment and feedback

Teaching assistant/ teacher collaboration – pupil feedback

 Context

Teaching assistant (TA) support is most effective when TAs are adequately prepared for the lesson, are well trained, and collaborate with the teachers. TAs usually know pupils well and work closely with individuals; this can be very useful in informing subject or class teachers about the progress that pupils have made during lessons. Pupils are influenced by the way the TA and teacher model behaviour in class. If the TA has status in class, there can be a positive impact on behaviour, as pupils will see the TA as having equitable authority with the teacher. The teacher can influence the way pupils perceive TAs, and good modelling of communication shows the class that the TA and the teacher are working together and can't be divided!

Feedback about pupil progress is extremely valuable to teachers, as it can inform planning. Teachers can use TA feedback to judge progress, and this can be used to plan next steps for the individuals or groups within the class. Feedback can be verbal or written and should be part of the communication between teachers and TAs. Feedback should focus on **pupils'** learning and well-being.

Making time to develop a relationship with a TA is time well spent. If you are a subject teacher, you may have infrequent TA support, but it is still worth investing some time in getting to know the SEN team in school so that you can effectively use their expertise. SEN teams usually welcome staff who drop in after school or during lunchtime to talk about a pupil or ask for advice. The SEN department will have lots of information about pupils and may be able to help you tap into pupil interests or strengths or give you some more background detail on a pupil's challenges, which will help you modify your teaching style accordingly. As a caveat, TAs vary in their experience and they are just as fallible as teachers, so be open minded about the feedback, listen to the evidence they provide and ensure that you as the teacher, remain the lead in decisions about teaching approaches or curriculum.

Accessible assessment and feedback

Consider

- Teachers and TAs should talk together at the start of the lesson, however briefly.

- Teacher's expectations to be made clear to TA, i.e., seating, target pupils, tasks, key words/concepts/level of questioning.

- Teachers should have clear learning objectives for pupils for whom the whole-class objectives may need modifying. This can be communicated verbally or written on any teaching plans.

- Teachers can ask TAs to communicate throughout the lessons about how pupils are progressing – call teacher over, point to successful pupils, use gestures to show who is doing well or not, use sticky notes or write on work to share how much a pupil did independently, how long particular tasks took or to share pupils' verbal ideas.

- Teachers should approach the TA and ask about how pupils are getting on. The teacher may want to work with target pupils, and in this case the TA can be directed to monitor the progress of the class.

- Feedback on progress can be written in exercise books or assessments by the TA and signed or annotated, so the teacher knows what the pupil has done independently.

- Feedback after a lesson can be through a conversation or in written form.

- Feedback from TAs will focus on pupil progress and be a discussion about what the pupil has learned or achieved. The pupil can be the focus of phrases, i.e., 'I have noticed that x works best when . . .', 'The pupil understood x and . . .', 'The pupil really struggled with the key words . . .', etc. It may be useful to share strategies which work well with pupils that TAs have gleaned from other subjects. All feedback should be delivered in a neutral, nonjudgemental way. TAs should be sensitive in the way they feedback and consider the impact of feedback on less confident teachers.

- Feedback about poor behaviour can be immensely helpful for the teacher, and TAs can be briefed to pick up on specific pupils or groups. It is helpful for pupils to see the TA on the same level as the teacher when it comes to applying policies. The teacher and TA can communicate how best to do this.

Accessible assessment and feedback

- If a TA does not offer feedback in a lesson, teachers should ask. The better the communication and trust between TAs and teachers, the more useful the feedback becomes.

 Reflect

As a teacher, are you able to model the kind of feedback that is useful? Are you able to confidently direct your support staff?

Possible template for feedback

Pupil(s): Lesson objectives for pupil(s)	Date: Teacher: TA:
What was the most successful part of the lesson for them? Why?	Pace Language Relevance Independence Understanding Level of scaffolding Interaction Progress
What did they need most help with?	Literacy Numeracy Practical Concept Instructions Knowledge Expression Interaction

Chapter 5
Outside the classroom

SOCIAL INTERACTION 146

CLUBS AND ACTIVITIES 149

BAGS AND EQUIPMENT 152

Outside the classroom

Social interaction

 ### Context

It is very common for pupils with additional needs to have social interaction difficulties. Sensory issues, language and communication difficulties and emotional regulation difficulties all impact pupils' abilities to develop reciprocal relationships. Some pupils prefer spending time on their own or seek out adult company. Sadly, pupils with additional needs tend to have fewer friendships than their peers. This can lead to social isolation. Bullying can be a big issue, especially in adolescence, when the need to fit in means that teenagers are less willing to spend time with more vulnerable pupils. The stigma of feeling different is a huge issue. Some pupils dread unstructured time, as they do not know what to do and feel stressed about the lack of routine. Vulnerable pupils often fail to pick up information about clubs or are too anxious to go to club meetings, as they don't know what it might be like or who will be there.

Friendships tend to develop amongst those who spend time together and who share common interests. If pupils with SEN spend time with support staff, or have lessons with other SEN children, they will seek out adults or gravitate towards other pupils with needs. This results in these pupils having fewer opportunities to practise the important skills needed for their emotional, cognitive and social development. Skills like how to manage conflict, rivalry and disappointment are modelled through friendships. Empathy and kindness develop through reciprocal peer interaction.

We all have a role in supporting pupils to develop social and communication skills, not only in the classroom but also on the playground, canteen and in unstructured time inside. Any time spent on whole-class teaching of emotional regulation, friendships and well-being will hugely benefit vulnerable pupils and protect learning time in class that might be spent unpacking issues left over from a tricky break time. Developing a classroom of kindness and empathy will help mitigate the issues faced by many pupils with additional needs.

 ### Consider

- Set up buddy systems – with peers or older pupils.

- Provide a safe indoor space such as the school library, corner of the form classroom or pastoral office.

- Set up a check-in so that a pupil knows where to find you.

Outside the classroom

- When suggesting places to go, take the pupils there as a trial run so they know exactly how to get there and what to expect.

- Provide games, cards, craft activities, computer club so that likeminded peers can meet.

- If pupils with additional needs socialise together because they feel safe, encourage friendships.

- Teach games – some pupils may have missed opportunities to learn childhood games.

- On the playground, set up a safe space such as a bench or play equipment space.

- Make time, on occasion, to eat lunch with pupils.

- Structure a part of the playground for role play 'lessons' such as a mini stage.

- Use visual reminders such as boards with timings on, activities to choose.

- Be proactive in observing interaction/tone of pupil talk.

- Preempt conflict by asking a pupil to do a chore or job or taking them for a walk.

- Encourage physical/tactile pupils to join lunchtime sports or outdoors clubs.

- Have headphones and sensory toys available.

- Pair up pupils who you have spotted that you think might gel.

- **Really listen** when pupils come to you with issues.

- Learn how to use a restorative approach for conflict and misunderstandings.

Reflect

How do you balance time needed for catching up with planning and marking, against investing time to support social interaction outside class?

Outside the classroom

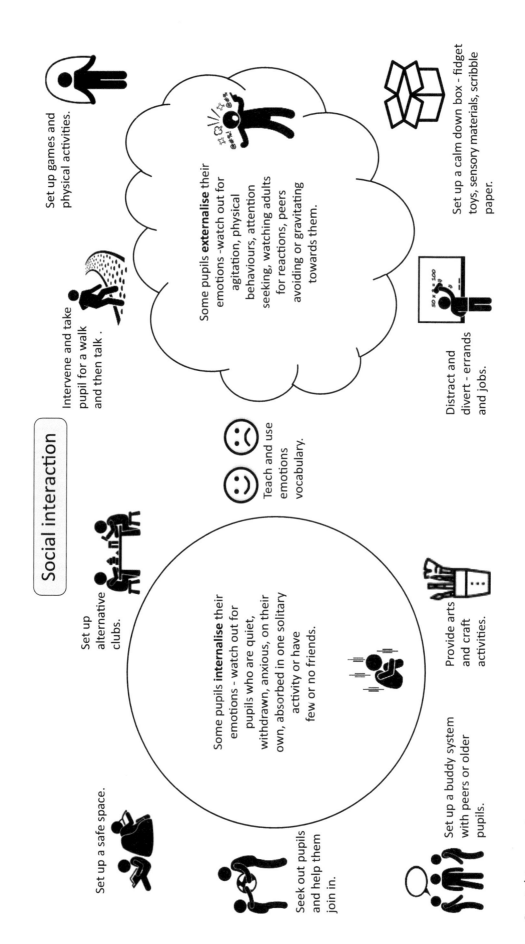

Outside the classroom

Clubs and activities

Context

Extracurricular activities and clubs play an important role in the development of young people. To be part of a group sharing common interests or to participate in a school trip provides opportunities to build social skills and confidence. Sadly, it is common for pupils with additional needs to miss out on what schools offer. These are some of the possible reasons why pupils may miss out:

- The paperwork gets lost or is squashed in school bags; parents/carers are uninformed.

- They don't pick up on whole-class or assembly announcements.

- They are unsure what and who is involved in an activity, and so are reluctant to go.

- They want to go but forget the time or venue.

- They want to go but don't want to go on their own.

- Home cannot afford the cost.

- There are barriers (e.g., physical disability or sensory issues), and discussion about how to work around them hasn't happened.

- Bullying or fear of bullying.

- Feeling different and that they won't fit in.

- They may need adult support to access activities, and plans haven't been discussed with pupil or home.

- They may not do activities or have interests outside school.

- They don't have a friendship group to go with.

- Many clubs include competitive or highly competent pupils, and so may appear elitist to others.

Often staff notice that some pupils haven't brought the slips back in for trips, etc., but don't always dig to find out the reason. In a busy school day, we can make assumptions about why pupils might not want to join a choir or go on a trip.

Outside the classroom

Vulnerable pupils require school staff to go out of their way to ensure everyone has a chance to join in, whatever is on offer. It may be that certain pupils need lots of support to get to an activity – extra adult support, planned transport, medical contingencies, etc. – and staff need to explicitly look at this to ensure equality of opportunity.

Consider

As a class or subject teacher, be aware of the pupils in your class who may need more support to be able to take part in extracurricular activities. Talk to SEN or pastoral staff about potential barriers and find out a bit about what they do outside school, how the family setup works or what kind of support has worked well. Be proactive.

- Call home before giving out paperwork or signposting pupils to online information –parents/carers can help organise pupils if they have the right tools.

- If you are planning a trip, find out any accessibility needs **before** costing or staffing so you can ensure equality of access.

- Have trip or club letters copied so when pupils lose them, you can provide spares.

- Set up routines about trips – i.e., frequent reminders, having a plastic wallet for trip letters, emailing home, having visual deadlines.

- Explain activities in detail – show pictures of what is involved, get peers to explain to others what to expect, walk and talk the day to reduce anxieties around the unknown.

- Take a pupil along to activities to settle them – you may need to do this for a few sessions until they are confident.

- Set up buddy systems to encourage pupils along to activities with a peer.

Reflect

Does the range of activities on offer provide enough choice for everyone, or would it be helpful as a school to look at offering a more diverse range of activities?

Outside the classroom

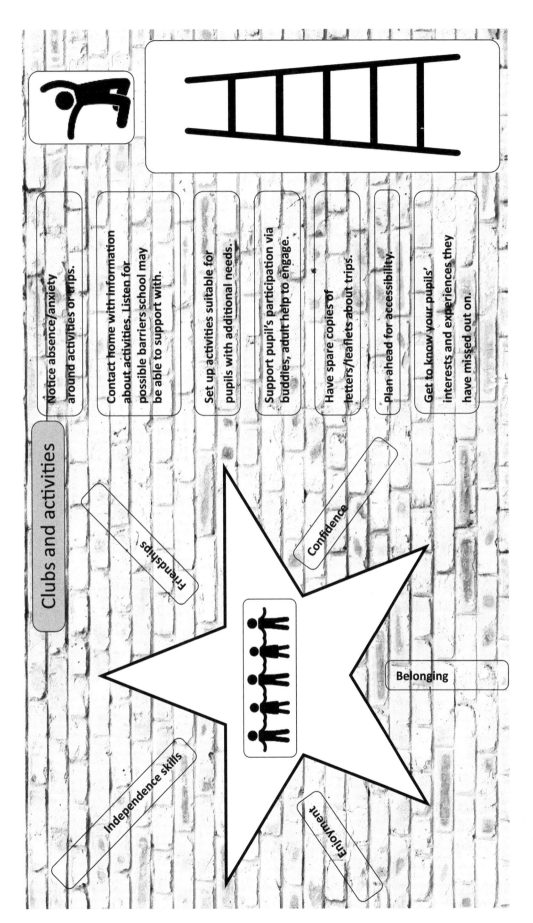

Clubs and activities

Outside the classroom

Bags and equipment

Context

Taking care of personal belongings and being responsible for organising your own items for school is an important life skill that we want all pupils to develop. However, children vary in their development, and some pupils reach secondary school still very much reliant on adult support to manage their possessions. This can cause frustration for everyone! Pupils with additional needs may struggle to organise themselves for many reasons – they may not be developmentally ready for this step, they may be distractible and forgetful, they may be in a heightened state emotionally or they may have physical or sensory issues which hamper their independence in school. For some pupils, home life is busy or chaotic, and families may lack capacity to support the day-to-day organisational hurdles needed to be well prepared for school. Some pupils also lack opportunity to learn these skills because their parents and carers have done things for their children and have continued to support in a way that inhibits a child's chance to develop independence. Sometimes pupils with significant needs have a lot of help in school and become dependent on adult support. They lack skills, confidence or motivation to self-manage.

Consider

It is worth spending time observing pupils to see if they are ready to take the next steps towards personal organisation. It may be a good idea to talk with parents or carers to see what their expectations are. Sometimes parents are frustrated because their child keeps losing things or won't pack their bag for school. Together you can look at what you think the child could achieve and work collaboratively towards a shared goal by dividing it into smaller steps and taking literally one step at a time.

- ◆ Be organised in the classroom and with your routines – set places for books, coats, lunch boxes, etc.

- ◆ Have spare labels handy.

- ◆ Visual prompts as checklists are useful for packing up, sorting a PE kit or for taking home to stick on a front door as reminders of what to bring to school.

- ◆ Have spare pens and stationery for vulnerable pupils who don't come to school with equipment, or who lose it during the day.

Outside the classroom

- Some pupils may like the feel of their bag or coat on their backs for sensory or emotional needs – be sensitive and find a suitable compromise, rather than sanction.

- Stick loose sheets in books or have a plastic wallet to put information in, to help minimise lost paperwork in bags.

- Have 'organisation' sessions where you teach and practise skills for packing bags, hanging up kit, tidying up after lunch, etc.

- Use music countdowns in class for tidying and packing up.

- Allow time at the start and end of a lesson for pupils to organise themselves without rushing.

- Have laminated visual prompts stuck on desks.

- Allocate well-organised pupil helpers to support others.

- Agree with any support staff on how much support is needed (learned helplessness is a risk, and pupils need to have prompts faded over time).

- Reward efforts by pupils to do things for themselves, even if the result isn't perfect!

Reflect

How do your own organisation skills impact your class? If you are super organised and like things just so, watch your need to hurry pupils up by helping them too much. If you are less organised, try to find time to put some of your own strategies in place so the classroom is more ordered to model the outcomes you expect from the pupils.

Outside the classroom

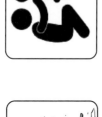

Bags and equipment

Suggestions for teachers to do in school that reduce stress

Some pupils will need support - fade support by encouraging them to do a little bit of the task and supporting the rest.

Routines in class. Be organised. Set places for items. Pupil helpers.

Make sure everything is labelled.

Avoid nagging! Use visual prompts, non-verbal gestures and if talking- keep voice neutral and avoid showing frustration.

Timed targets - use a countdown with music.

Avoid negative comments but praise any attempts to help themselves, however small.

Routines in class. Be organised. Set places for items. Sequence for laying out clothes when getting changed for PE. Pupil helpers.

Suggestion teachers can make to parents/carers that reduces stress - the book box!

Small plastic box (big enough to fit A4 books upright) - keep downstairs (**not in pupil's bedroom!**)

Stick colour coded timetable above.

All books, loose sheets, spare equipment goes in box.

Pupil empties bag into box and repacks from the box.

If parents/carers find loose homework lying about-it goes in box.

Encourage parents/carers not to come to rescue when older pupils forget lunch or homework.

For pupils in split families - box can be taken between homes.

Bags and equipment

Chapter 6
Working with parents and carers

WORKING WITH PARENTS
AND CARERS   160

Working with parents and carers

 ## Context

Engaging well with parents and carers is an important part of a teacher's role. Schools know that the engagement of parents and carers in their child's learning is critical to the child's achievement. If parents and carers are informed about processes in school such as curriculum design, how progress is measured and how their child is supported to achieve, this creates a collaborative approach where the school and parents/carers can work together to do the best for the child. Communication can be through various channels and you may find that you need to vary the way you contact families, by way of varying the time of day, using email or using online school communication platforms, reaching out by phone or in person informally or formally. Get parents and carers onside as soon as possible by being proactive and calling or emailing home as soon as you have a concern, or even better, when there is something positive to report. If we wait for families to contact us when they have a problem, our interaction is likely to be reactive rather than considered. Don't assume that pupils tell parents about what is happening in school, and don't assume that all messages or documents given to pupils make it back to parents or carers.

Many teachers are involved in review meetings that are in addition to brief subject or class consultations. Review meetings may be called to look at special needs or additional provision, attendance issues, pastoral concerns or planning around medical issues. Parents and carers might request a meeting to talk about their concerns in or outside school.

Some parents have an ambivalent relationship with school. They may have struggled at school themselves, they may not feel confident talking to teachers and they may be reluctant to come to meetings if their child is often in trouble. Many parents of children with special needs have had to battle to get their child the support they require and can come into school feeling that they might need to stand up to staff. Other parents and carers may just be very worried about their child. Their expectations about what their child can achieve may be in line with the school, or they may be unrealistic or less aspirational. A review meeting can be tricky to navigate, especially if you are at the start of a working relationship. Traditional parent/teacher meetings may be too one-sided, with the teacher doing most of the talking and using language related to school systems that may be confusing or full of jargon. There have been many changes in exam structure and assessment over the years, and teachers can sometimes forget that people outside the education system are not always up to date with the current systems or language. If we want to develop a collaborative relationship with families, we need to be aware that we may need to explain how things work. The keys to a successful progress or review meeting are planning, setting and listening.

Working with parents and carers

If you work with parents and carers who find communication with school difficult or who can be challenging, ask colleagues to support but be persistent, as it will be worth it for the pupil if you can eventually establish a positive line of communication.

Consider

Planning

- Ensure the time and venue of the meeting is shared and that everyone knows the time allocation – i.e., if the meeting is during the school day, make sure everyone knows if you must leave to teach at a certain time. Try to find a time when you can give the illusion that you are not in a rush.

- Collect some information for the meeting by downloading data, requesting comments from staff or talking to colleagues. If the pupils have high SEN or safeguarding needs, it may be appropriate to have a colleague with you to support the meeting. Find out what support the pupil is already receiving.

- Do some research prior to the meeting so that you are informed about what you as a teacher can and can't suggest – for example, check with the SEN or pastoral staff if there is an intervention that the school can put in place for this pupil or if there are any other activities on offer that you know are available.

- It is helpful to have the pupil at the meeting, but how you do this will depend on the age of the pupil and the focus of the meeting. It may be appropriate for the pupil to attend the whole meeting or part of the meeting. You can either collect the pupil later so the parents/carers can have a private discussion first, if needed, or you can let the pupil leave the meeting before the end. You will know your pupils and can talk to the parents and carers about what they think is best as well.

Setting

- Stand to greet parents/carers, or go and meet them at reception to bring them over.

- Ensure that the room has some privacy and that pupils can't look in.

- Listening is the most important part of the meeting. Set the meeting up in a way that is conducive to a comfortable discussion; i.e., avoid sitting behind a desk, or if this is not possible, position the chairs so it doesn't feel like an interview. Watch out for chairs that are not all the same height. If the venue is in

Working with parents and carers

a classroom, try to avoid holding the meeting in the middle of the space, as this can feel exposing.

- Ideally, have some water available. Tissues are also useful to have on hand. If the family are bringing younger children, having some safe toys or paper is helpful.

Listening

- Think about a parent/carer meeting as a two-way conversation. The purpose of any meeting is to share information about how things are going and to look explicitly at the needs and experiences of the pupil. Have some evidence to share, such as teacher comments, behaviour log or data so that everyone can see what is going well and where the areas for development are.

- Showing attention is vital – i.e., looking at the person, being relaxed, using non-verbal gestures to show you are listening, not fidgeting and using an open posture. Switch mobile phones off and avoid other distractions, so that your full concentration can be given to the conversation. Make sure other staff do not 'pop' in to give messages.

- Listen. Try to ask open questions. What is working well? What has worked well in the past? What is the pupil or parent/carer worried about? What do we think might be the barriers to progress? What do we already know? What are the hopes and aspirations?

- If parents/carers are not happy with provisions at school and are upset or angry, try not to be defensive but instead focus on listening, and clarify to them what you have understood they are saying.

- If the meeting becomes uncomfortable or you feel at all unsafe, do not hesitate to call it to a conclusion and politely ask the participants to leave, or leave yourself to fetch a colleague for support.

- Key goals – What can we focus on that will make a difference? This may be a specific area such as literacy or numeracy, or it might be a broader focus such as attendance or friendships.

- Plan – What do we all need to do next? What support does the pupil need to work on the key goals? Who in school might provide support? What can people at home do to provide support? What can the pupil try to do differently? Small steps work best. Sometimes it is helpful to work backwards from a goal and look at the steps needed to get there.

Working with parents and carers

- Don't make promises that you are not sure can be put in place. It is better to gather the information and make a further date to make the plan.

- Clarify – Here you can summarise the key points, clarify next steps and check that everyone understands and agrees. At this point it is often helpful to ask if there is anything that hasn't been covered. The more you allow the parent/carer to talk, the more information may be forthcoming, allowing a better insight into how the school can help. It is often at these late stages of a meeting when something crucial comes to light.

- If you are unsure about how to move forward, explain that you need to seek further advice and that you will be back in touch.

- Set a date for a follow-up meeting or agree how progress will be monitored. It may be that an email or phone call will be appropriate.

- Every setting will have a different policy, but I think it is good practice to record the meeting in some way – by jotting down key points on a paper template or typing up brief notes during the meeting and sharing a copy with parents and other key staff.

- Ensure that any safeguarding concerns are passed on in the appropriate way for your setting.

Reflect

Listening is a skill that needs practice. Are you aware of your own listening skills? Ask a colleague to observe you and give feedback, so that you can learn more about your own style and how to develop skills.

Working with parents and carers

How to get pupils and parents/carers talking

Tips for prompting pupils	Tips for prompting parents/carers
Use a whiteboard to write up key points, such as words to describe how things are going, successes, key concerns.	Write up agenda for meeting with times.
Use a 1–10 line and ask pupils to rate themselves on anything from a subject, skills, happiness, etc.	Offer to read out teacher comments or explain any data clearly and describe how it relates to expected levels.
Use a visual timetable to prompt ideas about lessons or subjects. Draw a mind map with the pupil with images and words about school.	Open questions work well. How are things going this year? Could you tell me a little more about . . .? Is there anything else we should know about? How could things be different? What would you like X to be able to do?

Working with parents and carers

Ask, how would things be different if? What would that look like?	Help prioritise by using ranked questions. What would you like to talk about first? On a scale of 1–10, where would this be? How could we move this up the scale?
If you had a magic wand and you could change things, what would you change? How would you know? What would be different?	Help clarify by paraphrasing and guessing. Can I just check I've understood so far . . . That must feel . . . I think . . . I wonder . . . It sounds as if . . .
Use emotional literacy cards to get pupils to rate how they are feeling.	Focus on ways forward. How could things be different? Shall we talk about how we might help X move forward with this? What can we do to help X become more involved in this? What do you hope will happen now?
Get pupils involved making a drink for everyone or offering out biscuits.	Ask about extended family and friends who could support.
Have some activities available if the pupil wants to stay but needs something to stay occupied – colouring, tablet, modelling clay, etc.	Reassure parents and carers if they bring younger children to the meeting.

Chapter 7
Strategies for learners – the nuts and bolts

ANGER	165
ANXIETY	168
ATTACHMENT	171
ATTENTION-SEEKING BEHAVIOURS	174
CHRONIC FATIGUE AND PAIN	177
COMPREHENSION	180
DIABETES	183
DISORGANISED PUPILS	186
EASILY DISTRACTED PUPILS	189

ENGLISH AS AN ADDITIONAL LANGUAGE	192
EPILEPSY	195
FIDGETING	198
HEARING IMPAIRMENT	201
LEARNING SABOTEURS	204
LIMITED LIFE EXPERIENCE	207
LISTENING SKILLS	210
LOOKED AFTER AND PREVIOUSLY LOOKED AFTER PUPILS	213
PHYSICAL DIFFICULTIES	216
PUPILS WORKING WELL BELOW AGE-RELATED LEVELS	219
SENSORY PROCESSING DIFFICULTIES	222
SIGNIFICANT LITERACY DIFFICULTIES – READING	225
SIGNIFICANT LITERACY DIFFICULTIES – WRITING	228
SLOW PROCESSING	231
SOCIAL INTERACTION	234
TRAUMA	237
VISUAL IMPAIRMENT	240
WORKING MEMORY	243

Strategies for learners – nuts and bolts

Anger

Context

Anger is an extreme emotion that impacts not only individual pupils but peers and staff as well. Anger is at the end of a continuum of other emotions like annoyance and frustration. In school, anger is what we see when pupils have lost control and are in an 'emotional hijack'. Most of us get angry sometimes, and it's important to understand that anger is a normal response to certain situations that can serve to motivate or protect us. In school, anger that causes concern might be anger in a pupil that is frequent and uncontrollable; lasting longer than normal; major tantrums still occurring after 7 or 8 years of age; causing danger to themselves or others; causing social isolation and/or triggering distress in the pupils because they can't bring themselves down from anger or because they feel ashamed of themselves.

When a pupil loses control in an angry outburst, what is going on for them? Anger can protect us from less comfortable feelings of sadness, fear or anxiety. What might the pupil be saying subconsciously? 'I am not in control'. 'I can't cope in this environment'. 'I can't do this task'. 'I'm embarrassed'. 'I feel threatened'. 'I'm ashamed'.

Pupils with ADHD struggle to manage their emotions and may be quick to anger. Pupils on the autistic spectrum may not cope with changes in routine or may be triggered by sensory overload. Pupils who are struggling with the lesson may build their frustration up to a point where they then blow. Pupils who struggle to express their needs verbally often get exasperated because they can't say what they are thinking. Pupils who have experienced unresolved trauma will have a highly sensitive fight-or-flight response.

Staff can respond in ways that either *escalate* or *de-escalate* the behaviours.

To escalate the behaviour – shame the child by ignoring them, confronting them or directly and aggressively questioning them. To de-escalate the behaviour – understand the reasons behind the anger by making the child feel safe, making the task doable, giving a choice, reducing shame and using cool off and calming strategies.

Consider

- All pupils have right to be taught in a safe environment – ensure that pupils know that the adults are dealing with behaviours and can protect everyone.

Strategies for learners – nuts and bolts

- Observe the pupil, work 1-to-1, ask colleagues for observations and try to work out the triggers.

- Reduce triggers where possible and where you can adjust for the pupils without impacting learning (i.e., if tests trigger outbursts, don't remove the test but find a quiet space and support to do a test).

- Learn to spot signs that the pupil is brewing for an outburst and pre-empt where possible; change the task; offer support; take a time out.

- Model anger in appropriate ways in class – narrate your frustrations and show pupils how you deal with anger.

- Teach the pupils about the biology of an emotional hijack. The more they can recognise their own body sensations, the more they can learn to self-regulate.

- Use a range of self-soothing and co-regulation strategies, e.g., breathing 10 breaths together, exercise, glitter jars, colouring.

- Use cool off time – inside or outside the classroom.

- Use social stories to normalise emotions and demonstrate how others express their emotions appropriately.

- Seek advice if the anger involves threats to harm themselves or others and you are concerned about safety.

 Reflect

How are you coping with extreme emotions in pupils? Dealing with angry outbursts can be emotionally draining, so always ask colleagues to take over or for support. Look after yourself.

Strategies for learners – nuts and bolts

Anger

Help pupils become self-aware by using visual strategies to identify feelings. Images, emojis, colours can also be used to make their own scale.
Use model of the brain to show emotional hijack.

Scale (low to high intensity):
- I am in control
- I am irritated
- I am getting frustrated
- I'm very annoyed
- I am about to lose control

What to do with an outburst

1. If a pupil is having an angry outburst - remove anything in the way, try distracting with playful approach, firmly redirect the pupil using minimal language, protect other pupils. Focus on the behaviour not the pupil. Try and use cool off or time out to minimise impact. Try using techniques like breathing slowly together.
2. If the pupil is out of control - try to get them to a safer place away from an audience to reduce possible shame.
3. If the pupil won't remove themselves - ask for support to remove the pupil.
4. If the pupil won't respond, remove the class.
5. Observe from a distance in the class or just outside.
6. Make sure the pupil is safe.
7. Wait out the outburst to run its course.
8. Tactically ignore any verbal remonstrations or insults. Most pupils can't remember what they have said later.
9. Once the crisis is over and pupil is calmer (they might cry) spend some quiet time without talking. Some comfort may help - toy, blanket, drink.
10. Talk it through once everyone is calm if the pupil is able to. Otherwise defer the conversation to a later time.
11. When the storm has blown over completely, talk through what could have been different and discuss strategies to try.
12. Think about a restorative approach for mediating with peers or staff affected or remediating any damaged property or mess.

Intensity of emotions builds up over a period of time. The time to calm down varies between pupils (and adults) but the whole cycle could take up to 2 hours. During the escalation and crisis phase the expressive language part of our brain is compromised, so avoid trying to have a conversation with the pupil during this time as they cannot explain or rationalise.
Dealing with anger can intensify emotions for the adults supporting the pupil, so you or your support staff may need a break before returning to class again.

Anger cycle: Calm → Trigger → Getting agitated → Escalating → Crisis → Calming down → Calm again (Intensity of emotion vs Time)

Strategies for learners – nuts and bolts

Anxiety

Context

It is normal to worry and have fears, and some anxious feelings can be useful to us as part of our response to threats. However, these anxious thoughts can become a problem when they interfere with everyday activities. Anxiety is unfortunately quite common in school-aged pupils and is preventing some pupils from accessing normal opportunities. Anxious thoughts arise when we expect that something bad is going to happen. Genetic factors, adverse experiences and learned fears can contribute to a pupil's anxious behaviours. Anxiety can manifest as anxious thoughts, uncomfortable sensations in the body or behaviours such as avoidance, anger and the need for control. Anxiety can be reinforced by adults' responses. Pupils with significant anxieties may have support from health professionals who can advise on the most appropriate approaches, but teachers can also have a role in preventing early anxieties in school from escalating.

The language we use around pupils is important: the word anxiety can be overused, when we might really be talking about normal worries. For example, many teenagers are worried about failing exams. Exams are genuinely stressful, and normalising this experience can help. Many pupils have negative thoughts that can grow into anxious thoughts; they may have unrealistic expectations of themselves; they may exaggerate the likelihood of something bad happening; they may put themselves down; they may think peers are judging them. Letting worries control actions can affect mood, feelings of worthiness, appetite and sleep. Many pupils express their worries subconsciously through bodily sensations like stomachaches, restlessness or nausea. Many adults working with anxious pupils instinctively want to reassure and reduce or remove the activity triggering the anxiety, because we don't like to see a pupil in distress. This can inadvertently **reinforce** the anxiety, because the pupil internalises the fact that their fear must be real if the adult has acknowledged it. If we always make it okay for the pupil **not** to face everyday school activities, they will never learn that they *can* manage them. Small anxieties snowball into more fears they cannot face, resulting in their comfort zone decreasing further.

Consider

- Listen to the pupil and gently challenge their logic or provide alternative positive thoughts – what are the facts?

Strategies for learners – nuts and bolts

- Teach the biology of the fight-or-flight response and how the brain responds to threats.

- Encourage pupils to face their fears – express confidence in their ability to have a go.

- Role model overcoming your own fears or refer to role models in real life or fiction who have done so.

- Don't ask leading questions such as 'Are you worried about . . .?'

- If they are anxious and upset, allow them to cry or feel uncomfortable. Stay by their side and show them that in time, these feelings will pass.

- Minimise the waiting time before an activity – the more time spent cogitating, the worse the fear becomes.

- Distraction and diversion can work if appropriately timed. Try humour, a fun activity, peer interaction.

- Movement is a great calmer – try going for a short walk.

- Gradual exposure to a trigger involves working backwards from the goal – e.g., aim for assembly by standing in the corridor, watching from the door, sitting right at the back, staying for a few minutes. etc.

- Teach calm down strategies – such as deep breathing, using a visual such as a glitter jar.

- Encourage pupil to spend time outdoors.

- Collaborate with parents/carers to have a common approach.

Reflect

How do you manage your worries and fears? Are you setting a good example to your pupils?

Strategies for learners – nuts and bolts

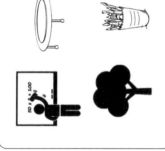

Anxiety

Signals
Tense.
Tummy ache.
Butterflies.
Dizzy.
Negative thinking.
Fast breathing or pulse.
Angry.
Tired.

Get busy
Do jobs round class.
Write in a journal.
Have a snack.
Colouring.
Walk or run.
Bounce.
Get out and about.
Sing or dance.

Talk about it
Talk to a pet.
Talk to friends.
Talk to a trusted adult.
Make a plan.
Find a friend or adult to help.
Set goals.
Take small steps.
Celebrate success.

Relax and think
Stop and think.
What helped last time? Am I thinking the worst?
Positive thoughts.
Listen to music.
Find a quiet space.
Hot drink.
Safe place thoughts.
Breathe.

Leaning into the worries and fears, rather than avoiding them, helps pupils build resilience.

Anxiety

Strategies for learners – nuts and bolts

Attachment

Context

It is helpful for classroom teachers to have a feel for the way early childhood attachment works and how it can affect the way pupils connect with others. If children have had their needs met by their caregivers, they will be able to form other healthy relationships. They will probably have the confidence and focus to learn new things and be emotionally resilient. Children who have experienced unpredictable care, have not had their needs met or have experienced trauma in their childhood may struggle with relationships and behave in ways that are difficult to understand. You may have pupils who mistrust adults, who refuse help or who sabotage work. You may have pupils who need constant reassurance and who are overly dependent on adult attention. Some pupils may blame others and find it hard to take any responsibility for their actions. Occasionally you may work with pupils who swing from wanting your attention one minute to pushing you away another minute. As teachers, we may notice some of these patterns being played out in relationships in class. Pupils may want connection but haven't always learned how to develop healthy reciprocal relationships, or they may struggle to relate to others, seem to be fearful of connection or be controlling of others.

School often represents a safe, secure base for pupils, as school is generally predictable and staff are consistent. School staff often represent key attachment figures for pupils. Reliable boundaries and set routines and spaces help pupils feel grounded, and a restorative, nonpunitive approach can help pupils learn to manage their emotions and develop trust in relationships. Teachers who are aware that the way we form relationships with ourselves and others is linked to prior experience, are often able to notice behaviours in a nonjudgemental way and recognise how a pupil is making them feel. Teaching is reciprocal, and staff represent key relationships for children. It is important to notice the attachment patterns that a pupil is presenting so that appropriate strategies can be used to help them feel safe. When we care about our pupils, it is hard not to take behaviour personally on occasion; it is important to share concerns with colleagues or any professionals working with a pupil. It can be emotionally exhausting to work with pupils with insecure attachment patterns, as sometimes whatever we provide isn't enough.

Consider

- Seek advice from the SEN team if you are concerned about a pupil's relationships in class. If the pupil has a key worker, liaise with them.

Strategies for learners – nuts and bolts

- Use empathic listening – acknowledge and label their feelings, empathise.

- Be predictable and consistent as far as possible – don't threaten or promise things you can't honour.

- Make the classroom a welcoming space and have places for belongings.

- Let a pupil keep their books or bag in the classroom.

- Sometimes a pupil needs a transitional object to know you are keeping them in mind – a special pen from your desk, a book, etc.

- Transitions can be tricky, so plan for changes of staff, pupils, room, class – explain changes, visit the new teacher, find a space in the new room, etc.

- If a pupil is developing an intense connection with you, speak to colleagues and discuss how to manage it safely and appropriately.

- Work hard to prevent behaviour escalating, as exclusion will damage any sense of belonging.

 ### Reflect

Do you find you are taking home worries about your pupils? How can you stay compassionate but not be overwhelmed?

Strategies for learners – nuts and bolts

Attachment

What might we see in class?
- Difficulties coping with change.
- Concentration difficulties.
- Trouble at unstructured times.
- Acting out.
- Clingy or controlling behaviours.
- Not understanding personal boundaries.
- Unpredictable outbursts.
- Being unkind to others.
- Defiance with authority figures.
- Hiding or running off.
- Not trusting adults to help.
- Sabotaging work or breaking things.
- Lying, minimising, blaming, raging.
- Difficulties expressing feelings and explaining their behaviour.
- Reverting to immature behaviours at times.

- Look after yourself.
- Try to not to take a pupil's reactions personally.
- Set your own limits and boundaries.
- Don't allow yourself to be solely responsible.
- Lean on colleagues for support - work as a team.

Pupils with attachment difficulties may be dealing with fear of rejection, sense of helplessness, low self-worth, survival instinct to protect themselves and to control their environment, overwhelming emotions and confusion in whether or how to relate to others.

Don't underestimate the role of schools in providing reassuring attachment figures and modelling healthy social relationships.

- Try to be predictable and constant.
- Routine and structure.
- Empathy and curiosity. Never anger.
- Scaffold learning to lower stress of tasks.
- Be patient and persistent - change takes time.
- Calm down space.
- Use creative arts to help pupils express themselves.

Attachment

Strategies for learners – nuts and bolts

Attention-seeking behaviours

 **Context**

Attention-seeking behaviours can be some of the most frustrating behaviours to deal with. It is exhausting to teach a pupil who seemingly can never get enough of your attention whatever you try. Attention seeking can come in many guises, but the most common behaviours are calling out or talking over people, getting out of a seat, physically or verbally annoying peers, making noises or tantrum-type behaviours. For the attention-seeking pupil, any attention received is meeting a need, so if negative behaviours get a response from adults or peers, these will be repeated. A predictable cycle of behaviour – reprimand – behaviour can become entrenched because staff feel they cannot let disruptive behaviours go unchallenged.

Underlying attention-seeking behaviours is a need for attachment and connection. A pupil may not have had their early needs met; they may be hypervigilant due to traumatic experiences; they may have low self-esteem or little sense of belonging; or they may be at a stage of development where they have not learned self-regulation skills. Attention seeking is often reinforced at home, and so pupils may enter your class having learned that if they don't get what they perceive they want, acting out will put them back in control. If lessons are unpredictable or staff change, the pupil may be more demanding because they feel less safe.

Reprimanding or putting in place punitive sanctions will be ineffective because the root of the problem – i.e., the pupil's need for attachment, is not being resolved. It can be very disempowering for staff trying to work out what to do with attention-seeking behaviours, and too easy to reinforce the negative cycle because you feel you need to respond. A good place to start is by asking a colleague to observe the behaviours and responses in action, in order to identify how they manifest in class and what is reinforcing them. Invite parents or carers in to find out how the pupil is at home and work together to put a plan in place. Once you have decided which strategies to try, be consistent and patient – change will not happen overnight, and things may get slightly worse before improving.

Strategies for learners – nuts and bolts

Consider

- Try and work out what the pupil needs – validation, reassurance or connection.

- Focus on the behaviour, not the pupil – avoid using 'you are' negatively.

- Set classroom boundaries so that everyone knows that positive behaviours are expected and praised.

- Praise pupils who are seeking attention in the right way – 'thank you for waiting and asking politely'.

- Set up a system whereby you give the pupil early attention at start of the session.

- Schedule 1-to-1 time with the pupil – explain when it is, reassure them when it is going to happen nearer to the time slot, spend time with them and find things to praise, let them know when it is going to end.

- Make time to listen to their feelings – use drawing, modelling or toys to help them express themselves.

- Try and catch them BEFORE they do their attention seeking – check in frequently, get eye contact, thumbs-up or smile, pat their shoulder as you rove around class, position your teaching space near their desk at times.

- Give them responsibilities or leadership roles.

- Ask them directed questions first to pre-empt calling out.

- Don't ignore them when they are not attention seeking – give them MORE attention at these times.

Reflect

Be aware that the behaviour may be pushing your buttons.

Strategies for learners – nuts and bolts

Attention-seeking behaviours

Remember that attention seeking is attachment seeking.

Teach social skills.
Teach alternative ways to seek attention; traffic lights, hand on teacher's shoulder, hand up, being helpful, doing well with the task.
Use social stories.

Give it time – if you are running out of patience, ask another adult to take over for a moment.
Take advice if you feel controlled by the behaviours.
Use a visual chart to help younger pupils see positives.
Talk to older pupils about any improvements they have made to show their progress.
Track progress over time so you can notice small gains.

Pre-empt by catching them on task – frequent check ins, diversion and distraction, pass them a sticky note with encouragement, use humour with older pupils, use drama and role play to give chance for performance, give thumbs up, send them on an important job, sit with them for a minute – **BEFORE** they attention seek.
Vary lesson structure so tasks have pace and interest.

If **behaviours escalate** – stay calm and remove anything to keep them safe, including other pupils if needed.
Speak calmly to them to let them know you are there.
'When you are calm, we can…'
'I will be here when you are ready to do the task.'
'I am just keeping you safe.'

Tactically ignore low-level attention-seeking behaviours but **don't ignore** the child – give reassurance attention such as close proximity; ask them if they need help; sit near and offer support; give a choice; try distraction. Be playful and distract them into making appropriate choices. Praise others who are on task or not responding to the behaviour.

Attention-seeking behaviours

Chronic fatigue and pain

Context

It is important that schools have an awareness of how chronic fatigue and pain conditions affect pupils' access to learning. Chronic fatigue is usually diagnosed in secondary-aged pupils but can be identified in younger children. Symptoms can be mild or severe and include painful limbs and muscles; headaches or stomachaches and migraines; sore throat or fluctuating temperature; general fatigue; sensory intolerance; and pain that is not relieved with analgesics. Pupils with this condition often have a very disrupted sleep pattern and are often awake at night. Constant fatigue or pain hugely affects mood; consequently, pupils can develop mental health problems.

The causes of chronic pain or fatigue have not been emphatically identified by the medical profession, so treatment varies but can involve exercise programmes, medication, graduated activity and cognitive behaviour therapy or pain management. Mindfulness interventions can be helpful. Recovery is variable, and pupils who are significantly affected may be unwell for a long time. The illness is incredibly stressful for the family as well as the pupil because the prognosis is often vague. If the pupil is not able to attend school, families need to work out how they are going to look after their child around work or other commitments. The pupil may need to start or finish school at different times involving tricky transport logistics. Some pupils will be absent for long periods of time, making it hard for their teachers to maintain a relationship. Pupils who are at home lose touch with their peers, and social isolation is a real issue.

Chronic pain and fatigue are emotionally as well as physically exhausting; memory and concentration skills are often affected. As pupils can usually only focus for short periods of time, they are constantly switching tasks, which disrupts their focus further. Motivation can be affected, as the pupils find themselves getting further behind and missing out on class teaching. Home tuition is often put in place, or ICT can be used creatively to stream lessons into the home. Even with home tuition, it is unlikely that a pupil can access a full package of subjects, so pupils often face the possibility of reducing their curriculum options.

Strategies for learners – nuts and bolts

 Consider

- If you are a form tutor, try and keep in contact with the pupil and family and if appropriate, encourage peer contact.

- If you are teaching a pupil, manage cognitive overload by chunking the task, reducing content, providing support with planning and allowing rest breaks. Using a laptop may be less tiring than handwriting.

- If you are supplying work for the home tutor, provide explanations or the scheme of work with the tasks. It is hard to find time to prepare work for pupils who are not in school, but just providing a textbook is not going to help the pupil. Tutors need some structure and guidance from the subject teachers, as they may not know the curriculum specifics.

- Let the tutor know when class assessments or exams are taking place, and send papers for the pupil to try. Mark and return so the tutor can identify next steps.

- Be supportive of parents/carers and remain nonjudgemental. Many parents and carers are struggling with the pupil's diagnosis, as there are so many unknowns and the condition is 'hidden'.

- Be understanding about reduced activity such as PE.

 Reflect

Is it hard to keep a pupil in mind when they are out of sight? How can you ensure that you don't forget to keep in contact during your busy school week?

Strategies for learners – nuts and bolts

Chronic fatigue and pain

- Help peers understand. Seating with friend.
- Take up time for questions - extra processing needed.
- Understand their anxiety about managing in school. Remember symptoms vary day to day. Respect their limits; if they say they can't, they can't.
- Quality over quantity - reduce content but maintain level. Manage homework quantity.
- Cut down writing - provide notes, group work scribes, ICT.
- Quiet working noise level. Movement breaks. Backed chair, cushion, footstool. Reduced light. Comfortable temperature.
- Continue to encourage participation. Invite to class trips, send notes home, email class news.
- Welcome pupils back from absence as if they come in every day and don't ask questions about absence. Discretely fill them in on what's been missed.
- Quiet space outside class to work. Rest breaks. Visit pupil outside lessons if working in inclusion room.
- Don't rush pupils. Gradual developing of confidence and stamina works best.
- Quiet time for lunch or time out of class.
- Focus on the positives. Manage expectations about what can be achieved while still aiming high.

Chronic fatigue syndrome remains a controversial illness, as the medical professions have not been able to determine a specific cause nor agree on the best way to treat patients. It can be very debilitating and isolating. It is a hidden condition, so it is difficult for peers and staff to understand. This makes it even harder for pupils and parents/carers to manage and for this reason staff need to be supportive and empathetic.

Many of these strategies will be effective with pupils with other long-term illnesses.

Chronic fatigue and pain

Strategies for learners – nuts and bolts

Comprehension

Context

Pupils who have weak comprehension skills have real difficulties accessing the curriculum. The main barriers to comprehension of concepts will be poor language skills, difficulties with memory and poor auditory processing. These pupils will struggle to process verbal information and may also struggle to pick up the meaning of text, even if they can decode well enough. Weak comprehension skills are relatively common in school and may adversely impact pupils who have not been identified with a learning need. Poor comprehension not only hinders academic progress but can also affect social interaction. Social skills rely on initiating conversation and play and picking up social cues which are often language based.

Things to look out for if you are concerned about pupils not comprehending the lesson include poor listening; looking blank or not responding when asked a question; giving off-topic answers; being slow to start work; and watching others for cues and being passive, for example, not asking questions and not taking the initiative. Sometimes you will notice older pupils finding ways to mask their poor comprehension by copying out all the questions before adding answers; never putting their hand up; waiting for the teacher to go over the answers and then writing them in; copying their friend's work; or taking ages to cut up sheets to stick in or lay out their work in a certain way that takes up time. Some older pupils are embarrassed, so when a teacher offers support, they may say they are fine. If they can't articulate what they need help with, they haven't engaged with the work. Any avoidance of a task while looking busy is a warning sign that the work is incomprehensible.

Consider

Getting the content delivery right for everyone will help the percentage of pupils who need support in this area. If you know the range of ability in your class, you can pitch the content so that everyone can grasp some of it, and then **build up** the complexity to extend others. If you always use strategies such as pre-teaching vocabulary, using visual backup for concepts, chunking information into short sections and repeating and revising key points, this will increase accessibility for everyone.

- ◆ Teach the facts before introducing the concepts – if pupils are familiar with the key words or key skills, they can then process the way the concept works.

Strategies for learners – nuts and bolts

- Some pupils need extra time to develop understanding – revisit the topic over time and build understanding bit by bit.

- To check level of understanding, help pupils articulate what they understand using drawings, scribing ideas, scaffold talk using sentence starters, open-ended questions or choices of answer. Often pupils may have an idea of something but can't put it into sentences. They may need sentences to match and sequence and then be given a chance to explain in their own words.

- Avoid ambiguous language or complex sentence structures and stick to key points.

- Steer away from idioms or sarcasm or provide explanations.

- Teach scanning and skimming strategies for reading and encourage use of highlighters for pupils to mark words they are unfamiliar with.

- Read out loud and paraphrase to highlight the meaning.

- Don't talk too long.

- Build confidence by praising effort or seeking support.

- Rephrase poorly constructed sentences back to the pupils to model correct grammar.

 ## Reflect

Are you sometimes swept up with your own great explanations because pupils are smiling and looking at you intently? Always check their understanding!

Strategies for learners – nuts and bolts

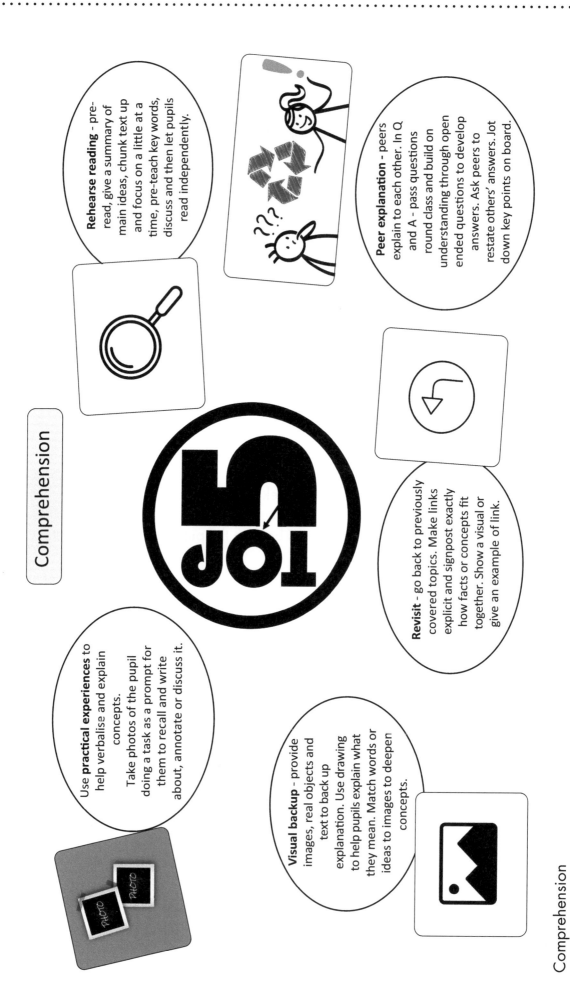

Comprehension

Rehearse reading - pre-read, give a summary of main ideas, chunk text up and focus on a little at a time, pre-teach key words, discuss and then let pupils read independently.

Peer explanation - peers explain to each other. In Q and A - pass questions round class and build on understanding through open ended questions to develop answers. Ask peers to restate others' answers. Jot down key points on board.

Revisit - go back to previously covered topics. Make links explicit and signpost exactly how facts or concepts fit together. Show a visual or give an example of link.

Use **practical experiences** to help verbalise and explain concepts. Take photos of the pupil doing a task as a prompt for them to recall and write about, annotate or discuss it.

Visual backup - provide images, real objects and text to back up explanation. Use drawing to help pupils explain what they mean. Match words or ideas to images to deepen concepts.

Comprehension

Diabetes

Context

Diabetes is a relatively common condition among pupils in school. Each pupil will have a medical plan which outlines treatment and emergency procedures, which will provide you with specific details of who in school is trained to support the pupil. This section is intended to develop awareness of the impact of diabetes on school life.

Diabetes is caused by lack of insulin production, which results in the body not being able to control blood sugar levels. Children with Type 1 diabetes can't produce any insulin, which means they must take insulin and frequently check their blood glucose levels. Insulin needs to be injected or given via an insulin pump. Pupils with diabetes need to check their blood sugar levels regularly throughout the day. Snacks may need to be eaten during the day to maintain blood sugar levels.

If a child's blood glucose levels are too high or too low while at school, they might start to feel unwell. Some general symptoms are feeling shaky, pale skin, sweating, hunger, tiredness, blurred vision, lack of concentration, headaches, feeling tearful or bad-tempered or moody behaviour. Low blood sugar should be treated with sugary food straight away. High blood sugar needs treating with extra insulin.

Diabetes affects pupils in different ways, and families vary in their ability to manage the physical and emotional effects of the condition. Parents and pupils can struggle with the diagnosis and can become anxious about the treatment or having to trust school staff to be vigilant. Many pupils struggle with the injections or the pump and may not be mature enough to self-manage, or may even sabotage the treatment. It can seem overwhelming, as managing the day-to-day monitoring and treatment is a big commitment. The pupil with diabetes can feel that they stand out as different. There is a lack of understanding around the treatment which can make it embarrassing or awkward. For example, older diabetic pupils may have to deal with peer comments about drugs, because of injecting the insulin.

Diabetes can affect learning. There may be times when a pupil is absent from school due to medical intervention or because their blood sugar levels are unstable. Anxiety can be a real issue for some pupils, especially if they have had experiences of being very unwell. Fluctuating blood sugar levels affect concentration and memory, and pupils may have mood swings when their blood sugar is not managed well. They may get restless or tired and you may notice irritability before lunch.

Strategies for learners – nuts and bolts

 Consider

- No child with Type 1 diabetes should be excluded from any part of the school curriculum or extracurricular activities.

- Read the medical plan so you are fully up to speed on emergency procedures and treatment.

- Set up a routine/support for checking blood sugar. If the pupil can be helped to feel comfortable to check in the classroom, they **miss less learning**.

- Explain diabetes to peers and set up a buddy if appropriate.

- Teenagers can become less vigilant in treating their diabetes – pass on any concerns.

- Allow snacks and water in class. Have spare snacks in a drawer as a backup.

- Be aware and understanding of the effects of fluctuating blood sugar, e.g., tiredness, lack of focus, short temper.

- Plan for active lessons and trips, i.e., PE when pupil may need to take extra snack and check sugar levels before and after; discuss medical plan for trips.

 Reflect

Are you anxious about managing the needs of a diabetic pupil? Where can you get support in school to help build your confidence?

Strategies for learners – nuts and bolts

Diabetes

Work as a team at school.
Include the pupil in the planning.
Build trust with the family.

(stressed figure)	Stress can affect blood sugar. The weather and illness can affect blood sugar. Monitor anxiety. Plan for support in tests - e.g. toilet breaks, supervision, rest breaks, snacks available.
(lunch bag)	Snacks when needed - in class. Early lunch pass. Communicate with home re dietary needs e.g. food diary. Know where spare snacks are kept in school. Plan for what pupil can eat at school parties.
INSULIN PUMP	Check and treatment where they are. Make sure staff are with them. Take pump with them to sports. Educate peers. Encourage participation in all activities wearing the pump.
(insulin syringe)	Safe place to inject insulin. Peer explanation. Check and treatment where they are and not have to move. Make sure staff are with pupil if they need to go to medical room.
(blood glucose meter)	Reminders to check sugar levels. Timer. Visual checklist. Support staff can help younger pupils. Allow safe place in class to do test. Remember PE, exams, snacks etc need extra testing. Notice changes in mood and concentration.

Diabetes

Copyright material from Rachel Cosgrove (2020), Inclusive Teaching in a Nutshell, Routledge

Strategies for learners – nuts and bolts

Disorganised pupils

Context

Lack of organisation seems to cause incredible frustration and worry. Being able to organise ourselves improves as we mature, and we would expect younger children to need a lot of physical and verbal prompting when they start to want to do things by themselves. However, many pupils with additional learning, physical and emotional needs really struggle with organisation, and this impacts school life to varying degrees.

Organisation is about being able to plan and sequence activities. We use our brain's executive functioning processes to pay attention to what needs to be done, hold it in our working memory and then plan and carry out the steps needed to complete a task. We need to be motivated to organise ourselves. We need to allocate time to organise ourselves. What contributes to the difficulties some pupils have in organising their books, belongings or themselves?

- They may be immature and not ready developmentally.

- They may struggle with working memory, and so forget the steps after instructions are given or lose track of a task part way through.

- They may struggle to focus on the task in hand, and so lose track or give up as they have moved onto something else or been distracted.

- They are not motivated to organise themselves – they may not prioritise the task, think it isn't relevant to them or not notice it needs doing.

- They rush with everything, and so don't allocate enough time to do a task, make mistakes or run out of time.

- They are trying to focus on other things, and so can't divert attention to the organisation task.

The results of disorganisation in school are shown in poorly presented work; lost or incomplete work; missing coats and bags; homework issues; lateness; pupils being reprimanded; missed opportunities because appointments or letters for trips are missed; and finally, fruitless nagging from adults which is often tuned out by the pupil! Disorganisation can be a huge barrier for pupils' engagement and participation and can contribute to feelings of low self-worth. We tend to stereotype

Strategies for learners – nuts and bolts

people on how they present themselves, so pupils who are dishevelled, poorly organised and producing work which is scrappy and incomplete may be viewed as having less potential than other pupils. Some disorganised pupils may be very creative or be deep thinkers. Untapped potential may be missed.

Consider

- Be organised in the classroom, don't rush and have set places for equipment. Have a routine for counting in scissors and glue and take time to start and end lessons.

- Support book work by preparing sheets ahead of time – i.e., doing the cutting or numbering for individual pupils. Go around and help stick in sheets for pupils who can't manage in the time. Help pupils with layout by finding the page for them, writing a heading or drawing open boxes for formatting their work.

- Get pupil close for practical demos. Set up practical equipment on table ready for them.

- Give homework in plenty of time before the end of lessons.

- Keep exercise books in class for pupil. Have spare pens available.

- Use writing frames and diagrams to help pupils see the big picture.

- Checklist for tasks – stick to table!

- Use email or call home to inform about trips or letters.

- Aim for some **quality work** incomplete, rather than rushed, poorly completed work.

- Help pupils organise their school bags.

- Be patient and understanding, as nagging probably won't work!

Reflect

Do you need to improve your organisational strategies when workload is heavy?

Strategies for learners – nuts and bolts

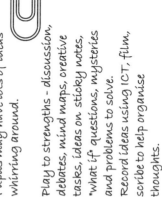

- Chunk the lesson into timed sessions.
- Give reminders when time is up.
- Stop task and check progress frequently to recap and refocus.
- Remove any books or sheets for previous task so desk is clear.
- Use checklist on whiteboard.
- Helpful peers to support organisation in task.

Pupils may have lots of ideas whirring around.

Play to strengths – discussion, debates, mind maps, creative tasks, ideas on sticky notes, "what if" questions, mysteries and problems to solve. Record ideas using ICT, film, scribe to help organise thoughts.

Disorganised pupils

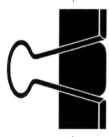

- Set routines and place for everything in class.
- Have individual drawer/box for pupil.
- Keep exercise books in school and use wallets for spare sheets. Colour code or cover books.
- Use ICT and help pupils make and organise files – prompt the saving of work into file before they lose it.
- Lay materials on desk in sequence.
- Help pupil find right place to start in exercise book.
- Provide checklists for packing up, school bags, what to bring to school.
- Help pupil with headings and starter sentences and guide layout with writing frame, grid or floating boxes to write in.
- Pupil leaders on tables – to help organise their group.
- Pre-cut sheets to avoid scissor distraction.
- Use different coloured card for card activities so pupils only have to find one colour.
- Have pots on desks for glues and scissors.
- Invest time in calmly modelling task.
- Use individual peg or box for PE changing.
- Teach pupils how to organise their bags and clothes.
- Label belongings.

Disorganised pupils

Strategies for learners – nuts and bolts

Easily distracted pupils

Context

All our minds wander frequently, as we are attracted by anything noticeable in our environment. Classroom distractions are aplenty – noises and windows, displays and resources, heaters and lights humming, stresses of the tasks or other pupils. Outside class, things happen in corridors, sirens pass by and insects go about their business – occasionally arriving in the classroom, resulting in short-term chaos and at least 5 minutes of regaining calm!

Some pupils have a fragile attention span. Pupils diagnosed with attention difficulties, poor working memory or with weak comprehension skills may struggle with maintaining attention or switch off if lesson content is wordy. Pupils in emotional or physical distress will be focussing on their own bodies or thoughts. Pupils on the autistic spectrum may look as if they are distracted if they are stimming (self-soothing repetitive actions or noises), when in fact they are using their stimming to focus on lesson input by blocking out other stimuli. Some pupils daydream but can appear focussed.

It is easier to focus when we are interested, when we feel the content is within our capability and when the environment is conducive to quiet thought. Realistically, most of us can only maintain sustained focus for short periods of time, and attention spans also vary over the course of the day. For example, you may have noticed that getting attention after lunch break takes a while to establish, that a fire alarm practice kisses goodbye to focus or that anticipation of lunch causes pupils to become unsettled. Being aware of the ecology of attention spans in your class and how external factors influence it will help you adapt the pace, content and working atmosphere of lessons to minimise distractions.

Consider

- Establish and practise routines for task transition, so that events like handing out textbooks don't disintegrate into 5 minutes of socialising and potential peer arguments.

- Give clear guidelines for times – e.g., how much work you expect in the time.

- Observe pupils and try and work out reason for distraction – i.e., work is too hard or too easy, peer issues, stress, pupil anticipating something worrying to them. Time out of class for a talk may help.

Strategies for learners – nuts and bolts

- Sit by a pupil or move near them to refocus gently.

- Be proactive with your seating plan so you split distractible combinations apart. Seating distractible peers right at the front can backfire, as they may keep turning around – sometimes seating them at the back to one side, by a wall, works better.

- Chunk the lesson or task into clear components, so pupils can feel a sense of pace but allow flow if the class is immersed.

- Use attention-grabbing activities to generate interest.

- Develop a system where you can cue in the class without talking a lot – hand signal, single-word instructions, visual prompt on board.

- For teacher talk, try gathering class in horseshoe or dimming the lights.

- For sustained pieces of work, plan with a pupil, provide key words, give them support to make a mind map or list, so they can get straight on with the task once set.

- Workstations can help – pupils can face away from peers.

- Try settling routines like quiet time, breathing exercises or movement breaks.

- If a certain classroom works better for focus, try and get it timetabled.

- Music may help focus if it prevents chatting or muffles outside noise.

- Try something different occasionally – invite a guest, set up a campfire circle. Difference can sometimes aid focus.

 Reflect

Do you distract pupils by intervening when they are focussed?

Strategies for learners – nuts and bolts

Easily distracted pupils

Try these ideas for pupils needing individualised strategies

- Keep instructions positive, rather than using **don't** all the time.
- Check they are not hungry, thirsty or need to talk though something that is upsetting them.
- Provide time to **get calm** if needed - walk, time outside the class, breathing, listening to music for short time etc.
- Make sure tasks are pitched to appropriate level of understanding - give extra explanation 1-to-1.
- Give short **timed targets** - bursts of a few minutes to get a sentence done, do 3 calculations, read a page etc.
- Be really positive as soon as they are focussing, but use **non-verbal gestures** rather than distracting them with talk!
- Provide sequence of activities visually.
- Use support staff to redirect pupil using close proximity or verbal and gestural prompts.
- Redirect focus with short sessions of chosen activities or talk about pupil interests to resettle before introducing task again.
- **Cue** pupil by name, get eye contact and ask directed questions to get them to think.
- Seat near front so you can prompt with eye contact or gentle touch to refocus and give 1-to-1 support (unless they are distracted by peers behind them).
- Seat near peers who can ignore any off-task chat or annoyances and who can **role model** good focus.
- Provide movement breaks.
- If pupils are distracting others - use non verbal actions to minimise - i.e. gently remove distracting items without reprimands.
- Plan ahead for potential distractions in tasks - i.e. scissors and glue can get in the way of learning!
- **Remove** potential distractible items from view.
- Provide lots of help for planning tasks.
- Working away from peers may be good for individual pupils who need total quiet - **workstations** or table on their own.
- Observe pupils who might be stimming excessively (repetitive self-soothing like rocking, tapping, humming) - is the lesson stressful? Are they distracting others? Ask them what they need to feel more comfortable.

Easily distracted pupils

Copyright material from Rachel Cosgrove (2020), Inclusive Teaching in a Nutshell, Routledge

Strategies for learners – nuts and bolts

English as an additional language

Context

Written and spoken language is a barrier for pupils who are learning English. When fluency is more secure, pupils whose home language is not English may still struggle with nuances in English such as idioms, colloquialisms and subtle meanings. Some pupils may have additional learning needs alongside their English language needs, and it is often harder to identify these as they may be masked by language comprehension.

Vocabulary recognition is learned first, and pupils may be able to pick up the gist of explanations if they have the right vocabulary. It is much harder for pupils to formulate their own sentences, as this relies on recall rather than recognition of words. Recall is tough, as there may be limited clues provided; the brain must search for the appropriate vocabulary and grammatical structure to produce a phrase with meaning. Pupils may be hesitant to read aloud or initiate conversations. They may struggle to keep pace with teacher or peer talk. They may nod or smile, when in fact they haven't picked up meanings. They will probably find independent writing harder than speaking. Reading comprehension is going to be a challenge, as texts may include a huge variety of less common words, slang or specific technical vocabulary. Any text that is about an abstract concept will be hard to decipher. Pupils may understand concepts such as science experiments or mathematical calculations but may find it hard to express it in a way that schools can assess and mark. For example, they may describe a concept correctly but use simplistic language which will not gain them the appropriate marks. Pupils with English as an additional language may also miss out on unspoken rules and gestures that are learned culturally.

Consider

- Build a relationship straight away so you can get to know strengths and weaknesses.

- Learn a bit about their home language and ask how to pronounce their name or learn some greetings.

- If there are other pupils who speak the same language, allow use of the home language where appropriate – pupils will feel much more comfortable and less isolated.

Strategies for learners – nuts and bolts

- Use translation strategies such as bilingual dictionaries or computer translators for written work or looking up specific words.

- Use visuals as much as you can – images, graphics, real objects.

- Speak clearly at a slower pace. Repeat points. Use expressions and gestures to emphasise what you are saying. Avoid using too much descriptive language or anecdotes.

- Avoid idioms and slang, or explain them if they come up.

- Narrate as you are showing them a task.

- Model correct pronunciation and grammatical structure back to pupils if they have attempted a sentence.

- Use vocabulary strategies such as pre-teaching, key word banks, focussing on high-frequency topic words.

- Always check understanding with open questions.

- Scaffold writing – choices of words, phrases, writing frames, verbalise before writing, scribe key ideas, provide model sentences they can adapt.

- Buddy with peers.

- Active listening and speaking in role play, drama, presentations, group work and games.

- Allow extra thinking time and support pupils to rehearse what they are going to say before they speak.

- Adapt some tasks to help accessibility, i.e., lower the cognitive demand of tasks involving lots of language.

- Use subtitles in home language and/or in English for video clips.

- Include some culturally accessible materials and liaise with parents to think creatively about bringing the home language into the class.

Reflect

What is your role in helping pupils adjust to school life?

Strategies for learners – nuts and bolts

English as an additional language

Support reading
- DARTs (directed activities related to text such as gap fills, tables, cloze).
- Paired reading with older reader.
- Read aloud daily.
- Flashcards with sentences to reorder/sequence into paragraphs.
- Summarise plot before reading, pre-teach vocabulary.
- Choose relevant texts.

Continue to encourage development of home language
- Liaise with parents/carers to read at home.
- Ensure homework is accessible and relevant.
- Value and include home language at school.

Collaboration with peers
- Barrier games requiring speaking skills; pair activity where pupils cannot see the other's materials e.g. mastermind, battleships.
- Scaffold talk with speaking template and props such as sentence flashcards, connectives, question words.

Talk before writing
- Practice key phrases.
- Try language drills.
- Use songs and chants to consolidate key language.
- Stock phrases will help hook the learning.

Continue to support even when pupil is verbally fluent.
- Writing will need scaffolding and subject-specific vocabulary explained.
- Exam support – bilingual dictionaries.
- Teach command words, provide checklists of connectives and exemplar phrases.

Strategies for learners – nuts and bolts

Epilepsy

Context

Epilepsy is a relatively common neurological condition in which seizures start in the brain. Not all seizures are caused by epilepsy. An epileptic seizure happens when there is a sudden and intense burst of electrical activity in the brain which temporarily disrupts it. There are many types of epileptic seizure, and each has different symptoms. Common symptoms are shaking, falling to the floor or periods of loss of awareness. Some pupils feel strange sensations like tingling, seeing lights or noticing smells. Some pupils don't take medication but are monitored. Other pupils take medication designed to prevent seizures. You will be aware of pupils with diagnosed epilepsy from their medical plan: they may need an emergency protocol. Some children grow out of childhood epilepsy.

Epilepsy that occurs in childhood may have long-term impacts on children. Epilepsy can affect memory and may contribute to learning difficulties. Medication can have side effects which can affect a pupil's ability to concentrate and focus. Epilepsy may influence a child's developmental milestones and can affect language skills, fine and gross motor skills and behaviour. Some children may not have their long-term learning affected but may be affected by day-to-day disruption due to their epilepsy, such as missing instructions due to 'absences' or fatigue from sleep deprivation due to nighttime seizures. The aftereffects of seizures may impact attendance, as the pupil may need to go home to rest or stay at home to recover. Schools need to be aware that seizures may be triggered by environmental stimuli or changes in the pupil's routine. Common triggers are photosensitivity (e.g., light) flickering screens, stressful situations, overexcitement or boredom or poor sleep. Classroom atmosphere, disruption caused by peer behaviour or stressful or exciting events such as exams, presentations or school performances may affect a pupil with epilepsy.

Pupils should not be discriminated against because of their epilepsy, and plans need to be made to ensure that pupils with epilepsy are included in everything other pupils do. Pupils with epilepsy may be anxious or embarrassed about having a seizure in school and may be very worried about how their peers may react. If agreed with the pupil and family, it is a good idea to raise awareness amongst peers to improve their understanding and empathy.

Strategies for learners – nuts and bolts

 Consider

- Read information provided by health professionals and parents/carers so you are fully informed.

- If high-need pupils have support staff working with them, speak to them about the specific needs and discuss how to make the classroom environment work best.

- Be aware of any risk assessments needed – e.g., for practical work or PE.

- Talk to the pupil and family about individual triggers or concerns.

- Encourage whole-class ethos around supporting the pupil sensitively.

- Ensure that you have good classroom routines in the event of a seizure – i.e., peers know how to vacate the room quietly and promptly.

- Scaffold learning using strategies to support memory and attention.

- Seating away from screens; limit screen time.

- Be aware of the emotional impact of epilepsy – look for ways to boost self-esteem.

- Make plans for lost learning time – i.e., printed notes, prioritise certain topics and leave out non-essentials, catch up time.

- Support or quiet room for assessments and tests.

- Monitor and make allowances for tiredness.

- Get to know the pupil so you can look out of changes in behaviours – or signs of potential seizures.

 Reflect

How can we balance the goal of full participation with health and safety needs?

Strategies for learners – nuts and bolts

Epilepsy

DO'S

- Familiarise yourself with pupil plan and emergency protocol. Ask questions if unsure.
- Seat pupil where staff can see pupil's face to monitor.
- Notice behaviours before and after a seizure as behaviour may be affected.
- Provide plenty of quiet time to recover from a seizure.
- Support memory, concentration and language - revisit previous topics repeat key points, chunk content, use images an checklists and check understanding.
- Cue pupil in by name. Allow extra time to process instructions and questions.

DON'TS

- Don't refer to seizures as fits/attacks etc. Use correct language.
- Don't refer to a pupil as epileptic - seizures are epileptic.
- Don't ignore any bullying or isolating behaviour from peers. Don't take time removing a class - maintain dignity of pupil.
- Don't rush a pupil - recovery can take a long time and they may not be themselves for a few days following a seizure.
- Don't let a pupil miss out on activities - find a way to adjust for safety.
- Don't underestimate the influence of the environment - be aware of triggers and prioritise class cooperation in maintaining a calm room.

Strategies for learners – nuts and bolts

Fidgeting

Context

Some level of fidgeting is totally normal and even beneficial to learning! Young children need to move regularly and are less inhibited, or less used to, sitting still. Children generally need to move about to stay focussed. Older pupils also need to move, but most can adapt to classroom expectations and will either fidget discreetly or find other ways to keep themselves focussed. Notice how much *you* fidget and observe other adults, because you will see that most of us will be shifting our position, fiddling with our hands, or playing around with digital devices. We all need movement breaks when listening to another person for longer than 10 minutes. Some pupils fidget excessively, and this can impact their own learning and distract others.

Excessive fidgeting may be due to boredom, hunger or sugar excess, anxiety or anger, or just part of an individual pupil's own level of activity. Many children who have experienced traumatic experiences will be hypervigilant and may be like meercats in class – constantly turning around, leaving their seat or poking and prodding others verbally or physically. Pupils who have had an argument with a peer during a previous lesson or break time may be unsettled and fidget in class. Pupils who struggle with learning may fidget, as they are anxious about failing or are bored. Certain pupils are big thinkers and may have busy brains, constantly whizzing around ideas, which makes it hard for them to settle. When a task involves difficult concepts, pupils may struggle to process the information, and so switch off and start moving physically.

The parts of our brain involving speech also involve movement; speech is often accompanied by gestures, automatically. If they want to talk, they may fidget – pupils who look as if they want to explode with an idea and blurt it out before waiting.

Some pupils need lots of sensory input to keep them focused. They have a low arousal setting, so they fidget in order to keep themselves alert. Other pupils need to calm themselves down and may stim or tap constantly. Rhythm is very calming and self-soothing, so tapping is a nice experience, although annoying for others!

Strategies for learners – nuts and bolts

 ## Consider

Planning your lessons ahead of time to cater to the needs of pupil fidgets is a good idea and will help you consider the structure of the tasks – i.e., how much sitting still is needed and where you can build in movement.

- Short, well-paced tasks.

- Get full attention before giving instructions.

- Adjust level of task if too difficult, or chunk into manageable bits.

- If tasks are repetitive, pupils tune out, so try and vary something.

- Tasks with some movement involved – moving around groups, collecting info, peer evaluating with sticky notes around tables, etc.

- Timed tasks/competitive tasks/choices of tasks.

- Tasks that involve a variety of activities – e.g., drawing, writing, discussion, games.

- Play to strengths – ideas generator, enthusiastic team member, leader.

- Find time at start of lesson to talk to pupils who enter the lesson agitated – if they need time to calm down or talk things through, this may save disruption later in the lesson.

- Calm routines – teachers can model calm behaviour.

- Write up the route through the lesson on the board so the sequence is visible.

 ## Reflect

How fidgety are you as a teacher? High-energy teachers can create energy in class, which may be great but also may lead to chaos! Find ways to vary your energy styles.

Strategies for learners – nuts and bolts

Fidgeting

Play rhythmic music with no lyrics during practical work sessions.

Try calming and settling routines…

- Allow some wandering.
- Use close proximity to redirect.
- Accept pupils and talk to them about what works.
- Use eye contact and cue by name.
- Provide quiet thinking space.
- Be predictable and cue routines.
- Teach breathing techniques and practice.
- Be calm and use varied voice volume.
- Over the shoulder marking is immediate.
- Be positive and praise their efforts to focus.

Keep a box of sensory toys or soft fidget items in the classroom.

When pupils **need** to fidget, let them, but manage it…

- Seating 'fidgetters' on outside edge of desk clusters or near staff for gentle redirection.
- Movement breaks / little jobs, errands.
- Provide appropriate fidget toys – paperclip, pipe cleaner, peg, stress toy.
- Some pupils need to tap feet or hands - can they do this on a quiet surface?
- Sensory cushions/wobble cushions.
- Allow doodling, using mini white board, writing on big board.
- Repeat instructions, display instructions.
- Use gestures to redirect rather than nagging by name.

Fidgeting

Strategies for learners – nuts and bolts

Hearing impairment

Context

Hearing loss in school-age pupils varies. Significant hearing loss should be identified in early childhood but hearing loss can be temporary due to glue ear or ear infections. Hearing loss can be caused by problems with the way the brain processes sound, or it can be caused by the transmission of sound being blocked in some way inside the ear structure. Some pupils will have issues with sound amplification, and other difficulties include specific loss of different sound frequencies or distortion of sound. Hearing loss can fluctuate in some pupils.

If a hearing loss hasn't been identified but you notice any of the following signs, it is worth talking to the parents/carers of the pupil to have it checked out: turning ear towards a sound, not following instructions, distraction and confusion, turning volume up, delayed or unclear speech, and concerns about language development. Hearing loss can have an impact on expressive and receptive language development – both of which are the foundations for successful literacy and numeracy learning. Most of us pick up language by listening to others, and pupils with hearing loss miss out on this incidental learning. Some pupils may be passive in class because they are not listening to general conversation, which normally makes lessons motivating. Hearing loss can also affect social interaction skills and increase the possibility of social isolation; teachers and support staff have a key role in ensuring that school is as inclusive as possible.

Consider

If a pupil has a specialist worker, it is worth making time to meet with them prior to teaching the pupil.

- Seating – generally it's best to seat the pupil near the teacher. If they have some hearing, 1–2 metres' distance is best, and then you can also use gestural cues.

- If the pupil has a wireless hearing device with a microphone for the teacher to use, practise using it, and remember to turn it off when you are not addressing the class or the pupil directly!

- It sounds obvious, but don't speak with your back to the pupil. Many teachers talk while writing on the board, forgetting that the pupil with hearing loss is relying on visual cues from you or using lip reading to aid word recognition.

Strategies for learners – nuts and bolts

- Use subtitles for videos.

- Speak clearly at normal pace. Stick to the point.

- Provide lots of visual backup – images, checklists on board, mind maps to illustrate a discussion.

- Watch out for background noise. It can be hard to distinguish talk from a mixture of other low-level noises.

- Use gesture. Some pupils may have learned signing. If you can learn some signing to support, then this may be helpful.

- Repeat instructions or key points – don't rephrase.

- Cue in pupil by their name.

- Explain new vocabulary and give examples in context of a sentence or example.

- Allow extra time to answer questions or respond to instructions.

- Check comprehension by asking open-ended questions.

- Adapt instructions in PE or practical lessons so the pupil knows signals for safety or next steps – e.g., coloured cards, gestures, system whereby peers stop so pupil can use class cues.

- Some pupils with hearing loss may need support with social interaction – teach turn taking, set up group work in the round, encourage buddies.

 Reflect

Do you sometimes feel awkward talking to someone with hearing loss, as you feel you need to speak differently? How can you upskill?

Strategies for learners – nuts and bolts

Hearing impairment

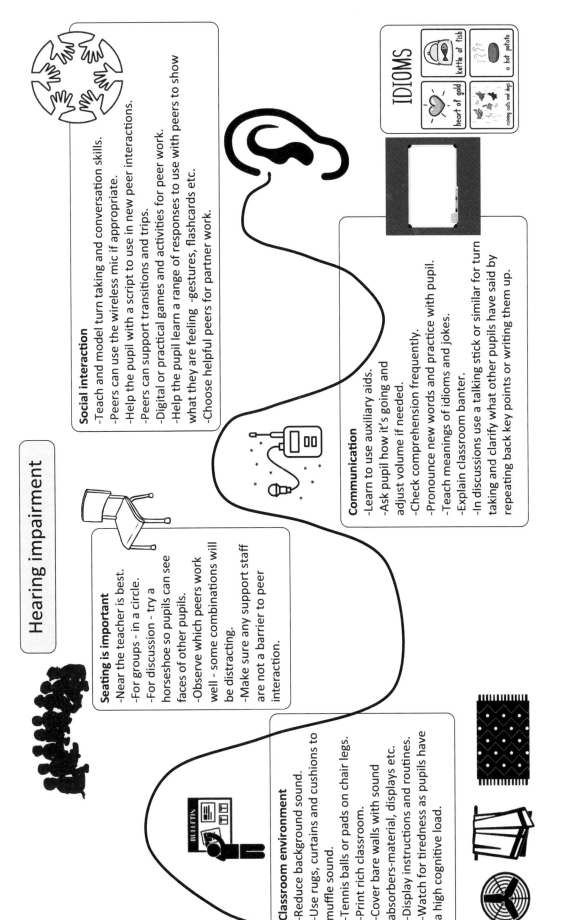

Social interaction
- Teach and model turn taking and conversation skills.
- Peers can use the wireless mic if appropriate.
- Help the pupil with a script to use in new peer interactions.
- Peers can support transitions and trips.
- Digital or practical games and activities for peer work.
- Help the pupil learn a range of responses to use with peers to show what they are feeling – gestures, flashcards etc.
- Choose helpful peers for partner work.

Communication
- Learn to use auxiliary aids.
- Ask pupil how it's going and adjust volume if needed.
- Check comprehension frequently.
- Pronounce new words and practice with pupil.
- Teach meanings of idioms and jokes.
- Explain classroom banter.
- In discussions use a talking stick or similar for turn taking and clarify what other pupils have said by repeating back key points or writing them up.

Seating is important
- Near the teacher is best.
- For groups – in a circle.
- For discussion – try a horseshoe so pupils can see faces of other pupils.
- Observe which peers work well – some combinations will be distracting.
- Make sure any support staff are not a barrier to peer interaction.

Classroom environment
- Reduce background sound.
- Use rugs, curtains and cushions to muffle sound.
- Tennis balls or pads on chair legs.
- Print rich classroom.
- Cover bare walls with sound absorbers-material, displays etc.
- Display instructions and routines.
- Watch for tiredness as pupils have a high cognitive load.

Hearing impairment

Copyright material from Rachel Cosgrove (2020), Inclusive Teaching in a Nutshell, Routledge

Strategies for learners – nuts and bolts

Learning saboteurs

Context

Learning saboteurs are those pupils who appear to disrupt the learning of others – seemingly on purpose. They are the pupils who arrive late and make an entrance, who call out in class, who sabotage their work and who appear to be doing everything they can to get negative attention or assert power over the adults. Staff can feel very tested by these behaviours and sometimes feel it's a battle to get these pupils onside.

Pupils who are sabotaging lessons may be doing so because it meets an unmet need in some way. For example, many pupils fear failure and would rather be sent out, so they have a valid reason not to participate. Others may lack social skills and are not able to self-regulate, so they may disrupt a lesson with a confrontational outburst. Pupils with sensory processing difficulties may be overwhelmed in class, so they may act out in a subconscious attempt to manage their anxiety.

The response from the adults and peers is key to the continuation of the behaviour. Attention can fuel the behaviours, but conversely, ignoring the behaviour can result in escalation. Some pupils seek power over the adults in the room as this helps them feel in control, so they will sustain the behaviour *until* the adults react. The behaviours are a sign that the pupil is not comfortable in class and may be a symptom of unmet emotional or social needs, learning difficulties or problematic learned behaviours.

Consider

- Recognising the behaviour is a start. Step back and observe the interactions playing out. Try and work out what the pupil **gets as a result** of the behaviour. Look for patterns such as triggers or responses after the behaviour. This will help you work out how to help the pupil change the behaviour. Relationships are the key, so get to know the pupil in and out of class – connection will help build up trust. Once a pupil trusts that you will follow up, keep them safe and consistently deal with their behaviours – you can start to make changes.

- Know the triggers and try to reduce the risks in class.

- Stay calm, and keep your body language and voice neutral, so you avoid showing frustration or anger.

Strategies for learners – nuts and bolts

- Use positive language in class – for example, say what you would like to see, not what you don't see.

- If other pupils are affected, give them appropriate attention.

- Use proximity to try and reduce the behaviours – if you have support, get another adult to give positive attention/distract/divert before behaviours surface.

- Sell the task in way that reduces anxiety – chunk it, explain it well and make it sound achievable.

- Remove the audience – have a quiet space to talk to the pupil.

- Have alternatives set up – i.e., time out card, agreed time to talk outside class Agree on these with the pupil ahead of the lesson.

- Try a script for helping the pupil – name the emotion and give choices.

- If an outburst has resulted in sabotage of work or classroom equipment, find a way for the pupil to recompense others by helping tidy up. Do this discreetly without shaming the pupil.

- Never shame a pupil.

- Recognise if the pupil is using power to threaten and seek support and advice from colleagues.

Reflect

Do you have a pupil you dread teaching? Fake it till you make it: practise assertiveness, have your script and build trust with the pupil over time.

Strategies for learners – nuts and bolts

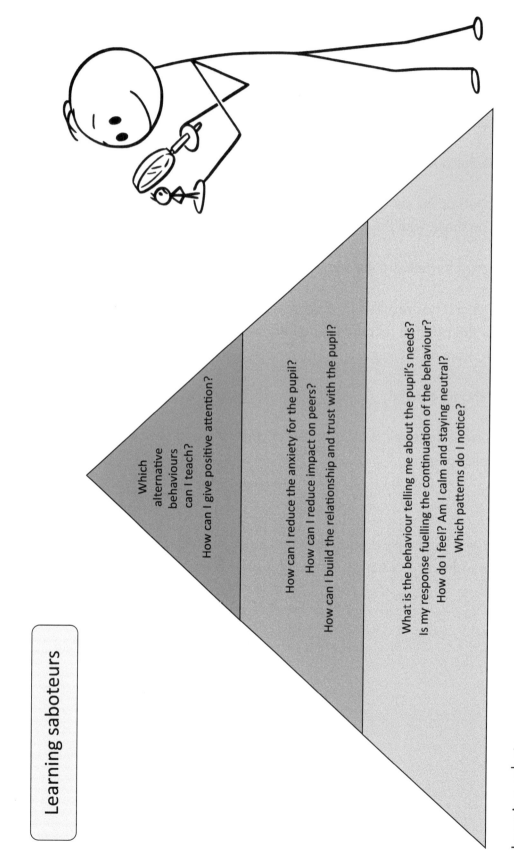

Strategies for learners – nuts and bolts

Limited life experience

Context

Our experiences in life shape our learning. Pupils who have had opportunities to experience a wide range of enriching activities will have developed knowledge of their world. These experiences build up into schema (mental maps) and provide connections to hook subsequent learning onto. The kind of experiences that help build successful learners might include being read to, collaborative play or sports, looking after a pet, exploring nature or visiting different places. If children are in families where adults have had time to share activities such as discussions, music, cooking, gardening or arts and crafts, these pupils will have developed a rich vocabulary and confidence to try new things.

There will be pupils who, for all sorts of reasons, haven't had access to this kind of learning outside school. Some may not have travelled outside their hometown. Many pupils spend time indoors on screens rather than playing outdoors. There will be pupils with additional needs who find it hard to explore outside the home due to medical or social/emotional barriers. Parents might have anxieties about allowing their children independence, as they are overly protective. Children may not be expected to do chores or go to the local shop, so they don't develop confidence to do things on their own or use their initiative. Pupils who have this limited life experience will have less developed neural connections and will find it harder to assimilate new information. Often these pupils don't know what they don't know and consequently, they won't necessarily show curiosity or ask questions. They may write in brief because they don't have the depth of experience to extend their ideas. Any task involving critical thinking will be very hard, as this requires general and background knowledge which these pupils may lack. Confidence may be affected because when peers are ahead, motivation to persist may be a hurdle.

Consider

- Find out what pupils know at the start of a topic – use questions and mini quizzes, drawing or word matching to establish a baseline. Ask pupils for examples and probe their experiences by using open questions.

- You may have to do a lot of foundation teaching to get some pupils to a starting level – sometimes going back to facts that were covered in earlier years.

- Widen pupils' experiences if you can by using the local community for trips, asking speakers to talk about their lives, using video and film clips

Strategies for learners – nuts and bolts

of experiences or places, exploring any outside space or arranging a trip connected to a topic.

- Use real objects where you can – clothing, artefacts, etc.

- Use models to illustrate a concept – e.g., junk model of digestive system.

- Stories and analogies can be used to bring a topic to life and make it familiar.

- Give real-life examples if you can, from your own life – pupils love to hear stories about their teachers!

- If you are teaching an abstract concept, try and link it with something concrete that they do understand or recognise.

- Have starters with photos or illustrations of the topic, so that pupils can see something familiar to hook into.

- Provide a sensory experience if it can fit into your plan – share music, smells, bring in foods associated with a topic, try a piece of art that conjures up a theme.

 Reflect

Do you wonder why some pupils lack depth in their writing? It may be that they don't have a lot to say.

Strategies for learners – nuts and bolts

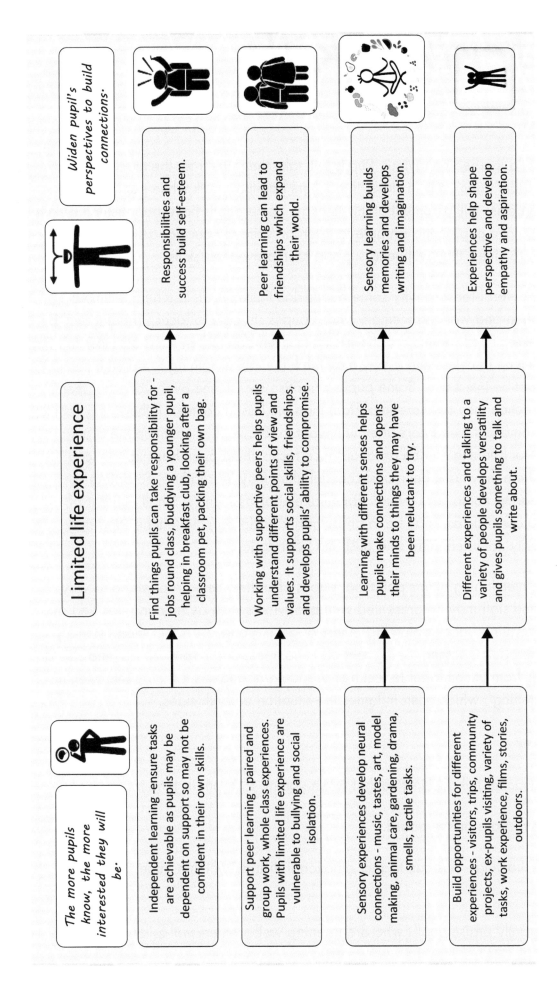

Strategies for learners – nuts and bolts

Listening skills

Context

Listening is a learned behaviour. Pupils will take their cue from the teacher about how important listening is in class. If teachers habitually talk while pupils are still talking, the class will assume that this is okay. Some pupils have poor listening skills and if you have pupils who struggle to listen, in spite of your good silent listening classroom routines, they will need support to improve their skills.

There are several reasons why some pupils don't listen well. Listening is linked with attention and working memory and if pupils struggle to focus, listening will be compromised. Pupils on the autistic spectrum often don't listen to whole-class talk, as they don't tune in unless cued; they may think the talk is nothing to do with them or may just not be interested. Some pupils prioritise social time over work. For them, peer interaction may be more important than the lesson content. If there is a conflict going on amongst their peers, they will want to resolve it or continue the drama in class. Not listening can be an avoidance tactic. If the pupil has experienced lessons where they have been unsuccessful, they may fear failure, so opting out and appearing not to care avoids potential embarrassment. A small number of pupils you come across may be in an authority battle with the teacher and may determinedly not listen to try and push the boundaries.

It is worth mentioning at this point that pupils often find being reprimanded very difficult, and staff may be presented with behaviours such as smirking, looking at the floor, arguing back or blaming others or getting angry – rather than listening to what the adult is saying. Being told off is not nice, and pupils will try and shield themselves from uncomfortable feelings of shame or anger. Staff may interpret this as 'not listening', which often inflames the situation on both sides.

Consider

- Keep teacher talk succinct so that when you do talk, pupils tune in.

- Put instructions on the board.

- Avoid shouting – this can trigger emotional distress which hampers listening further.

- Exuberantly praise pupils who are listening well – others will follow!

Strategies for learners – nuts and bolts

- When questioning, use strategies whereby everyone is expected to respond – i.e., think, pair share, one answer per pupil round the class, mini whiteboard responses, thumbs up or down, etc.

- Model the process of listening to pupils – narrate what is going on in your head as you listen.

- Demonstrate a task using no words at all – and then clarify verbally afterwards.

- Try seating pupils in a horseshoe or circle without desks or try a boardroom setup.

- Seat chatty non-listeners away from their friends. If this causes issues, plan it ahead and discuss with the pupil.

- If you have support staff, make sure they do not automatically repeat the instructions to the pupils, because the pupils will continue to rely on the adult to do the listening for them.

- Stories are a great way to make teacher explanation more accessible to pupils who struggle to listen to and process new information.

- Set up group work so that you can talk to a smaller number of pupils more directly rather than addressing the whole class.

- When dealing with pupils who struggle to listen to redirection, stick to the facts, use a calm voice and let them talk first so they feel listened to.

Reflect

Have you ever timed how long you talk for?

Strategies for learners – nuts and bolts

Listening skills

Build the skills

Listening skills activities ideas

- Mindfulness scripts, dead lions, relaxation sounds.
- Sound recordings - guess the sound.
- Outdoor learning - nature walk to collect sounds.
- Talking stick. My turn, your turn.
- Silent time in class - for duration of a piece of music, timer.
- Peer interviews - hot seat, ask the expert, pupil presentations and questions.
- Withhold instructions for a task so pupils have to ask and then listen.
- Barrier games - pair listening to get info such as battleships.
- Partner describing games - describe shapes to partner to build or draw.
- Teach whole body listening - mouth closed, feet on floor, hands in lap, eye contact.
- Describe and draw. Draw a simple picture with details like a beach setting. Read a description of it in stages. Pupils draw what they hear. Compare pictures!
- Memory games - I went to the market, alphabet shopping, describe a picture from memory to a partner.

Modelling good listening to pupils

- Build the relationship.
- Reflect back - 'So what you are saying is...' 'So let me check that this is what happened'.
- Label the feeling - 'You sound angry', 'That must be hard'.
- Take time to listen. Body language neutral. Involve pupil in doing a job side by side. If the pupil is angry or upset - wait.

Listening skills

Looked after and previously looked after pupils

Context

Looked after children are those who are being looked after by the local authority – this could be in a foster placement – either for the long term or temporary, or in a residential placement.

Each child has an attached social worker, and regular reviews are held to make sure the home situation is working well. Adopted children and children living in special guardianship have previously been looked after.

The majority of looked after and previously looked after children will have experienced many transitions in their lives and may have had to cope with several home and school moves and significant adverse childhood experiences. They may be aware of their life story, or they may not know their family history. There are many reasons why children are taken into care. The most common reasons are that they have experienced abuse and/or neglect, but there are other circumstances that may lead to care, such as bereavement, family breakdown, lack of parental capacity, long-term illnesses or significant disability where parents can't meet a child's needs. Children at risk of criminal or sexual exploitation may trigger a care episode, as may parental imprisonment or being an unaccompanied asylum seeker. Looked after and previously looked after pupils are a vulnerable group. They are vulnerable to academic underachievement and school exclusion and at risk of developing mental health problems later in life.

As a class or subject teacher, it is helpful to have some background on your looked after or previously looked after pupils so that you can plan effectively to meet their specific needs. If you are a form teacher, it's very useful to attend any review meetings arranged so you can develop a relationship with the carers or parents and get a view of the big picture for that child. Knowing that pupils may have been impacted by early attachment issues or trauma helps you understand their behaviour and interactions in school. It is hard for pupils who have moved regularly to invest in school and trust new adults. If they have moved schools, they may have gaps in their learning or missing assessments. If they are new to your class or school, they will definitely need time, nurture and additional support to settle well.

Strategies for learners – nuts and bolts

 Consider

- Have high expectations – these pupils may have obvious gaps in knowledge but have high potential.

- Fresh-start approaches every lesson – try to offer an open door even when things have not gone to plan previously.

- Reassurance, building trust and getting to know strengths, likes and dislikes.

- Find time to provide some 1-to-1 time in class to check understanding.

- Provide a safe space in class or alternative – bean bag, book corner, etc.

- Have extra equipment available and don't give sanctions for not having PE kit or pens, etc.

- Communicate with carers/parents about homework and explain curriculum. Some carers may not be familiar.

- Avoid reprimanding in a confrontational way or lecturing pupils. Listen to the pupil's account of an incident and focus on consequences rather than sanctions.

- Be sensitive to language and activities that revolve around families and be vigilant in language you use about meetings or social workers as most looked after children dislike the institutional abbreviations commonly used and do not want to be singled out.

- Find resources that represent a diverse range of family setups or stories featuring heroes and heroines from a care background.

- Monitor peer interaction and deal with any comments that stigmatise the child.

- If the child is unaware of their background, be vigilant about overheard conversations.

- Support potential flashpoints such as transitions and unstructured times.

 Reflect

Can you find time to go the extra mile?

Strategies for learners – nuts and bolts

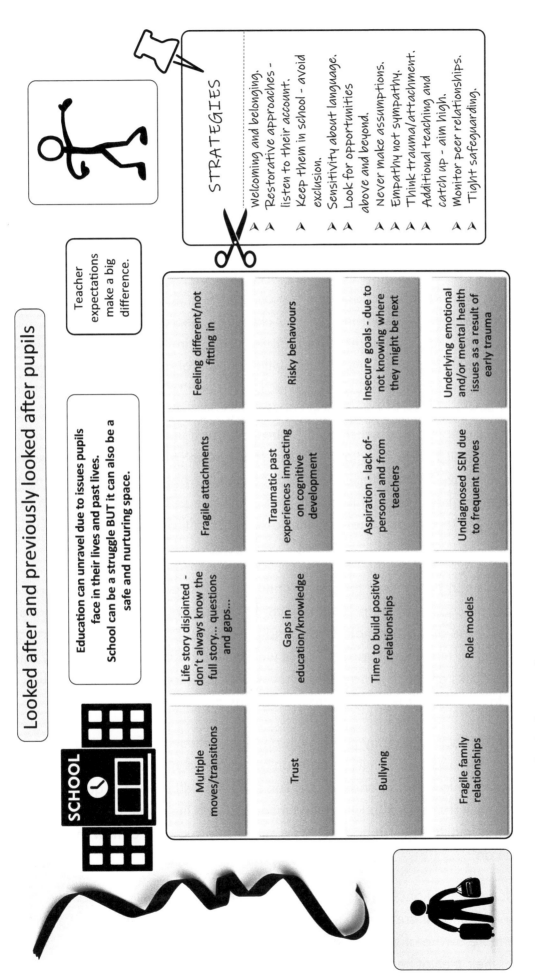

Looked after and previously looked after pupils

Education can unravel due to issues pupils face in their lives and past lives. School can be a struggle BUT it can also be a safe and nurturing space.

Teacher expectations make a big difference.

STRATEGIES
- Welcoming and belonging.
- Restorative approaches – listen to their account.
- Keep them in school – avoid exclusion.
- Sensitivity about language.
- Look for opportunities above and beyond.
- Never make assumptions.
- Empathy not sympathy.
- Think trauma/attachment.
- Additional teaching and catch up – aim high.
- Monitor peer relationships.
- Tight safeguarding.

Multiple moves/transitions	Life story disjointed – don't always know the full story… questions and gaps…	Fragile attachments	Feeling different/not fitting in
Trust	Gaps in education/knowledge	Traumatic past experiences impacting on cognitive development	Risky behaviours
Bullying	Time to build positive relationships	Aspiration – lack of – personal and from teachers	Insecure goals – due to not knowing where they might be next
Fragile family relationships	Role models	Undiagnosed SEN due to frequent moves	Underlying emotional and/or mental health issues as a result of early trauma

Looked after and previously looked after pupils

Copyright material from Rachel Cosgrove (2020), Inclusive Teaching in a Nutshell, Routledge

Strategies for learners – nuts and bolts

Physical difficulties

 **Context**

Pupils with physical difficulties will need staff to be aware of mobility, spatial and motor abilities and social emotional development. Some pupils will have associated medical intervention, which may impact attendance.

Mobility around school can be tricky, as not all schools are designed for good accessibility. For any pupil using a wheelchair or a walking frame or who needs to manage their balance, school sites can be daunting. As a teacher, you can support accessibility by reorganising your classroom and acknowledging the efforts that pupils are taking just to get in and around school. In the section of Chapter 3 entitled 'The physical environment', you will find general classroom adaptations. Especially important for mobility is posture. Desks need to be the right height and if the pupil can sit out of a wheelchair, insisting on appropriate seating is key – a supportive cushion, a backed stool, a footrest or an angled slope. Some pupils may be reluctant to use these adaptations because they don't want to appear different, and you will have to encourage them to prioritise their posture without drawing too much attention. It is important to ensure that pupils are seated where they can be with peers. Make sure practical activities are set up so that everyone can participate equally.

Spatial skills can be an issue for some pupils with physical difficulties. Some pupils have poor perception of the position of their body or have difficulties with spatial orientation. Fine and gross motor skills, and personal care tasks such as dressing or cutting food, may need support. Pupils with dyspraxia may appear clumsy and bump into desks or knock things off as they move. You may also notice that they struggle to lay out their writing or draw diagrams accurately.

Tiredness is a factor for many pupils with physical difficulties. Everything takes more effort and time and as a result, energy can get depleted during a school day. Most pupils are keen to be independent, and some will be determined to get around on their own even if this is exhausting. Communicate with the pupil, as well as with parents and health professionals, to make sure you are aware of how much the pupil can do.

The social and emotional needs of pupils with physical difficulties can be overlooked by schools. Being different can knock self-confidence, and as pupils mature and become more aware of the realities of their own situation, they may need staff to be aware of their mental health needs.

Strategies for learners – nuts and bolts

Consider

- Train the class to put bags well under desks and keep routes clear.
- Use a clean format on slides and worksheets – uncluttered.
- Think about position in class – don't always teach from the front, or teach a group at the table. Getting down to a pupil's level is more inclusive.
- Encourage independence even if the pupil could complete a task with support – self-esteem improves with personal successes.
- Help pupils lay out work by drawing a template.
- Pre-prepare some tasks that are unrelated to the learning – i.e., cutting out, weighing out, setting up equipment.
- Lay out practical activities in sequence.
- Adapt assessments and provide appropriate support.
- It is also worth watching other pupils around wheelchairs. Some pupils can be overly helpful; others can take advantage.
- Vary length of tasks so pupils can manage fatigue.

Reflect

Do you find it difficult to watch a pupil struggling and find yourself tempted to step in and help? Be aware that there will always be a balance between independence and support.

Strategies for learners – nuts and bolts

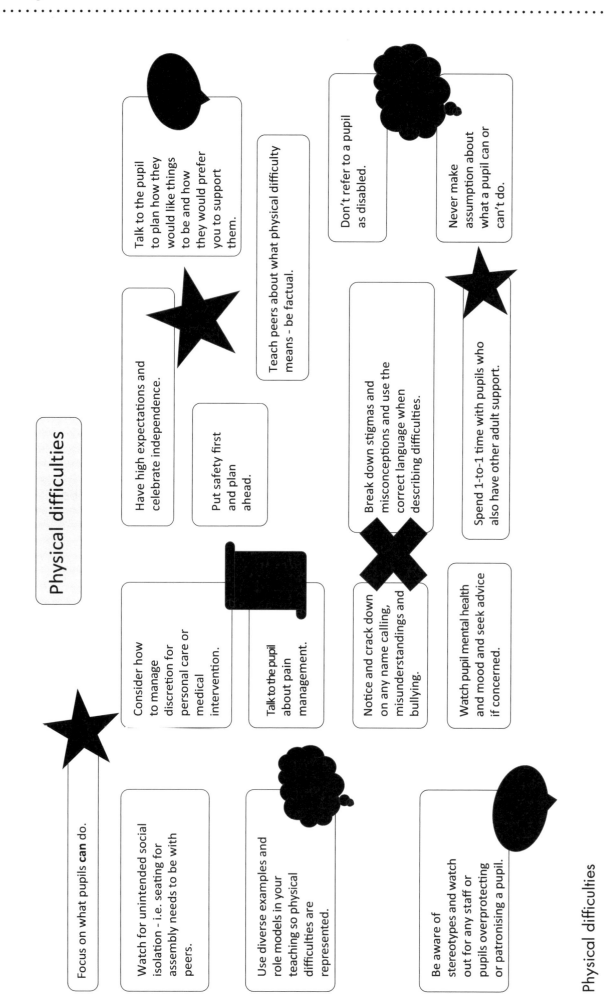

Physical difficulties

- Talk to the pupil to plan how they would like things to be and how they would prefer you to support them.
- Teach peers about what physical difficulty means - be factual.
- Don't refer to a pupil as disabled.
- Never make assumption about what a pupil can or can't do.
- Have high expectations and celebrate independence.
- Put safety first and plan ahead.
- Break down stigmas and misconceptions and use the correct language when describing difficulties.
- Spend 1-to-1 time with pupils who also have other adult support.
- Consider how to manage discretion for personal care or medical intervention.
- Talk to the pupil about pain management.
- Notice and crack down on any name calling, misunderstandings and bullying.
- Watch pupil mental health and mood and seek advice if concerned.
- Focus on what pupils **can** do.
- Watch for unintended social isolation - i.e. seating for assembly needs to be with peers.
- Use diverse examples and role models in your teaching so physical difficulties are represented.
- Be aware of stereotypes and watch out for any staff or pupils overprotecting or patronising a pupil.

Strategies for learners – nuts and bolts

Pupils working well below age-related levels

Context

Mixed attainment groups include a huge variation in knowledge and skills. You may have groups containing individual pupils who are working at a hugely different level from their peers. These individuals may have more significant learning needs and will need a more bespoke curriculum.

This represents a challenge for the class teacher. Do you plan a parallel curriculum for the pupil? How can you include the pupil in the class learning objectives when they may not be ready for this level? How do you assess their progress when they can't access your standard assessments? There is no easy answer to these questions, but with a positive attitude, an inclusive ethos and a bit of creativity, it is possible to adapt the curriculum to open it up for these pupils.

Firstly, you need to know the level the pupil is currently at in your subject or year. Which key skills do they have, and where does that put them in terms of an appropriate set of objectives? This is your starting point in terms of skills and knowledge to aim for. Have high expectations but think about how you provide pupils with successful leaning experiences. If they cannot understand the whole-class topic, time will be wasted unless you can adapt tasks to their level.

Can you include the pupils in whole-class teaching? For literacy and numeracy, tasks could be differentiated by topic or level of support. It also may be appropriate for the pupil to work on an individual curriculum that meets their specific needs. In wider subject areas, pupils should be able to work on factual and practical knowledge and naming and describing things. Introduce vocabulary which will help them recount what they have learned. For some pupils, it may be suitable to establish a parallel set of valuable literacy, language, practical or social skills which can be developed alongside the whole-class content – for instance, a pupil working on learning to label science equipment alongside peers who are developing their investigation skills. When pupils are exposed to the rich language of the classroom, they pick up social skills and vocabulary alongside their peers and are exposed to higher-level learning opportunities which they may or may not access.

Strategies for learners – nuts and bolts

To assess progress, meet the pupil where they are. It may be inappropriate for them to do the end-of-topic assessment even with adult support, so come up with alternative ways to measure progress and record the journey in an individual way using visuals, adapted assessments or adult observations.

Consider

- Research or ask colleagues for ideas for activities from year groups below.

- Mix up the way you group the class so that these pupils can work with role models, get support from peers and have opportunities to take a lead in the skills they feel confident in.

- Direct the teaching assistant so they are clear about what your aims are for the pupil. Make sure that you, as the teacher, spend 1-to-1 time with the pupil.

- Scaffold questions so the pupils get to answer alongside the class.

- Evidence progress using photographs, work annotated by adults supporting, adapted assessments, recordings of discussion with pupil, diaries, etc.

Reflect

Are you concerned about adapting the curriculum content for individual pupils or having to show progress via exercise books, which doesn't give the whole picture of the pupil's progress? How can you make a case for what is the best progress for a pupil and how to demonstrate this?

Strategies for learners – nuts and bolts

Pupils working well below age-related levels

Assess foundations - what do they know? Which skills have they got? Are the foundations solid? Can they use the foundation knowledge in different contexts or have they just rote learned facts without comprehension? Look at curriculum and decide where to **start** and what to **leave out**. Where would like the pupils to get to?

Build confidence by getting a few things secure in factual memory or as a skill.

You can focus on a few steps each lesson rather than trying to deliver all the content.

You can change the end point as you assess over a few lessons. Keep raising the bar.

Don't put a ceiling on where they can get to.

Hitting the Sweet Spot

- Too hard - goes over heads- not absorbed at all.
- In the zone between a little hard and just right- the **sweet spot** - just within level of skill or comprehension-builds on what they know and moves them on.
- Too easy - pointless unless it's a confidence boosting tactic.

Simplify lesson concept and focus on one idea, fact, description or concept.

Recognition is easier than recall. Multiple choice, exemplars, cues.

joules	You measure energy in joules
power	How much energy is transferred to the appliance.
watt	We measure power with watts
appliance	Something that uses electricity to work
Electricity meter	In your home- it measures how much electricity you use.
kilowatt	1000 watts

Key words focus

How to adapt lessons to hit the sweet spot for individual pupils?

Pictures - draw ideas, draw comic strip, add images using computer, match and sequence pictures, take photos of work and skills demonstrated by pupil.

Parallel objectives - improving general literacy, numeracy skills alongside lesson topic.

Real objects - handle them, describe, experience, learn key words.

Concrete learning. Experiential learning builds schema.

Repetition - revisit several times

Art, model making, collage, make own display on topic.

Pupils interview peers to get answers. Find someone who knows…? Peer buddies. Group work with different roles.

Life skills tasks.

Pupils working well below age-related levels

Strategies for learners – nuts and bolts

Sensory processing difficulties

 Context

We make sense of our world by processing the sensory input and attending to what we need to. We sort, order and attend to stimuli so that we manage the input without feeling overwhelmed or underwhelmed. Pupils with sensory processing difficulties have low or high sensory thresholds and find it hard to manage the volume of input or to discriminate between types of stimuli. Sensory processing difficulties are common in children on the autistic spectrum.

Pupils with sensory processing difficulties find it hard to extract the right information from their environments. If lots of people are talking, it's hard to tune into who you should be listening to. Pupils may be drawn to certain visual stimuli and therefore miss other information. They may be triggered by smells. Some pupils need a high level of stimuli to enable them to respond. They may love loud music or enjoy tapping or shouting. Other pupils are startled by loud noises. Pupils often struggle with coordination and balance because it is hard for them to integrate the information coming into their vestibular and proprioceptive senses (position and balance senses).

What might you see if a pupil is struggling with sensory integration? Pupils may either tune out or overreact. If they are under-aroused, they may need lots of prompting to get going. If they are over-aroused, they can't filter the sensory input and too much information may cause a fight/flight/freeze response. For example, they may show poor focus; they may withdraw and put their head on the table or hands over their ears; they may have an emotional outburst which appears not to have a trigger; or they may try to self-soothe through stimming (repetitive movements or sounds) actions like swinging, rocking, humming, banging their head, flapping their hands, chattering or hopping on their toes. Some stims are helpful to pupils and aid focus, because they help the pupil manage the sensory input. When pupils are stressed, you may see stims that are harmful, such as hair pulling.

 Consider

- ◆ Try to work out the difference between 'won't' and 'can't'. Pupils on the autistic spectrum often find it hard to recognise their own bodily sensations and find it even harder to express why they might be reacting to something. They may

Strategies for learners – nuts and bolts

run off, sit still or have an outburst when they are overwhelmed. Understand the trigger and don't reprimand the pupil; they may not have control of their response. Over time, you can support pupils to recognise their triggers and use strategies to self-manage.

◆ Be sensitive to pupils who are reluctant to touch certain textures – some pupils find painting, using chalks or touching dough uncomfortable. Offer implements or gloves to manipulate the media.

◆ Keep the sensory environment as predictable as possible – a calm working classroom.

◆ Have a plan for unpredictable events, such as the fire bell going off.

◆ Allow pupils to wear noise-cancelling headphones.

◆ Be sensitive to scarves, backpacks or hoodies. A pupil may feel comfortable having their head covered or enjoy the weight of the bag on their back. Compromise with the rules or aim towards removing the hood or bag in their own time.

◆ Be vigilant about sensory-seeking pupils – especially younger pupils, as they may put things in their mouths. Try alternatives to give them an appropriate sensory experience such as a crunchy piece of apple, a cold drink or a safe chewy stick.

 Reflect

Do you notice that pupils manage better some days than others? Why might that be?

Strategies for learners – nuts and bolts

Sensory processing difficulties

Examples of sensory-seeking behaviours

Licking, eating, keeping things in the mouth, wets, looks intensely at things, fascinated by reflections and shiny things, bangs objects, likes vibrations, tears paper, moves a lot, spins, rocks, likes the playground, crawls under things, enjoys rough and tumble, fiddles with objects, leans on others, squeezes hands, prods, coat on, plays with sand.

Examples of sensory-avoiding behaviours

Poor eater, uses tip of tongue to taste, avoids smells, moves away from others, startled by flashes of light, closes eyes, covers ears, dislikes crowds, avoids haircuts, fear of climbing on things, cautious, difficulties walking on uneven surface, avoids messy play, doesn't like wearing tight clothes, avoids washing, anticipating of touch causes flight.

Sensory ideas to use in class

Sensory toys	Weighted things	Firm touch on shoulder or head
Arm rubbing	Jumping on spot	Spin on teacher's chair!
Move and sit cushion	fiddle with objects	Headphones with music
Bean bag	Run around 	Straw to suck
Crunchy food	Bear hugs	Peer back/shoulder rub
Energisers	Pushing activities	Chewy things
Resistance exercise	Weight-bearing exercise - push- ups, wall sit, plank	Wearing rucksack with bean bags inside
Musical instruments	Cuddly toys	Chunky pens
Sand trays	Silly putty or modelling clay	Elastic stretch bands
Visual reminders	Stress/calm down box	Bouncing on exercise ball
Mini trampoline	Swaddle with blanket	Crawling through tubes
Pre-warning of change	Minimise peer noise	Put blinds down
Get changed in quiet place	Sunglasses	Gloves
Glitter jars	Ear defenders	Calming smells
Routines	Leave class early or late	Seating plan
Sit near wall or door	Doodling	Turn down glare on screens

Sensory processing difficulties

Strategies for learners – nuts and bolts

Significant literacy difficulties – reading

Context

You may have pupils in your classes who have struggled to grasp basic reading skills in line with their peers and who have significant difficulties with literacy. These pupils may have gaps or delays in their learning, or they may have problems processing phonological sounds. These pupils will need targeted intervention to help them make steps towards improved decoding and comprehension of text. As a class teacher, you will need to be aware of their reading difficulties and try to support their needs in lessons. There are three ways to think about how you can support significantly weak readers. Firstly, you can **teach word building** in your subject or literacy lessons by sounding out key words, modelling how to break words into syllables and teaching specific sight words and sounds at a level appropriate to your learners. Secondly, you can **adapt and support reading tasks** using scaffolding, adjusting tasks or using peer or adult support. Thirdly you can **work around the reading difficulties** by offering alternative tasks or delivering content to these pupils verbally, pictorially or by using concrete experiences. Pupils who have reading difficulties may also have poor working memory capacity, which can impact hugely on day-to-day learning. We develop lots of our vocabulary through wide reading, and as pupils progress in school they may widen their vocabulary gap further if they cannot access texts alongside their peers.

Pupils who have struggled to read early on in their school life will be at risk of developing poor self-esteem, as reading forms such a large part of the school learning experience. Many older pupils may have coping strategies to mask their difficulties, and it is important to be aware of this. It will be helpful to build strong relationships with the pupil and family and to accept advice from the SEN staff so that you know how to best provide support.

Consider

- Pair reading – buddy up in friendships so that stronger readers can read out loud to their partner.

- Learn the correct phonic sounds so you model the correct phoneme.

- Provide fiction texts prior to lesson, so pupil has a chance to read at home.

Strategies for learners – nuts and bolts

- Avoid italics, words in capitals or underlining text – use **bold** to highlight.

- Pastel-coloured paper can be helpful.

- Read out loud in class to all – repeat sentences that carry the key information.

- Clarify and explain the text to help poor readers verbalise and more deeply comprehend the meaning; they can't reread in the same way as others.

- Turning text into bullet points or mind maps on the board may help weak readers by distilling the amount of reading needed.

- Read with the pupil; they attempt the text out loud, and you read alongside quietly with a second's delay, so they hear the correct words. They may have a go if they know you are prompting with accurate text.

- Reduce text – use icons, images and diagrams instead.

- Chunk the text to be read into strips or cards – with prompts such as images.

- Use a reading pen or text-to-speech on tablet or computer – pupil can read independently.

- Adapt texts so they include themes of interest to the pupil.

- Alternatives to reading – audiobooks, cartoon stories, picture books, experiences, talking, film and TV, drama, can all be used to deliver content.

 Reflect

Do you remember reading out loud in class? How did it feel? Never force a pupil to read out loud.

Strategies for learners – nuts and bolts

Significant literacy difficulties - reading

Minimise distractions. Quiet working environment. Extra time for processing. Consider background colour - soften colour. Use black text in easy-to-read font in lower case. **black text**	Modelling reading - learn the correct phonic sounds. Use expression and gestures. Reread. Choose pupils to read who can read with intonation. **th, ee, oi, a**	Pre-teach key words that are in chosen text - use images and examples. Point out sounds in words or roots of words. Provide pupil with small number of key words to look for.
Provide visual prompts - key words with images or symbols. Story board of sequence of events. Photos or pictures to respond to.	Use ICT to support reading - highlight text for computer or reading pen to read. Film or record teacher reading. Record key sentences from text on recording device for pupil to play back. 	Pair and group reading support - give roles. Adult readers to support in class - rove and read enough for the pupil to get on and then check in again. Know their reading age and level of text.
Deliver information avoiding reading - act it out, explain it, demonstrate it, video clip, tell a story, discussion, bring in objects, provide visual cues.	Help pupils look for key words or initial sounds in text. Teach pupils how to look for cues such as pictures, headings, diagrams. Use sticky notes or card strips/cut outs to target text to focus on. **Look for three facts.**	Change the task for the pupil to reduce reading load - matching tasks, reduce the text, reproduce text at appropriate reading level, draw storyboard, make a model, paired discussion, devise a role play.

Significant literacy difficulties – reading

Strategies for learners – nuts and bolts

Significant literacy difficulties – writing

Context

For pupils who have struggled to grasp the basics of literacy in line with their peers, writing is an even bigger barrier than reading. When we write, we need to be able to hear or visualise the phonological sounds in a word in order to start to spell it out. Unlike reading, which has clues within the structure such as layout, images, headings or sight words, writing usually starts with a blank page. Pupils who have very poor reading skills will need a lot of support to develop writing skills. You may want to check back to the 'Alternatives to writing' section in Chapter 3 to see a range of ideas you can turn to when writing can be substituted with an alternative. In this section, you will find ideas for spelling and writing development.

Writing uses a lot of cognitive processing. Pupils who have lots of ideas but struggle with spelling, find writing incredibly frustrating. As pupils get older, they also become more aware of the discrepancy between their own writing and that of their peers; often, this results in even fewer attempts to write. These pupils need significant support in any writing tasks and specific intervention in spelling. Talk to the SEN team to find out the barriers to progress and how best to support the pupil. Learn the phonic sounds so that when you are sounding out words, you are using the correct phonemes. Bear in mind that the pupil may be able to show their knowledge in other ways, and vary your assessment so that you can help them demonstrate what they know in other formats.

Consider

- Verbalise before any writing – in pairs, with adult support or in groups. Make sure ideas are scribed for the pupil in a mind map, bullet point list or short sentences.

- Use sticky notes to record ideas – scribe them and then ask pupil to reorder the ideas.

- Use writing frames – provide key words or phrases and ask pupil to write in the space from the scaffolds.

- Use a recording device for the pupil to verbalise sentences – scribe or type for them.

Strategies for learners – nuts and bolts

- Use the dictation facility on a tablet or computer.

- Use mini whiteboards in class for adults or peers to jot down spellings.

- Teach spellings of key words to class using phonemes or etymology of words.

- Model ways to practise spellings in class.

- Use word banks, checklists, displays with key words for spellings.

- Use double-spaced writing so adult can write correct spellings for pupils to practise.

- Avoid marking for spelling accuracy with these pupils – focus on content ideas, or just one or two areas such as capital letters or initial sounds.

- Reduce writing task by adapting the class task to the pupil – a diagram to label, writing frame with part completed, partly annotated picture to complete, grid with statement cards to sort and copy in, storyboard to complete.

- If the pupil can type, this can be an accessible way to write, as you can use spellchecking and editing as well as use text-to-speech to check sense. Many reluctant and poor writers are much happier using word processing.

 ## Reflect

Are your weak writers finishing before the rest of the class because their peers are absorbed in a long writing task? You may need to plan in additional tasks for them to do independently or with an adult, such as illustrating their work, typing it up, making a collage, etc.

Strategies for learners – nuts and bolts

Significant literacy difficulties - writing

- Use **sounds** not letter names for spelling out.
- For testing use spellings in sentences rather than singularly.
- Pick a **small** number of **high-frequency** specific topic words to learn.
- In writing, put in correct spellings for the pupil and then highlight **2/3** words for them to learn.
- Display phonic sounds in class and make personalised dictionaries or play spelling games.
- Refer to words with similar sounds i.e. look for the 'ee' sound in 'cream' to spell 'leaf'.
- Practice using all the **senses** - look at the word, sound it out, break it into parts, spell it in the air, write it out, type it, read it, put it in a sentence.

- English spellings don't follow consistent rules.
- Sounds (phonemes) can be represented in several ways in writing (graphemes).
- Stand-alone spelling tests don't help pupils with significant literacy difficulties.
- Strategies such as mnemonics, pyramid, Look Cover Write Check are not effective for pupils with significant difficulties.

Significant literacy difficulties – writing

Copyright material from Rachel Cosgrove (2020), Inclusive Teaching in a Nutshell, Routledge

Slow processing

Context

When we receive information, we upload it, make sense of it and respond. Processing speed is the pace at which we do this. Individual processing speed varies. When we use a skill or information repeatedly, these neural pathways become stronger, making our processing more efficient.

Processing speed is not linked to intelligence, but it does have an impact on learning. It is possible to be of any ability but process information slowly. Slow processing means pupils respond to input at slower rate than others. Speed of information processing is not the same as physical quickness. It is important to recognise that the speed and fluency of processing information is the issue, **not** the child's knowledge and understanding.

Pupils with slow processing speed have a slow work pace because they need to make more mental effort to achieve the task. Pupils with fast processing speed will be quick to answer questions and will be first to offer ideas, whereas pupils who ponder may need to take time to figure out how they are going approach something or consider the answer before speaking.

Slow processing speed can be a big issue for pupils, as they may miss input or feel rushed. Tasks such as reading for meaning, numeracy, listening and note taking can be stressful if you can't process quickly. You may lose your thread in a calculation or place in a story if it takes longer to work through the text or steps. Being a slow processor can also affect tasks needing executive functioning such as time planning, making decisions and organising multi-step tasks. You may notice pupils with slow processing speeds struggling to start tasks promptly, drifting in and out of attention and sometimes lacking perseverance in completing complex tasks. It can be overwhelming and frustrating when you can't keep up. When teachers talk a lot from the front of the room, pupils spend so long taking in one bit of information that when the teacher has moved on to a new piece of content, they are still processing the previous information. You may notice that pupils with slow processing speed miss nuances in discussion and conversation.

Consider

- Be vigilant in recognising processing speed – pupils with additional needs may have slow processing as part of their profile, but other pupils with **no other**

Strategies for learners – nuts and bolts

apparent specific needs may have slow processing speeds, and staff may have attributed underachievement to lack of motivation or other reasons.

- Reduce quantity rather than challenge of work.

- Distraction can get in the way of focus – aim for a quiet classroom if content requires a high level of processing.

- Peers can be supportive – i.e., to discuss a task or idea, but watch out for peers who distract their neighbours from thinking.

- Repetition helps if the information is repeated but not rephrased.

- Additional time for any assessment or tests.

- Flipped learning – provide information to be covered prior to lesson so pupil can absorb in their own time.

- Allow a good amount of time for pupils to respond to questions – avoid jumping in and hurrying them up.

- Back up explanation and instructions with visuals or text, so the pupils can revisit the information by rereading.

 **Reflect**

We are used to linking quick thinking with successful learners. We want our lesson to be well paced, but at what cost? Do you find yourself stepping in to hurry pupils up or finish their sentences for them? Can you compromise pace for depth?

Strategies for learners – nuts and bolts

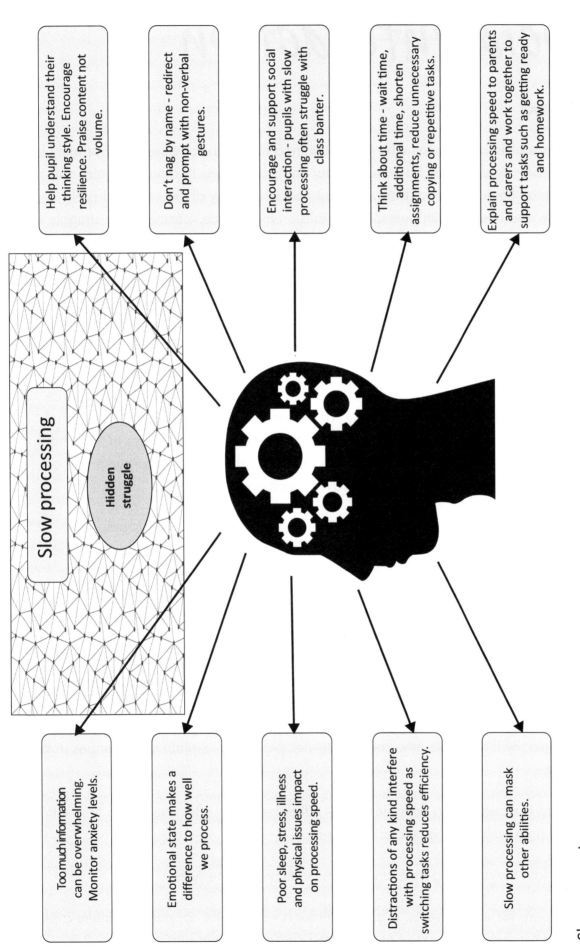

Strategies for learners – nuts and bolts

Social interaction

 Context

There are plenty of reasons why pupils can find it hard to socialise appropriately in school. Some pupils may have missed out on opportunities to develop social skills; others may have emotional baggage that gets in the way of their ability to self-regulate and interact with peers; and pupils on the autistic spectrum may struggle to understand the rules of social interaction or find socialising very stressful.

Socialising can be tiring for all of us. It can be difficult to read the intentions of others and manage the sensory load of a social situation. Many people put on a bit of a mask when in a social setting, as there are certain expectations of politeness or small talk that are required. For school-aged pupils, picking up these social nuances can be difficult and potentially very stressful. Schools are essentially very social places, and pupils are expected to spend a lot of time with others and participate in social activities throughout the day. These social times use up a lot of emotional energy. Many pupils are using all their emotional resources just being in the school environment. Add in a change of routine, a poor night's sleep, an argument or an assembly and pupils will either withdraw or melt down.

There are lots of things schools can do that help mitigate the social stressors in school and help the pupil develop their social understanding. Understanding each pupil's background, triggers and interests is a good starting point. It is always a good idea to stand back and try and work out what might be going on for the child before you step in or make a judgment. Imagining what it's like to walk in their shoes really helps staff to relate to a pupil's difficulties.

 Consider

- Display and explain routines so pupils know what to expect from the day, especially if there are new social activities planned – explain any changes in the day.

- Build in opportunities for quiet time – either before or after interaction time – this will help recharge the 'social batteries'.

- Explain the rules of games and the reasons behind the rules.

- Prepare for social events, e.g., talk through what might happen and make a plan with the pupil. Try a script or laminated cards to prompt pupil.

Strategies for learners – nuts and bolts

- Be sensitive about insisting that a pupil joins in an activity – if the day has already been busy or highly interactive, adding another stressful activity isn't going to go down well.

- Give choice of working in a pair or alone, rather than in a group.

- Teach and model social skills. You can use board games, social skills games, social stories and comic strips or stories.

- Teach names of emotions and how to recognise them. Photos and cartoons can be useful. Label emotions so pupils learn a wide range of words to describe their feelings.

- When things go wrong, use a coaching approach – look back at the situation and go through step by step. Talk about how it could have been different. Drawing speech bubbles for pupils to say what they were feeling or said makes it visual. Look at the consequences for everybody.

- A circle of friends may help some pupils.

- It's okay to offer alternatives to social time on days when the pupils are not going to cope.

 Reflect

Are you worried about pupils who don't always want to join in? A balance of encouragement **and** allowing down time is crucial.

Strategies for learners – nuts and bolts

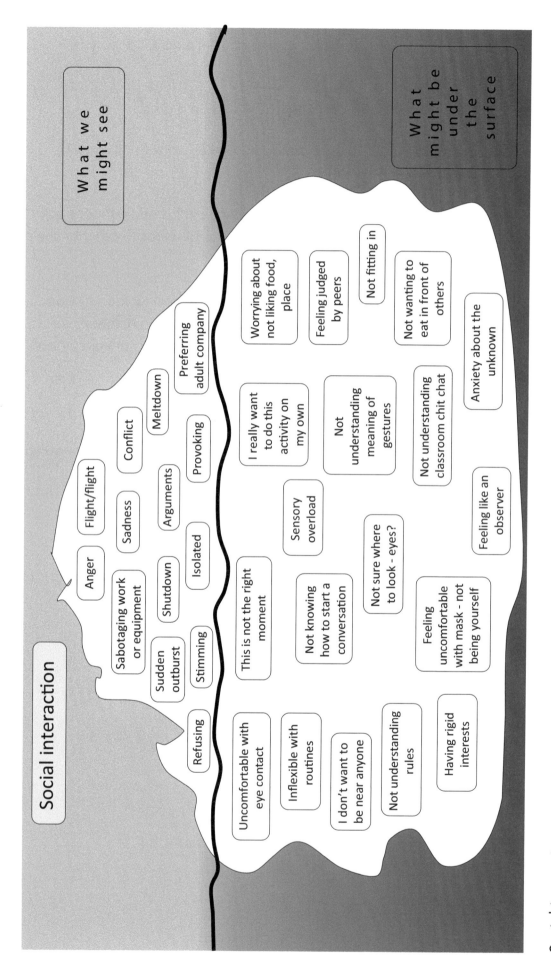

Strategies for learners – nuts and bolts

Trauma

Context

A traumatic event involves single, multiple or enduring experiences that overwhelm someone's ability to cope or process their emotions. When we cannot regulate our emotional response, the brain gets flooded with stress hormones which are toxic to the brain. This traumatic stress can lead to lasting damage and affects brain development. Children with adverse childhood experiences can recover **with support**. Without support, trauma can lead to mental and physical health difficulties in later life.

Many of us experience potentially traumatising events in our lives, but if we are able to safely talk about the events and get support from people we trust, we can process and minimise the impact of the trauma. When children experience traumatic incidents that are frightening and out of their control – they feel powerless. If, for example, the trauma is caused by a caregiver or if the trauma is hidden and not talked about, then the child is not able to process their feelings and may feel shame or confusion. Often, trauma is 'stored' in our bodies and even if memories are affected, the impact of the trauma is experienced as feelings and sensations. Trauma can stem from experiences of abuse and neglect; domestic violence; war; grief and loss; significant illness; or from cultural historical trauma. Children can block the traumatic experience from their memory to survive. Families may not be forthcoming with information or may not understand effects of incidents. Carers may not know their child's detailed history. As school staff, we may not be aware of trauma in pupil's life, but we may see signs of it in behaviours in school.

Pupils with trauma in their background may have a sensitive fight-or-flight response. When they experienced trauma, their brain switched to survival mode, flooding their body with adrenaline and other hormones. This response remains on high alert and affects their behaviours and the way they respond to peers, adults and situations.

Behaviours we may see in school include emotional swings; impulsive and risky behaviours; sensitivity to criticism or apparent lack of remorse; processing and language difficulties; mental health concerns; social exclusion; zoning out; physical complaints such as stomachaches; aggressive or sexualised behaviour; self-sabotage; avoidance, anxiety and attentional difficulties.

Pupils will need therapeutic intervention to help them process past trauma. It is not in the remit of teachers to do this kind of work, and there is a risk we can retraumatise a pupil if we delve into past experiences without specialist training. However, a

Strategies for learners – nuts and bolts

trauma-informed school staff can do a lot to nurture and support pupils to settle in school and feel safe and secure enough to focus on learning.

Consider

- Consult with your SEN or pastoral staff if you have concerns about a pupil you teach.

- Seek to understand what a pupil's behaviour might be about. Be consistent and persistent – sometimes the trigger for a certain behaviour will be unknown but will have related to something in a pupil's past.

- Don't take behaviour personally. Have clear boundaries but adjust for individuals if appropriate.

- Provide a safe withdrawal space, e.g., a blanket, toy, bean bag, headphones.

- Model self-regulation, teach names for emotions, help pupils to articulate day-to-day problems. Don't shout or use sarcasm.

- Learn some calming strategies such as breathing exercises, glitter jars.

- Use visuals like a coloured chart for emotions, emoticons, toys.

- Help pupils with peer activities – pair with good role models.

- If a behaviour is an issue, follow up with an immediate consequence but steer away from punitive sanctions. Think about avoiding further shame. A restorative approach is preferable.

School staff can build nurturing relationships and trust with pupils, which will give them every chance to feel safe and achieve.

Reflect

How do you balance the needs of the pupil with the needs of others? How can you become more trauma informed, and which colleagues in school would be useful mentors?

Strategies for learners – nuts and bolts

Trauma

Classroom strategies

Reassure *(Talk About the Issue)*
- Validate pupils' feelings.
- Use empathic listening.
- Make time for sitting in silence.
- Talk though using pictures.

Name the Emotion
- Emotion cards.
- Reflection sheets and diaries.
- Read stories with relatable characters or plots.
- Wondering out loud – 'I am wondering if you are feeling sad'.

Grounding Techniques
- Calm voice.
- Breathing together.
- Relaxing colouring.
- Feet on ground.
- Senses – smell, drink, sensory toy, soft material, hoodie, glitter jar.
- Self-soothing – weighted scarf, warm drink.

Plan for Triggers
- Visual timetables.
- Explain change of routines ahead.
- Plan for cover teachers.
- Time out space.
- Traffic light cards.
- Tactile area/calm down box.
- Seating plans – escape routes.
- Plan for assemblies/break times.

Model Self-regulation *(Deep Breathing / Count to Ten)*
- Explain your feelings and actions.
- Model self-calming.
- Reflect out loud.
- Show class breathing techniques.

Trusted Adult
- Be patient, warm, positive, nurturing, consistent, predictable and protective.

Trauma

Strategies for learners – nuts and bolts

Visual impairment

Context

Visual impairment is defined as the loss of vision that can't be corrected through the wearing of lenses. Visual impairments arise from neurological or genetic conditions or structural problems with the eye and vary in the degree and type of vision loss. Pupils with significant visual impairment may have specialist support.

Visual impairment can affect acuity of vison, field of vision and sensitivity to light. Every pupil is unique, but areas of difficulty can include distinguishing text or pictures, mobility around school, using equipment, facial recognition, picking up social cues, eating and drinking, following verbal instructions and explanations and taking part in practical activities. It can be overwhelming to be in a busy school when you have a visual impairment and everyday activities take time and effort. This can be tiring, both physically and emotionally. In addition, pupils with visual impairment may find it hard to communicate with their peers and can find themselves socially isolated especially if they cannot, or do not choose, to participate in all the opportunities on offer in school.

Consider

Teachers can make school a lot more accessible for pupils by thinking about the classroom space and the presentation of activities. Clearing the classroom of clutter helps mobility and reduces risk but also reduces visual distraction.

- Use your name as you greet pupils (some pupils can't see who you are as you approach), i.e., 'Good morning, it's Mrs X'.

- Verbalise when you want to demonstrate things – describe the position of an item.

- Seating – pupils need to be able to face the board but ask them how close they need to be, as up close or face on may not be visually best. The light source needs to be focussed on what they are looking at.

- White space is helpful – leave gaps between text and images on worksheets, slides and templates.

- Contrast is important – bold colours, dark on light.

Strategies for learners – nuts and bolts

- Help pupils distinguish writing layout by using squared paper, bold lined paper, coloured markers to show top and bottom, writing frames.

- Colour coding can be helpful – e.g., different-coloured books for subjects, tape on stair risers, labels for equipment.

- Tactile markers, e.g., for light switches, recording devices, cookers, science equipment. Tactile objects for concrete learning.

- Try an 'occluder' – this is a window cut out of card, used to focus on a key piece of text or image.

- Magnification – use magnifiers, magnify text or images on the computer, interactive whiteboard or on a tablet.

- Use speech-to-text software.

- Support assessment, e.g., scribe, modified test, enlarged graphs.

- Extra time may be needed to complete tasks.

- Offer alternatives for activities a pupil may be uncomfortable doing, such as a set place to sit for assemblies, lunch or unstructured time.

- Adapted physical tasks and/or equipment for PE and other practical subjects – be sensitive to how confident or safe a pupil may feel.

- Always offer support for mobility by holding out your wrist to guide – never try and guide without warning the pupil.

- Pupils may be anxious about social activities that depend on sight, and so may need support and encouragement to participate, or may prefer an offer of an alternative social activity with fewer participants.

Reflect

Do you feel awkward communicating with a pupil with visual impairment? We rely on visual feedback, so it can feel uncomfortable. Think about school from your pupil's viewpoint, as this should help you work with them to overcome barriers.

Strategies for learners – nuts and bolts

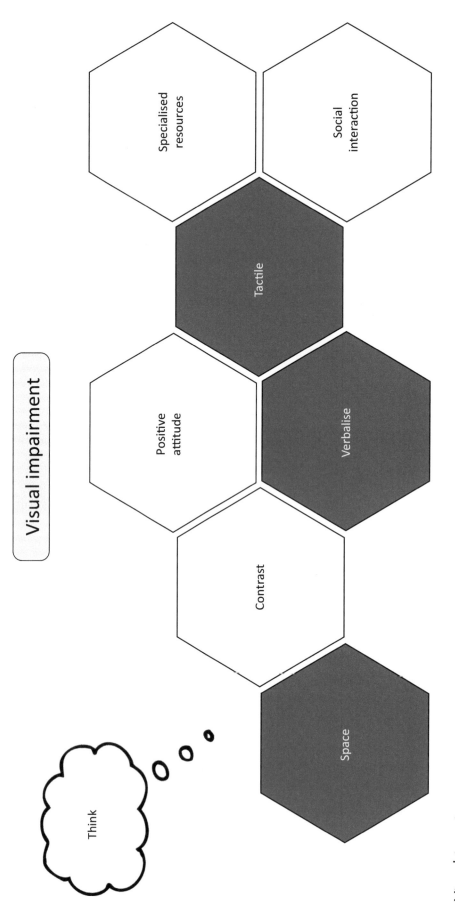

Strategies for learners – nuts and bolts

Working memory

Context

Working memory is like the sticky note of the brain. It allows us to temporarily store information for long enough to do something with it – before discarding it or moving it to another part of our memory store. Working memory capacity varies between pupils, and poor working memory capacity is a common barrier for many pupils who struggle with learning in school.

Pupils with poor working memory capacity will have great difficulties in retaining and manipulating information. They will struggle to follow teacher explanation and instructions and will have big difficulties with immediate recall; starting and completing tasks; answering questions and maintaining attention and focus. Because a lot of classroom practice requires pupils to absorb new facts, listen and read for comprehension and follow instructions, this can mean the pupil with working memory issues is constantly behind peers, wondering what to do, asking their neighbours for help or acting out/shutting down in frustration or boredom. Working memory issues can have a big impact on pupils' ability to grasp the basic building blocks of learning, such as literacy and numeracy.

You can recognise pupils struggling with working memory by looking out for some of these indicators: turning to talk to a neighbour straight after teacher instructions; inattention and distractibility; lack of initiative in group work; and losing their place in a task and not appearing to know what to do to start a task. Many of these pupil behaviours may be misinterpreted by staff as poor listening skills, lack of motivation or even disruptive behaviour. Pupils with poor working memory are missing a lot of learning on a day-to-day basis, and for staff it can appear that their efforts to teach are literally 'in one ear and out the other'!

It is worth noting that working memory capacity develops throughout childhood, into our twenties and thirties. Younger children will have less developed working memory capacity than older pupils – whatever their individual differences. In any class there will be a range of working memory abilities, and some older pupils may have developed ways around their difficulties. If you use strategies to support the pupils most in need, you will be helping others as well.

Consider

Anything you can do to back up teacher talk with visual prompts and key text, will help pupils receive the information in more than one way and make it more likely

Strategies for learners – nuts and bolts

to stick. The strategies of chunking information, repeating sentences and using images alongside text will benefit all pupils. Working memory is extremely easy to compromise through distraction or overload.

- Repeat instructions or key points (don't rephrase, as that is new information to recall!).

- Avoid a lot of filler language – trivia, anecdotes, etc. If you want to teach a few main ideas, stick to the main point.

- Get total silence when providing the class with information they need to recall.

- Revisit prior learning little and often – rehearse together and practise retrieving the key knowledge, return to the same topic a few times.

- Get pupils to repeat back to you.

- Put the lesson sequence on the board as a checklist.

- Use whiteboard to display instructions.

- Think about clarity of language you use in explanations and instructions.

- Link together verbal and visual material – avoid abstract images, as this creates more information to process and recall.

 **Reflect**

Have you noticed some pupils struggling a lot with instructions or focus? Refer the pupil to the SEN team for further advice.

Strategies for learners – nuts and bolts

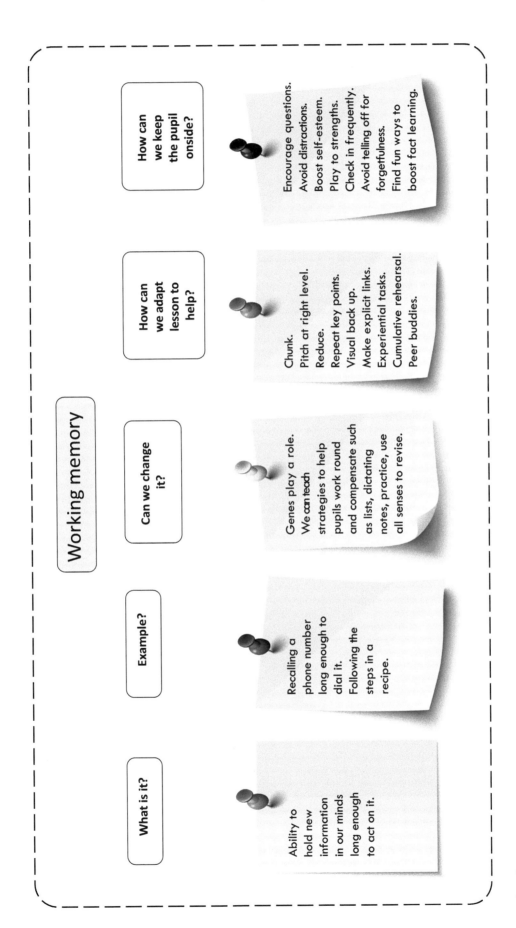

Chapter 8

Staff energy

STAFF ENERGY REFLECTION
QUESTIONS   251

Staff energy

Context

Working in a school is a demanding job. A teacher's role is emotionally intense and pressured. Several decisions must be made quickly during every lesson. We balance the learning and emotional needs of our pupils with the demands of paperwork, parents, colleagues and accountability pressures.

Schools are relational places. Everyone has some of their own emotional baggage, and we never know someone else's entire story. The job is much more enjoyable when we can build positive relationships, both with colleagues and with pupils and their families. Schools vary in their culture and working environments, but we can be much more effective in meeting the diverse needs of our pupils if **we** find ways to look after ourselves.

Emotionally resilient staff whom I have worked with share some of these common features: they value themselves and are self-aware; they enjoy challenges and use their initiative; they are open to new ideas and contribute; they show compassion; they ask for help; they know their limits and they can manage their emotions appropriately at work. Some staff are keen to learn about their own well-being and recognise that even though the workload is rather inescapable, many staff are very compassionate and will often put their pupils' needs first rather than take time for themselves. Recognition of our own well-being is crucial in managing the rigours of the job without compromising our own physical and mental health.

Working with pupils with additional needs adds pressure because planning can take extra time we don't have, and we may worry about our pupils or feel under-skilled when teaching them. There will be pupils who make us feel disempowered, angry or sad. We may be inexperienced or feel unsupported in school. To instil confidence in our pupils, we need to feel confident in our own abilities to teach our pupils. No member of staff should feel isolated, and perspective is sometimes needed.

Consider

- Use all the support you can – find a colleague who will listen to your concerns, collaborate with teaching assistants.

- Use a diary to time box when you are going to do tasks; **overestimate** how long you might need.

- Resources – ask colleagues before making your own.

- Spending ages creating resources that pupils use in 2 minutes is probably not the best use of time. Get pupils to do more or plan a task needing no resources.

Staff energy

- Find a work time that doesn't affect your sleep – work at school or stop work **way** before bedtime.

- Get organised – use checklists, have a good filing system, make time to create computer file names. If you make resources for individual pupils, store them to use again.

- If dealing with a challenging pupil who has rattled you, take time and space to reset by asking a colleague to cover.

- If you are working with a pupil with lots of issues, recognise when you are feeling overloaded emotionally. Pass on concerns and share the load.

- Be assertive with what you feel you can manage – don't feel you have to take on responsibilities you are not ready for or can't make time for.

- Ask for advice, use expertise in school, share worries with colleagues. Staff feel respected and valued when asked to give guidance.

- Notice how other staff are coping and ask them if they need support.

- Don't get drawn into negative staff room talk. Don't speak badly about pupils or use negative words to describe their personalities. Keep your integrity and value compassion.

Reflect

Are you aware of your own needs during the school day?

Staff energy

Staff energy

Inclusive teachers need to be at their best.

- Live in the moment - focus on what you can do now, rather than build up anxieties about the what-ifs.
- Remember that we make our own choices - get out of victim mindset and take positive steps.
- Set time limits and work smartly. Don't try doing 2 things at once. Switching tasks is tempting but inefficient!
- Have a positive outlook - watch the negative voice and steer clear of gossip and politics as this drains us.
- Try not to sweat the small stuff - teaching isn't about being perfect and having immaculate resources - share teaching materials and use your time for things that have the biggest impact.
- Talk to people you trust. It's helpful to be listened to.
- Monitor stress levels and know when you need to take a break, delegate or ask for support.
- Prioritise - focus on what is important to you at work and at home.
- Be realistic about what you can do and focus on completing things well rather than saying yes and then regretting it.
- Put aside time for yourself and make it happen.

Staff energy

Staff energy reflection questions

To think about	Your reflections
How often do I talk to colleagues at school? Have I got colleagues I trust?	
Am I able to switch off at the weekend? Am I thinking about school all the time?	
How am I using email? Can I turn it off at the weekend?	
How much time am I devoting to pursuing my own interests outside school?	
Am I worrying too much about individual pupils or classes?	
Am I managing to spend quality time with family/friends on a regular basis?	
Am I taking short breaks during the day? Can I relax a little?	
Have I had time to make appointments for my own health or life admin?	
What is my mood like? Am I feeling anxious about school? Am I tired?	
How many hours a week am I working? Could I work fewer hours and still manage my workload?	
How late in the evening am I working? Am I able to stop thinking about school enough to sleep?	
Have I been able to do any exercise on a regular basis?	

Staff energy

To think about	Your reflections
Am I spending too much time on things I could do more efficiently?	
Am I making time for planning ahead, or am I doing things at the last minute?	
Have I volunteered for too many extra things that I now regret?	
Can I find humour at school to share with colleagues and pupils?	
Am I feeling under pressure from some parents' expectations?	
Do I enjoy thinking about teaching and coming up with ideas?	
Am I comparing myself to others?	

Appendices

Inclusive teaching checklist

Seating carefully planned.	
Peers supportive of each other.	
Classroom well organised and pupils know routines.	
Clear lesson objectives appropriate to level of pupils using clear language (different individual pathways for pupils if needed).	
Visual backup – range of pictures, photos, drawings, diagrams on whiteboard or in front of pupils.	
Questions directed and pitched/scaffolded if needed; i.e., choices given, prompts.	
Instructions clear and pupils listen. Instructions supported on board, paper or by peer buddies.	
Teacher checks understanding through open questions and probes pupils further.	
Access to teacher – roving around prompting, explaining, questioning.	
Resources planned so text or level is accessible to all.	
Enough time given so pupils can process.	
Pair and group work planned.	
Concrete examples used – real objects, videos, everyday examples.	
Additional adults used to progress **learning.**	
Transitions signposted, tasks move on and pupils know they are starting a different task or concept.	
Ethos of 'have a go'; no worries about wrong answers.	
Alternatives to writing – diagrams, collage, speaking tasks, discussion, use of computer, etc.	
Scaffolds/props – key word lists, writing frames, tables or grids readymade, models, number lines, etc.	

Appendices

Seating carefully planned.	
Evidence that pupils can complete work independently – work completed in book.	
Pupils' need for explanation recognised – pupils can start if they are ready, others can wait for extra support.	
Tasks chunked into shorter tasks and pace managed.	
Tasks simplified, reduced, adapted or extended.	
Variety of feedback used – annotated, highlighted, stickers, verbal, peer, self, smiley faces – **feedback understood by pupil**.	
Appropriate behaviour and communication noticed and rewarded.	
Homework suitable and achieved – differentiated if appropriate.	

Appendices

The inclusive classroom

Speech and language needs
- Visual, visual, visual.
- Explain vocab including non-subject words.
- Minimise filler talk.
- Keep talk short and unambiguous.
- 1-to-1 explanation.
- Use concrete examples and everyday references to hang new information on.
- Revisit vocab often.

Emotional needs
- Structure, routine - be consistent.
- Plan lessons very well and have resources ready.
- Start lesson with pace.
- Positive body language and instructions.
- Calm voice - avoid shouting.
- Praise appropriate behaviour.
- Deal with pupils individually.
- Build rapport and positive relationships - prevention is best.
- Have a fresh-start approach.

For all pupils
- Arrange furniture so all pupils can see.
- Chunk information and explain clearly.
- Make Learning Objectives explicit and understandable to all.
- Minimal distractions for teaching - get them quiet, have learning routines to get them busy straight away.
- Have visual and concrete cues - mind maps, pictures, objects, demos.
- Have key vocab displayed, give prompts sheets.

Memory and processing needs
- Revisit topics.
- Chunk information.
- Back up verbal information with visual cues/ notes/ write on board.
- Pre-teach vocab.
- Reduce information/avoid too much chat.
- Extra time.

Literacy needs
- Alternative recording methods.
- Pair with good reader.
- Colour code - e.g. black for copying, blue for instructions.
- Allow ICT use/tablets.
- Supply key words.
- Scribe ideas before pupil writes.
- Verbalise before writing.

Sensory processing needs
- Routines/explain changes.
- Minimise sensory issues-noise levels etc.
- Give pupils extra time.
- Cue in by name.
- Quiet working areas/workstation.
- Treat behaviour as cognitive not behavioural issue.
- Groupings need to be sensitive or allow pupil to work on own.

The inclusive classroom Venn diagram

Appendices

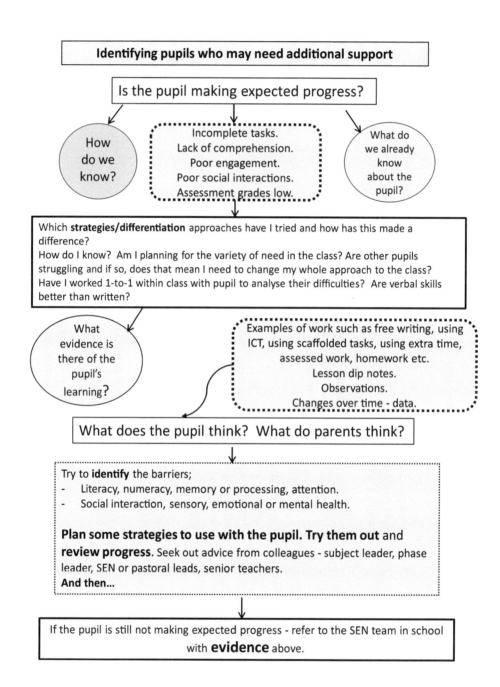

Identifying pupils who may need additional support

Menu of lesson task ideas

Short of planning time?

Need some inspiration to increase pupil engagement and add variety to adapted tasks?

Try this takeaway menu of possible activities for lessons.

Make a poster.	Make a leaflet.	Analyze graphs, data, tables.
Draw/make graphs or charts.	Draw tables/fill in tables.	Write a song, poem, rap.
Pupils plan and teach part of lesson.	Open-ended questions – what if . . .? How many ways can . . .?	Use/make puppets.
Observe another pupil.	Adult does task badly – pupils observe and correct.	Choice of activity – pupils choose.
Make a freeze-frame mime – tap pupil on shoulder and get them to explain concept.	Memory – give pupils time to memorise part or whole of a picture/practical setup. Draw it.	Make a worksheet into a jigsaw.
Mini whiteboard activities – show and tell, sequencing.	Washing lines: jumbled-up words on cards – hang on a line.	Speed dating – line up opposite a partner. Teach them a fact. Move on.
What is best – x or y? Vote by going to part of room – justify.	Take notes.	Mark each other's work.
Make a test for the teacher.	Hot seat – one expert or character gets interviewed by class.	Highlight text.

Appendices

Cloze activity.	Fill in gaps.	Write captions for pictures.
Here are the captions – draw the picture.	Teach to learn – research and teach each other.	Group project.
Make a word list/bank.	Make a Venn diagram showing links between ideas/words.	Word search/number search.
Quizzes – pupils make own quiz. Do teacher quiz in teams, on whiteboards, in pairs.	Here is the answer – what is the question?	Read aloud.
Write up or type in best. Illustrate work.	Cut and stick models or definitions.	Colour in/highlight diagrams, drawings, maps.
Draw/Pictionary/listen and draw.	Listening – story, poem, description.	Look at an object.
Spot the difference.	Spot the odd one out.	Spot the mistake.
Spot all the vocab, key words, etc.	List similarities/differences.	Matching tasks – words to definitions, words to images.
Make a news report – written or scripted/performed.	Dictation – good calming activity!	KWL chart (what you **know**, what you **want** to know, what you have **learned**).
Mysteries.	Make a collage.	Question grids.
Make a jigsaw puzzle.	Make a model.	Worksheet and questions.
Textbook and questions.	Group mind map. Individual mind map.	Debate or silent debate on whiteboard.
Carousel of activities. Learn a topic from pupil experts.	Make a storyboard/do captions for a storyboard.	Role play.
Make a flow chart.	Sentence starters – finish off, extend.	Make a slide presentation from scratch or with template.
Whole class explain – sentence by sentence/word by word.	Do a sketch.	Discussion – pair, group, class.

Appendices

Make up a play.	Do a survey, write a questionnaire.	Watch a film or video clip. Turn sound down and pupils commentate.
Photos as prompt for writing, discussion, etc.	Interview someone.	Find key words in text.
Bingo with topic facts/questions.	Make a whole class model with people.	Watch a demonstration – in silence.
Guess who/what – cards with facts – pupils ask questions to guess words.	20 questions.	Bag of objects – to introduce a concept, character, etc.
Writing frame – complete.	Research on internet – give parameters to focus.	Design a . . . (machine, invention, book cover, building, app)
Make a wall display.	Make an exhibition – pupils then 'visit' the exhibition.	Teacher models task.
Facts – rank them, sequence them, put in categories.	Jigsaw, envoy, snowball – group work.	Make an animation.
Group discussion with roles – chair, observer Q & A using props, i.e., talking stick.	Q & A with passing on questions to expand the answers.	Calculate – work out percentages, numbers, etc. from information.
Thinking skills – i.e., explain a concept using key or limited number of words.	Write a social media comment.	Silent debate.
Learning objective as question or gaps to complete.	Answers on a sticky note – stick on board.	Ranking facts or ideas tasks.
Selection of questions, facts on cards – pupils pick a card.	Find someone in the class who . . .: (can explain key fact; use a grid to record)	Stand up, sit down game – true/false statements.
Write from another's perspective.	Write a letter to . . .	Turn an explanation into a diagram.
Reproduce something accurately – could be a drawing, diagram, poem, etc.	Design an experiment to test something.	Highlight and sort what is fact or opinion.

Appendices

Pair up pupils – persuasion task – take turns trying to persuade partner.	Connect facts using a line on the page – make links between ideas.	Make a map.
Balloon debates – can use facts, words or concepts as well as people.	TV chat show/radio phone in.	Human continuum for opinions. Line up where you think you agree.
Picture on slide – answer questions to reveal picture.	Make comic strips.	Board game – design with clues related to topic.
Prompt sheet – 'how to' guide for lesson.	10 questions in 10 minutes.	Write a post card.
How are these words linked . . . ?	Pictures on slide – how are these connected?	Model exam answer.
Advert/sell an idea.	Use modelling clay to demonstrate an idea.	Make a timeline.
Make an acrostic or a mnemonic of a topic.	Hangman/Taboo/Just a Minute/charades.	Pairs: put words on board – pupils pair them up.
Stick tasks/facts around room. Pupils rove around and do task.	Mystery guest – give one pupil name of person linked to topic. Class guesses who.	Alphabet games – name a topic-related word starting with. . .
The no or yes game – pupils can only answer no or yes.	Write an equation to show your learning using symbols or images.	Pupils make an aide memoire to remember something.
What is it? Use a prop. Prop games – what could it be?	What's missing – leave gaps in sequence.	Questions and answers on cards – find person with correct match in class.
Two truths and a lie game – about facts in a topic.	Annotate text using codes like tick, cross,! according to teacher instructions.	Bring in a bag of objects related to topic. Pupils guess connections.
Dinner party: mill about, call a number – pupils get into groups of that number and talk about a topic.	Draw and tell. Make a 4 x 4 grid. Read text. Pupils draw in each section to retell information.	Hot seat – pupil or teacher in character or concept role. Class asks questions.

Bibliography

Some ideas for further reading and for delving into more detail about specific barriers or to find resources to support inclusive teaching.

Bird, Ronit (2007). *The Dyscalculia Toolkit*. London, Paul Chapman Publishing.

Bosanquet, Paula, Radford, Julie and Webster, Rob (2016). *The Teaching Assistants Guide to Effective Interaction: How to Maximize Your Practice*. Abingdon, Routledge Education.

Collins-Donnelly, Kate (2013). *Starving the Anxiety Gremlin: A Cognitive Behavioural Therapy Workbook on Anxiety /Management for Young People*. London, Jessica Kingsley Publishers.

The Communication Trust. Available online at: www.thecommunicationtrust.org.uk

Coulter, Susan, Kynman, Lesley, Morling, Elizabeth, Murray, Francesca, Grayson, Rob and Wing, Jill (2016). *Supporting Children with Medical Conditions*. Abingdon, Routledge Education.

Cowley, Sue (2018). *The Ultimate Guide to Differentiation*. London, Bloomsbury.

Department for Education and Department of Health (2015). *Special Educational Needs Code of Practice:0–25 Years*. Available online at: www.gov.uk/government/publications/send-code-of-practice-0-to-25

De Thierry, Betsy (2015). *Teaching the Child on the Trauma Continuum*. Guildford, Grosvenor House Publishing Ltd.

De Thierry, Betsy (2019). *The Simple Guide to Understanding Shame in Children: What it is. How to Help*. London, Jessica Kingsley Publishers.

Didau, David (2014). *The Secret of Literacy: Making the Implicit, Explicit*. Carmarthan, Independent Thinking Press; Crown House Publishing.

Didau, David and Rose, Nick (2016). *What Every Teacher Needs to Know About Psychology*. Woodbridge, John Catt Educational Ltd.

Bibliography

Dunn, Buron and Curtis, Mitzi (2007). *The Incredible 5 Point Scale; Assisting Students with Autism Spectrum Disorders in Understanding Social Interactions and Controlling their Emotional Responses.* Overland Park, KS, APC.

Fisher, Robert (1999). *First Stories for Thinking.* Oxford, Nash Pollack.

Gathercole, Susan and Packiam, Alloway (2008). *Working Memory and Learning.* London, SAGE Publications Ltd.

Hattie, John and Yates, Gregory (2014). *Visible Learning and the Science of How We Learn.* Abingdon, Routledge.

Honeybourne, Victoria (2016). *Educating and Supporting Girls with Asperger's and Autism.* London, Speechmark Publishing Ltd.

Lawson, Wendy (2011). *How People With Autism Learn.* London, Jessica Kingsley Publishers.

Ling, John (2010). *I Can't Do That: My Social Stories to Help with Communication, Self-Care and Personal Skills.* London, SAGE Publications Ltd.

MacKay, Neil (2015). *Total Teaching: Raising Achievement of Vulnerable Groups.* Wakefield, SEN Books.

Morrison McGill, Ross (2017). *Mark. Plan. Teach.* London, Bloomsbury.

Mucklow, Nancy (2009). *The Sensory Team Handbook: A Hands-on Tool to Help Young People Make Sense of their Senses and Take Charge of their Sensory Processing.* Ontario, Michael Grass House.

Packer, Natalie (2016). *The Teachers Guide to SEN.* Carmarthen, Crowne House Publishing Ltd.

Quigley, Alex (2018). *Closing the Vocabulary Gap.* Abingdon, Routledge.

Radburn, Ruby (2008). *The Feelings Artbook: Promoting Emotional Literacy through Drawing.* Milton Keynes, Speechmark Publishing Ltd.

The SEND Gateway. Available online at: www.sendgateway.org.uk

Wallace, Fiona (2007). *What Else Can I do with You? Helping Children Improve Their Classroom Behaviour.* London, Paul Chapman Publishing.

Willingham, Daniel (2009). *Why Don't Students Like School.* San Francisco, Jossey-Bass.